PROSECUTRIX

Fight for Justice

Ronald E Bowers

Former Senior Prosecutor
Los Angeles County District Attorney's Office

Some names and locations have been changed to protect the privacy of individuals connected with this story. Certain events and statements have been inferred from the facts of these cases and public articles about these cases.

Ronald E. Bowers, Publisher
losangelestruecrime@aol.com

ISBN 978-1-7325281-9-2

First release November 2016

INTRODUCTION

Why are we so fascinated by elite groups who are able to do extraordinary things? History is filled with special groups who were somehow unique and went on to achieve great triumphs. Some would point to **Jesus Christ's disciples,** who were a special group that went on to spread the gospel throughout the world. They were a diverse group in which their personal and collective accomplishments had a significant impact on Western Civilization.

Throughout history there have been so-called elite groups we all remember that accomplished amazing acts. In the military, there have been exceptional fighting groups who were recognized for accomplishing great feats. In World War II the **Band of Brothers** were held up as a group of soldiers who did remarkable deeds in the heat of battle. During the Vietnam War the **Green Berets** gained fame as an elite group that was able to achieve remarkable results by their daring military missions. We can't forget the **Top Gun** pilots who were recognized for their incredible skill in flying fighter jets. Their brave exploits were made famous by the Tom Cruise movie by the same name. More recently, the U.S. Army **Delta Force** gained the reputation of being able to carry out the most difficult rescue attempts and seemed able to do the impossible.

However, with the successful attack on Bin Laden, the US Navy **Seal Team 6** became a household word with so many young people eager to be a part of the Special Forces. The members on these teams became mentors to impressionable youths who want to attain greatness through intense training, practice, and dedication.

In addition to military elite groups we all have our favorite **sports teams** of all times, in which fans considered certain sport eras as made up of exceptional teams. The **1967 UCLA basketball team** (Your author may be slightly biased since UCLA was my alma mater), coached by John Wooden and lead by Lew Alcindor (Kareem Abdul Jabbar), was an example of unbelievable accomplishments. To be fair, the **1962 USC football team,** which won the national championship, coached by John McKay, can't be overlooked. (Since your author went to USC for Law School, I would be remiss if I didn't include them.)

Every old-time NFL fan can rattle off their beloved Dallas Cowboys teams and every cheese head can argue that the greatest Green Bay Packers team was coached by Vince Lombardi.

We admire certain elite groups for their extraordinary accomplishments. Many times we aren't aware of the actual members of these groups. Other times an individual is given the credit for the accomplishment rather than the entire group who made it happen. For years the public had the impression that Bill Gates and Steve Jobs single-handedly invented many of the great technological inventions of our time when in fact it was a group effort that actually accomplished these great achievements.

In many instances, these elite groups and their members become an enigma to the public. Often the members of the group are cloaked in secrecy in order not to interfere with the mission of the group. Although the group may be visible to the public, no one is in a position to reveal the inner workings of the group. No one, especially journalist or writers, ever gained the trust to go behind their secret veil to see what makes these special teams able to accomplish their exceptional feats.

For 43 years I was a deputy District Attorney in Los Angeles County and was personally aware of many of the famous cases that the public and the news media seem to have an endless fascination with. I remember back in the 1960s, the DA's Office would assign one of their experienced prosecutors to work on and try the publicity cases. As a result, certain senior prosecutors like J. Miller Leavy and Joe Busch became known as exceptional prosecutors who were recognized as the titans in the courtroom.

However, over time the concept of one prosecutor per case gave way to having a pool of experienced trial lawyers from one section in the DA's Office handle the publicity cases. Those lawyers would be assigned the big cases as they occurred. At first, this group was called the Special Trials Unit. Just like any group, for logistical reasons they had to be attached to an existing part of the DA's Office bureaucracy. Therefore, Special Trials was affiliated with Central Operations, where it received its clerical and support personnel. There was no formal head deputy who ran the Unit; however, one of the assigned prosecutors was given the responsibility to oversee the operation. For years, Sterling "Ernie" Norris was given the task to act as the so-called Deputy in Charge of this relatively small Special Trials Unit.

Later on, David Conn was placed in charge of the Unit and was in that position when the O.J. Simpson case unexpectedly landed on the DA's doorstep. Initially, David Conn and Marcia Clark were the two prosecutors assigned to the case. Since it was generating so much publicity, the Administration decided to place Bill Hodgman in charge of the Simpson case to assist Marcia with the preparation of the case. However, after the disastrous result with the Simpson case, the DA's Office recognized that an elite division was needed to be ready to take on the most difficult cases as they occurred. That was when the idea of having a **Major Crimes Division** was established. This Division would be fully staffed with a head deputy whose main task was to oversee the major cases and supervise the prosecutors assigned to them. The Division would handle the high-publicity cases as well as the complex cases requiring special attention.

This **Major Crimes Division** would consist of the best and the brightest attorneys in the DA's Office. Often the prosecutors were labeled Top Gun attorneys who had the experience and knowledge to prosecute the most difficult cases from the time of the filing of the charges through the completion of the trial and sentencing of the case.

Everyone agreed that creating such a special division was a great idea, but the implementation was much more challenging. First off, all attorneys by their very nature think of themselves as being exceptionally talented. This is especially true of the deputy district attorneys, who have incredible experience in the courtroom. Every prosecutor would consider themselves as being qualified to be a part of this so-called 'elite group' making up **Major Crimes Division**. At first some attorneys were resentful that they weren't selected to be included in this special group.

The Los Angeles County District Attorney's Office employs around 1000 attorneys at any one time. This DA's Office proudly claims to be the largest prosecutor's office in the nation. When attempting to staff the **Major Crimes Division**, the administrators had a large pool of trial attorneys to pick from. However, many of these deputies want to gain litigation experience to make themselves more valuable as prosecutors. Also, the main way the prosecutors advance through the ranks of the DA's Office is by being recognized for trying challenging and especially high publicity cases that the downtown administrators know about. Therefore, a large segment of the prosecutors in the Office want to have the opportunities to try noteworthy cases for their own career reasons.

With the establishment of the **Major Crimes Division,** the vast majority of the publicity cases went directly to Major Crimes, resulting in less opportunity to advance the average deputy's career. Many deputy District Attorneys felt some degree of resentment toward the **Major Crimes** prosecutors, who were perceived as taking away the publicity cases. However, within a short time this indignation turned to admiration. Many of the prosecutors were glad that the **Major Crimes** deputies took over some of the extremely complex cases that the rank-and-file prosecutors didn't have the time to properly handle.

The DA's Administration recognized that they needed to staff **Major Crimes** with highly talented attorneys who not only knew the law but had magnificent litigation skills before a jury. It wasn't sufficient that the prosecutor be bright or has a pedigree from a prestigious law school. The **Major Crimes** deputy had to have the ability to organize complex factual cases and be able to prepare such problematic cases for lengthy trials. However, in addition to those qualities the deputy had to be able to handle an inordinate amount of stress for the entire duration of the trial, which might take months. Perseverance, tenacity, resilience, and stamina were qualities that a **Major Crimes** deputy would need to possess. Also, there was a need for constant energy and ability to bounce back after setbacks in their cases which might be caused by judges, difficult defense attorneys, uncooperative witnesses, and low-energy detectives.

A **Major Crimes** prosecutor had to be willing to commit an unbelievable amount of time to the job. It wasn't an 8 to 5 job, since when engaged in a lengthy trial there may be times when the prosecutor has to be working day and night. In other words, one's family and social life had to be put on hold for months, especially during the lengthy trials. The word **DEDICATED** could be used to describe the level of intensity that every **Major Crimes** deputy was required to possess.

The next issue in establishing a **Major Crimes Division** was who would be the 'leader of the pack.' All these elite highly skilled deputies didn't want to take orders or direction from someone who wasn't as bright and experienced as they were. The leader had to have exceptional credentials that all the assigned **Major Crimes** deputies would recognize. They wanted a leader who they recognized as a consummate trial attorney who had endured the legal minefields of extensive trials and come out of them not only with battle scars but with a successful record of convictions.

However, all of the assigned **Major Crimes** deputies by definition are excellent attorneys with considerable experience of their own; they aren't fond of having a supervisor dictating what they should be doing or being told how to try their cases. This is why these **Major Crimes** deputies are thought to be like a group of thoroughbreds who don't want to be penned in. These deputies wanted a boss who recognized their worth and respected them for their unique abilities. This is why the head of the **Major Crimes** needed to be a person who didn't micro-manage the elite group. Yet this leader would provide them the support they needed, as well as a sympathetic ear to listen to them vent about the frustrations of their cases.

However, from the DA's administration prospective, they wanted a head deputy who could corral in these thoroughbreds so they didn't run wild and get lost in the 'tall weeds.' In other words, the leader had to focus the energy of these thoroughbreds into constructive actions. The District Attorney didn't want this incredible stable of horses to lose direction and run amuck and be an uncontrollable segment of the DA's Office.

By the late 1990s, the **Major Crimes Division** was struggling to take over the pending cases in the old Special Trials Unit. Several experienced prosecutors were assigned to **Major Crimes** without much fanfare. Eventually a no-nonsense head deputy by the name of **Curt Hassel** was assigned to head up this new group of highly skilled attorneys. His background was being the well-organized leader of the Major Narcotic Division, which concentrated on the narcotic dealers in Los Angeles County. His forte was being an expert on drafting complex search warrants and wiretaps in an attempt to cripple the large Drug Cartels.

Curt Hassel was transferred over to **Major Crimes.** He had tried his share of cases coming up through the ranks, he was looked upon as a solid, follow-the-line administrator. Curt recognized that he was being placed in a position to supervise attorneys who had a wealth of experience in litigation. His approach was to be a supportive leader who supplied the **Major Crimes** deputies all the resources that the DA's Office had at their disposal. This approach paid off since the **Major Crimes** deputies appreciated his '**hands-off style.**'

Hassel's main contribution to this Division was going on a hunt throughout the DA's Office to identify the highly talented trial lawyers who were scattered throughout the 21 branch and area offices. Since the Los Angeles District Attorney's Office was so huge, it was impossible for the headquartered administrators to be aware of each of the rising stars who were obscured by the mere size of the Office. When Hassel noticed such impressive attorneys he would take them aside to sell them on the idea of coming downtown to be part of the exclusive **Major Crimes Division**.

Within a year, he had assembled an incredibly gifted group of prosecutors who were more than willing and able to round out the elite circle of **Major Crimes** deputies. In 1999, the DA's Office went through a brutal election in which Steve Cooley replaced District Attorney Gil Garcetti, who was blamed for the O.J. Simpson fiasco. The new DA Steve Cooley wanted Curt Hassel to play a high-level position in his new administration, which meant that the head position in **Major Crimes** would become vacant. This move could have been the death knell to the **Major Crimes Division**.

Nonetheless, the DA's administration wisely elevated **Pat Dixon** to be the new leader of **Major Crimes**. Pat had been one of the most experienced trial prosecutors in the DA's Office. He had tried the ***Ninja Murder*** case involving the Woodman brothers, which took over a year to try. He was without a doubt the most knowledgeable and experienced trial lawyer in the DA's Office

When Pat Dixon took over as the head deputy in **Major Crimes,** all the prosecutors assigned there knew that he had tried the big ones and had incredible results. Since he had been assigned as a prosecutor to the old Special Trials Unit, he easily made the transition to **Major Crimes**.

Since he had advanced from being one of the attorneys to its leader, he understood how to treat his fellow **Major Crimes** deputies. He didn't try to inject his beliefs without first listening to the individual deputy's theory of the case. Pat had chafed at those supervisors who tried to micro-manage his cases. The **Major Crimes** deputies respected his approach of giving them wide latitude to try their cases as they saw fit. The few meetings he had with his elite group could be better described as a 'community bull session.' He didn't tell his prosecutors what to do but had them explain to their fellow deputies what issues they had in their cases and how they intended to handle them. These meetings turned out to be more of a passing on information to the others and certainly wasn't like the boss telling them how to try their case.

Major Crimes Division somehow evolved as though the planets, moons, and stars were in perfect alignment. It turned out to be a loosely configured group that consisted of extremely talented thoroughbred attorneys who were unleashed to take on the toughest cases. Those years from 2000 to 2010 were truly a remarkable time, involving exceptional attorneys who were able to make one of the greatest contributions to the American Justice System. They as a group were willing to charge and try some of the most difficult cases of all times.

The public was never aware of the awesome job performed by these **Major Crimes** prosecutors during this decade. The purpose of my new book series *DA Delta Force* is to give you, the reader, an opportunity to go behind the scenes to see one of the most remarkable periods of the criminal justice system in the busy Los Angeles court system. Often the public received a distorted view of the courts and no one is in a position to set the record straight.

To a large extent the **Major Crimes** prosecutors never talk about their cases, for various legal and practical reasons. On the other hand, criminal defense attorneys often like to generate media attention about their case for the benefit of planting 'reasonable doubt' seeds in the minds of potential jurors. However, prosecutors by their very position are restricted in their comments about the criminal cases that they are handling. As much as the prosecutors might like to reveal all the evidence they plan to present to the jury, they know that would be inappropriate. They can't do anything that could be interpreted as prejudicing the accused from receiving a fair trial.

Seldom do the prosecutors ever discuss their case with the news media except for giving mundane information that is contained in the courts' record. When the cases are concluded the news media moves on to the next big case and has no real interest in yesterday's news. Another reason why the public doesn't hear much about the **Major Crimes** cases is the fact that those prosecutors handling such cases have learned that talking to a news reporter is like touching the third rail of a subway. Every **Major Crimes** deputy has been burned by reporters. Talking to a reporter is like naively running through a minefield hoping not to be blown to bits.

As a result you, the public, seldom ever hear about the fascinating cases handled by the **Major Crimes Division** deputies. Long before the Division was formed, there were a few prosecutors who wrote about cases they have personally handled. Vincent Bugliosi quit the DA's Office to co-write ***Helter Skelter***, and Marcia Clark left the Office to co-write ***Without A Doubt***, which earned her $4.2 million. Those incidents concentrated on the one big case they personally had handled as a prosecutor. On other occasions, a free-lance writer has spent months sitting in various courtrooms trying to gain insight on how the criminal justice system operates. However, even with the enormous amount of time spent observing, these free-lance writers have no way of knowing what really happened behind the scenes. They receive a one-dimensional view of a three-dimensional landscape. These writers, even with the best intentions, only see a small portion of the picture.

Unfortunately, the public never gets a candid view of what really happens in the courts, especially in the elite section of the DA's Office. However, a unique situation occurred in which I, the author, had the opportunity to work directly with the various **Major Crimes** prosecutors for over a decade. For most of the time, I was the Head Deputy of the Trial Support Division. My job was to work with all the prosecutors to assist them in preparing their exhibits and visual aids for their jury trials. This included creating slide shows to be used in their Opening Statements and Arguments. I had a staff of attorneys and paralegals who did the hands-on work, while my job was to do the initial workup and develop the strategy for how to present the case to the jury. After I retired, I came back as a consultant working exclusively for **Major Crimes Division**.

In other words, I was like a fly on the wall in the **Major Crimes Division,** seeing and hearing all the interworking of the Division. In my 43 years as a prosecutor, I never saw so many talented attorneys concentrated in one place at the same time. I marveled at how lucky the DA's Office was in having such an elite team. I thought, *What a shame that the public doesn't know what an excellent job this group is doing for them.* I thought that some day when I had the time I would attempt to shine the spotlight on the **Major Crimes Division** and let the public know what these gifted attorneys have accomplished by making our Criminal Justice System work.

Years earlier, I had the opportunity to visit a Kentucky horse farm where I saw thoroughbred horses that were housed in a large corral. It was impressive to see these magnificent creatures perform special maneuvers with precision. They exhibited incredible speed and endurance that few horses possess. I had to admire what these thoroughbreds were able to accomplish. The trainer who cared for this group of horses knew how to let each horse develop to its full potential without stifling its ability to learn its limits.

When I think of the **Major Crimes Division** prosecutors, I think of them as a group of thoroughbreds who perform amazingly well with limited supervision. This book is an attempt by me to illustrate to you the reader what remarkable feats these **Major Crimes** deputies were able to accomplish during what I call the Golden Era Years (2000-2010). In order to tell the story about this incredible group, I have divided the material into a number of books. Each will follow the career of one of these prosecutors. This first book will examine the distinguished career of a female attorney by the name of **Eleanor Hunter**, who quickly moved up the ranks to **Major Crimes**. She is just one of several extraordinary, talented attorneys who made a major contribution to **Major Crimes Division**. I have selected just five of her cases, which will give you a picture of what a remarkable attorney she became.

The first case to be discussed is ***People vs. David Helms***, in which she took an unwinnable case and turned it around which resulted in a conviction that put a child abuser behind bars. Next we will discuss the case of ***People vs. Kathleen Soliah***, in which Eleanor along with her colleague Michael Latin was able to close the last chapter of the infamous SLA domestic terrorist group, who almost got away with Murder. Then we observe Eleanor's tenacity first hand in the case of ***People vs. Bruce Koklich***, in which she didn't give up on this No Body case, which seemed like the Perfect Murder until she proved otherwise. At the same time, she had to try the case of ***People vs. Sante Kimes***, which involved the notorious mother-son team that defrauded and murdered their way across the country. In the last case, we review the case of ***People vs. Peter Govin***, which involved a dispute over an alley between two motels owned by different Indian families. Everyone agreed this was a horrific case, but the question was how to convince the jurors to convict. Eleanor's dogged determination, coupled with her legal skill, put these killers on Death Row.

We will go behind the scenes to show you how these cases were solved by the detectives and how a highly skilled prosecutor walks these cases through all the obstacles embedded in the criminal courts system. By the end of this book, you will better understand what a magnificent job was done by the **Major Crimes Division** and why it is referred to as the *DA Delta Force*.

CONTENTS

CHAPTER 1 HELMS-FACTS OF CASE

The Major Crimes Division of the Los Angeles District Attorney's Office is the division where criminal cases are sent when they are deemed high-publicity matters or when it is a serious case fraught with unbelievable problems. For several years, between 1995 to 1998, there was an unsolved case involving the death of a two-year-old boy named Lance Helms, who had been beaten to death. On the surface, the case seemed to be the typical 'shaken baby' situation. Generally, the child abuse occurs when only the parents are present. In this Helms matter, the father, David, and his girlfriend, Eve Wright, (Pseudonym) were the only persons present in the Van Nuys apartment when the young child died.

Such tragic cases come to the attention of authorities by paramedics or emergency doctors who are asked to put life back into a child who has suffered traumatic injuries. The adults with the child claim they don't know how the child received the injuries. If the child is of walking age, the adult will claim that the injuries occurred when the child accidentally fell down some stairs or ran into some furniture.

The problem with these situations is that generally there is no independent witness who can verify the parent's story. In recent years, the emergency room physicians and nurses have been required to notify law enforcement whenever they treat a child with suspicious injuries. This has resulted in every parent of a young child being paranoid to take their child to receive medical attention in fear that they will be suspected of child abuse. What every parent knows is that all children will receive injuries from falls and other types of accidents that are a part of the growing-up process.

To understand the convoluted Helms case one has to know who the parties are. First we start with Lance Helms, who died of multiple injuries at the age of 2 ½. His father, David Helms, who had custody of Lance, was with him when he died. Next there is Eve Wright, who was a live-in girlfriend of David Helms who was babysitting Lance shortly before he died. Finally there is Gail Helms who is the mother of David Helms and the grandmother of little Lance.

David was 35 years old and a drug addict with a considerable criminal record. He had been living with a prior girlfriend, whom he impregnated. This prior girlfriend was a heroin addict and was sent to state prison for a robbery conviction. Unfortunately, when baby Lance was born neither parent could provide a good home for him.

However, David Helms' extended family was very warm and caring people. David's mother, Gail Helm, was concerned as to what was going to happen to the welfare of her grandson. With Gail's support, David's sister, Ayn Helm, asked County Children's Services to place Lance with her. As a result, Ayn and Gail were given full custody of Lance and basically raised him from the time he was five months old.

Since Lance's mother and father were heroin addicts, unfortunately, baby Lance was born addicted to heroin. Even though Lance had to receive special attention and treatment, Ayn was so proud of Lance's development. From a very young age of five months, it was Ayn and Gail who provided all the care and nurturing Lance required during his formative years. Consequently, Lance was fortunate to be a part of a very loving home that provided everything he needed.

In 1994, David Helms didn't have to be burdened down with raising his son Lance. He met Eve Wright (23) and the two of them started living together. For whatever reason, David decided he wanted to regain the custody of his son, Lance. His life style hadn't greatly changed except he had changed girlfriends. He filed papers with the County Dependency Court and requested full-time custody of Lance, who was now two years old.

David's mother and sister objected, saying that Lance was doing so well under their custody, which was supported by all the social worker reports. However, the Dependency Court judge said that under the law, the court had no choice but to give Lance over to his biological father, since the goal of the State is the reunification of a child with its parents. The child's welfare and safety was not a factor to be considered when deciding reunification.

So the Dependency Court ordered that Ayn and Gail Helms turn Lance over to his father, David Helms, even though he was a known drug addict. This was especially difficult for Gail Helms because she knew about her son's violent background. All agreed that Lance was a happy and healthy child when living with Ayn.

Then Lance moved back in with his father and Eve, the girlfriend. Gail and Ayn were permitted to have Lance spend the weekends with them. As time went by, Ayn and Gail noticed that Lance had bruises and discoloration on his face. At first they dismissed these injuries as mere accidents that Lance may have had during the week when he was staying at his dad's place.

As the months passed, Gail noticed that Lance's face and body contained more and more bruises. She became so alarmed that she told workers at the Department of Children's and Family Services. She tried to get someone to look into the welfare of Lance. However, this social bureaucracy didn't seem to be following up on what had happened to Lance that resulted in these numerous scrapes and bruises. In order to get the Children and Family Services to take notice, Gail decided to take photos of Lance's injuries. She also compiled a diary that spelled out in detail all the injuries she was observing. She used this diary to provide proof that Lance was being abused in his father's care. The Children and Family Services didn't do anything to reexamine the charges being made by Lance's grandmother. Lance continued to remain in the custody of his father.

The question became, Why wouldn't the Department of Children and Family Services investigate the charges of child abuse as evidenced by all the photos and documentation that Gail Helms supplied to the social workers? Some might dismiss the grandmother's concerns as though she were acting as a mere busybody who was jealous because she and her daughter, Ayn, had lost custody of the child, Lance. The agency may have dismissed her concerns because she didn't agree with the government's purpose of reuniting natural parents with their children.

However, all the complaining by Gail, the grandmother, didn't change the custody court order. Lance remained in the custody of his natural father. On April 6, 1995, the stage was set for a tragic event that changed so many lives. On that day Eve, David's new girlfriend, was home in the couple's North Hollywood apartment, caring for Lance and her own son, Calvin, who both had the stomach flu. Later that afternoon David came home and told Eve to go to a pawnbroker down the street, to redeem a few items for him. Lance was apparently talking to his father and sitting up on the couch after Eve had left the apartment.

Eve wasn't gone that long and returned in 15 to 20 minutes, and when she returned she found Lance slumped over and his lips had turned blue. Since he didn't seem to be breathing, the paramedics were called and they found that Lance had died.

The child's body was transferred to the Coroner's Office for an autopsy to determine the cause of death. Dr. Rizzo (Pseudonym) conducted the autopsy and concluded that the victim died of blunt force trauma to his abdomen. In Dr. Rizzo's opinion he believed the victim died 30 minutes to an hour after being beaten.

The police had conducted the initial investigation and learned that Lance's father's girlfriend was the person who was with Lance 30 minutes to an hour prior to his death. Eve admitted caring for Lance during the time period in which the coroner indicated the violence occurred. As a result, the detectives brought the case to the Van Nuys DA's Office for filing of a complaint for child abuse causing death. Lance's father, David Helms, indicated that he was not at home when the beating would have occurred. He said that Eve was the only adult in the apartment. He maintained that he had not struck or ever hit his son.

The DA's Office was faced with a situation in which, based on the coroner's opinion that the only person who could have committed the beating was Eve, the girlfriend, it seemed to be a 'no brainer' to file charges against her, which the DA's Office did. At time of the Preliminary Hearing, the Coroner made it clear that the victim was subjected to a violent attack at least 30 minutes before his death when Eve was caring for him. Eve was held to answer for charges and her trial eventually was set for December 4, 1995.

Something amazing happened on the day of trial. Eve's public defender asked the DA if there was any way that some type of plea bargain could be worked out. Apparently, Eve didn't want to be convicted of Murder, which could result in a sentence of 15 years to life in prison. Eve and her attorney were aware that jurors have no sympathy for anyone accused of beating a child to death. On the other hand, the DA's Office recognized that their case entirely rested on Dr. Rizzo's opinion as to the time of death, and that the father, David, named Eve as the only person present at the time of the beating.

For both sides to come out a winner it was agreed that Eve would plead no contest to the charge of Child Abuse with the special allegation that the abuse resulted in the death of a child. Judge Michael Hof accepted the agreement and Eve received a sentence of 10 years in state prison and could be eligible for parole after serving half that sentence.

Everyone was satisfied with the plea bargain except for Gail Helm, the grandmother of Lance, the victim. At a news conference after the disposition of the case she stated, "This was not a case of child abuse. She, Eve, killed Lance Helms." As the grandmother tried to hold back tears, she went on to say, "He was beaten brutally. This little boy was tortured until he finally died." In the grandmother's mind, someone should pay dearly for the unnecessary death of her grandson.

CHAPTER 2 HELMS-MOTHER'S REACTION

Gail Helms was mad as HELL. It was unclear where this grandmother's wrath should be directed. Should the Department of Children and Family Services be held responsible for negligence in not conducting an investigation? The County Dependency Court had as its top priority to reunite children with their natural parents so the child would feel a familial bond with the parent?

The grandmother was so outraged that she unleashed a tirade of criticism on the Dependency Court for returning the child to such a dangerous environment. The news media found this a compelling story, and reporters were assigned to interview the grandmother to obtain details. All of this caught the attention of the state legislature. The result was that State Senator Richard Polanco became interested in the allegations that the grandmother was making against the Dependency Court.

All astute politicians look for certain causes that have no down side to them. The two things that a politician can count on to gain public support are fighting against Child Abuse and fighting Cruelty to Animals. The State Senator set up a public hearing in Sacramento, the state capital, to investigate allegations that the Dependency Courts were placing children in dangerous situations. In order to rally around such a winning issue, the legislator called on Gail Helms to testify at his hearings.

At the subcommittee hearings, Gail related how she had explained to the Dependency Court that her son, David, was a drug addict and that her grandson would be at risk if he were returned to the custody of her son. Gail explained how the Dependency judge ruled that the policy of the court was to reunite the child with their natural parent. As David Helms was the natural father of Lance, the judge indicated that he had no discretion in this matter since the natural parent should always be reunited with his or her child.

There wasn't any dispute over giving Lance to his natural mother, because she wasn't available, having been convicted of robbery and sentenced to state prison. The Dependency Court's only stipulation was that David had to attend a drug rehabilitation program, which he did for several months.

The State Senate hearings did create considerable publicity about how the Dependency Court was so concerned with reuniting parent and child and that the child's safety was not a factor to be considered. Because the Dependency Court claimed confidentiality, the public and media didn't have knowledge about how the Dependency Courts were operating as to determining who should get custody of the child. Since Gail was the grandmother, she was privy to the Dependency Court's hearings. She could see how the welfare of the child wasn't as important to the court as reuniting the child with a natural parent. She had learned firsthand what the Dependency Court's policies were in regards to deciding custody.

Gail gave testimony at the legislative hearing that the Dependency Court was told about her son's violent behavior and the great danger of returning the child with the natural parent. The news media picked up the story and pressure was directed at the LAPD to take another hard look at the death of two-year-old Lance Helms. The detectives recontacted Dr. Rizzo, the medical examiner, as to his opinion that the fatal injuries were inflicted 30 minutes to an hour before the time of death. Dr. Rizzo re-examined the photos of the child's injuries and conducted further research.

Thereafter, he came to the conclusion that his original findings were in error. Because of the severe and massive injuries to the stomach area with the broken ribs, he believed that the victim would have died immediately at the time of the beating. This opinion meant that Eve Wright couldn't have committed the beating, because she would not have been at the apartment when the beating occurred. In fact, she would have been at a pawn shop trying to obtain some money at the direction of her boyfriend, David Helms.

With the new time of death, the detectives wanted to follow up on the possibility that David Helms may have been the person who had inflicted the beating on Lance. The detectives began interviewing other residents of the apartment complex and came up with a number of people who said they had seen the father, David, strike or hit Lance on prior occasions. The detectives contacted the DA's Office and related their findings that Eve Wright may not have inflicted the fatal beating to little Lance.

There was now the possibility that the DA's Office may have convicted the wrong person for causing the death of Lance. The DA's Office took such allegations very seriously. Gail Helms, the grandmother, claimed that she was very angry with the district attorney's office over the manner in which they had handled the case against Eve Wright. It became apparent that the DA's Office needed a well-experienced prosecutor to review all aspects of the case. After considerable discussions, the matter of Lance Helms' death was transferred to the Major Crimes Division to sort out all the new and changing facts.

By 1998, Lance's death had turned into a Pandora's Box. The LAPD detectives were taking the position that it was Lance's father who should be prosecuted and that the girlfriend had been improperly charged. The easiest way to handle this nightmare situation was to get the girlfriend out of prison and somehow make the entire situation disappear so there would be no more embarrassment for the DA's Office.

When the matter of Lance's death was handed off to the DA's Major Crimes Division, the first item of business was to assign one of its top attorneys to the case. It was Eleanor Hunter who apparently picked the short straw and inherited the case. At the time, she wouldn't be described as a seasoned prosecutor. She had impressed the DA's administration when she won a conviction on a tough case that had occurred in the Torrance area. She demonstrated potential and would be described as an 'up and coming' prosecutor. The Major Crimes Division was in search of a Grade III deputy to fill one of their slots. She possessed the intensity and zeal that the administrators were looking for.

Although Eleanor rose to the ranks of Major Crimes rather rapidly, she recognized that she needed to prove herself to her veteran colleagues. When she ended up with the Helms case, she could have resented being assigned such a controversial child abuse case; however, she was determined to make the most of the situation. Eleanor knew the only way to be successful in this Helms case was to win over the detectives. She needed them to find witnesses for her and check out certain stories.

Eleanor knew she had to build a foundation with the detectives, so she asked them to give her a condensed version of the facts of the case. The detectives continued to explain why they had made a case against Eve, the wrong person. They tried to justify it because the medical examiner had said one thing and now had changed his opinion. What was going through Eleanor's mind was, how was she going to get any jury to believe a medical examiner who gives inconsistent opinions as to the time of death?

As Eleanor sat listening to the detectives' tag-team presentation, she may have been wondering how did this weird case get dumped into her lap. She thought, whom had she offended so much that they would want to torpedo her career with this case? Eleanor, who liked to consider herself a winner, had to wonder why was she being saddled with such a mess. However, she had to reflect on what she was told when she came on board with Major Crimes. She was warned that most of the Major Crimes cases were going to be challenging and certainly wouldn't be a pleasant 'walk in the park.'

Her first order of business was to get Eve, the girlfriend, out of state prison. She wanted to obtain a truthful statement from her as to what happened to Lance that evening. An arrangement was worked out in which Eve plead no contest to a felony child abuse charge and the original murder charge was dismissed. Eleanor assigned the detectives to work on the concept to get Eve brought over to the prosecution side. Since the DA's Office had been instrumental in sending Eve to state prison, Eleanor felt it best to let the detectives work out the arrangements for her release and obtain the facts of what really happened to Lance.

With the detectives working on their task, Eleanor started to meet with Gail and somehow convince her that the DA's Office was truly interested in seeking justice for her grandson, Lance.

Gail's crusade had hit a snag when her daughter, Ayn, came down with Lupus. Unfortunately, Ayn died from the disease five months after Lance's death. Gail believed that Ayn had died from a broken heart because she so loved Lance and felt so badly that she wasn't able to fight to keep Lance safe with her and away from her violent father.

After Ayn's death, Gail reconstituted her energy to see that her son was convicted for the killing of her grandson. She may have been the only person who personally knew how brutal David could be. She knew his history of violence, including the telling characteristic that even as a boy he often would punch his brothers in the stomach. Eventually, Gail learned the true extent of the injuries that killed Lance. They included a broken rib, a liver that was split in pieces, a six-inch tear in the structure that anchors the intestines to the spine, and a bruised diaphragm. The logical conclusion was that these injuries came from vicious punches to the stomach.

Gail knew that it was highly unlikely Eve was physically able to inflict such injuries on Lance. It was much more likely that it was David who administered such violent punches to Lance's stomach. It was Gail's insistence that her son, David, was the only person who could have caused such abdominal injuries on Lance.

Now Eleanor had convinced Gail that the DA was on her side, and she was able to utilize Gail's knowledge of her son's violent past to help build a case against him. Soon the detectives had ironed out things between the DA's Office and the girlfriend. Eve had served 21 months in state prison before she was released, and seven months later charges were filed against David Helms for murder and child abuse likely to produce great bodily harm or death.

CHAPTER 3 HELMS-HIS TRIAL

As every real estate agent knows, the three key ingredients for selling property are LOCATION, LOCATION, AND LOCATION. For an attorney, the key to success in court is PREPARATION, PREPARATION, AND PREPARATION. Apparently, Eleanor had paid attention in law school when the professors tried to instill in every law student the vital need for old-fashioned PREPARATION.

Eleanor recognized that David Helms' defense attorney would try to poke holes in the prosecution's case. The changing position of Dr. Rizzo, the medical examiner, as to the time of death was a giant hole in the DA's case that the Defense would be able to drive an 18-wheeler through. To counter this, Eleanor was working with a pediatric surgeon who was willing to testify that Lance was hit so hard in the abdomen that his liver was split into pieces and he would have died within 10 minutes.

Related to this issue, the Defense was going to concentrate on the fact the DA's Office prosecuted the wrong person the first time around. The Defense would ask the jury, "How convinced are you that the DA is prosecuting the right person in this second case?"

There was another issue that had to be dealt with, and that involved the dislike for the actions of the Dependency Court. The jury might take the position that the real 'bad guy' in this matter was the Dependency Court, which created the situation by placing Lance back in custody with his father. Could some jurors place the blame on the Dependency Court and somehow exonerate David Helms for his violent behavior?

Eleanor knew that this David Helms case was one of those rare situations where the prosecution starts out on the defensive and slowly tries to gain the confidence of the jury. There was no way to hide the giant blunders that had been made in the original prosecution of Eve Wright's case.

When Eleanor gave her Opening Statement before the jury, she first tried to summarize the facts of the case; however, she was candid with the jury, telling them that mistakes had been made originally in the investigation of this case. Eleanor believed that by being honest with the jury, she could soften the attack from the Defense. She wanted the jurors to understand why these mistakes were made and how they were later rectified.

When it was the Defense's turn to make an Opening Statement, they didn't waste any time in attacking the prosecution's case. The Defense's position was that this was a simple case and the main issue was whether Eve or David had beaten the victim to death. They pointed out that their evidence would point out that Eve was the killer.

After the jurors had heard both Opening Statements, it was time for the prosecution to call their first witness. The prosecutor called the girlfriend, Eve Wright. By now she was 25 years old but gave the image of a frightened lamb. As she walked to the witness stand, she held her head down and seemed to be avoiding eye contact with anyone in the stark courtroom. It was obvious that Eve would have liked to have been anywhere in the world except testifying in front of all the unfamiliar people. Out of the corner of her eye, she could see her old boyfriend, David, sitting at the counsel table with his attorney. His piercing eyes were fixated on her, so she tried to avoid his stare.

As Eve sat uncomfortably in the witness chair, Eleanor looked directly at her and commenced with her first question. Eve tried to answer, with her faint voice barely audible to the jurors. Eleanor tried to ask Eve simple questions in order to build her confidence. As many times as Eleanor had worked with Eve to prepare her to testify, Eve reverted to acting like a person with extremely low self-esteem.

Even though Eve didn't come across as a strong witness, she did appear to be the type of person who could be easily manipulated by others, especially someone like her old boyfriend David Helms. The prosecution was able to get Eve to testify that David was the only person with Lance when she left to go to the pawnshop. Further, she described that Lance was in good health when she left. However, when she returned 20 minutes later she found Lance on the sofa and he didn't appear to be breathing.

Eleanor liked to use visual exhibits that helped the jurors understand when and where things happened. The first exhibit was a map of the various locations, showing how close they were together. She used this exhibit when asking Eve how far the pawnshop was from the apartment. The other exhibit shown to Eve was a series of photos showing the interior of their apartment. *Both these exhibits are on the next graphic page.*

Graphic Page

The purpose of this exhibit was to show the distances between the critical locations.

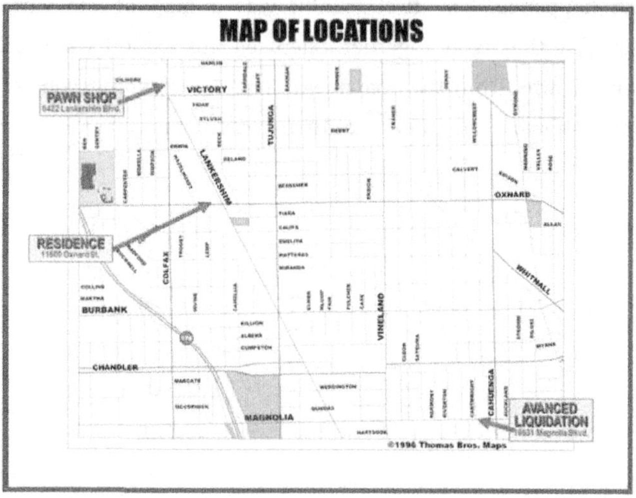

The prosecutor used this exhibit to show the jury David Helms' apartment.

After the prosecution had finished asking questions of Eve, the Defense probed her credibility and motive for testifying the way she did. What surprised Eleanor was how well Eve did in remaining calm and focused during the intense questioning. Now it was time for the prosecution to call Dr. Rizzo to the witness stand. Eleanor had been dreading this moment and felt that the Defense attorney was lying in wait ready to drop a bomb on him.

Dr. Rizzo took the witness stand and without any hesitation testified that he had made a mistake in calculating the time of death. He was frank and admitted that he had made an error based on incomplete information. He explained that he had later done considerable research and conducted a more thorough review of the injuries that Lance had suffered. He would now conclude that death would have occurred immediately. It would be like a car striking someone.

When it came to the Defense's cross-examination, the jury had already heard about the mistake, so there was no giant 'got you' moment. Surprisingly, Dr. Rizzo's testimony went as well as could be expected. Eleanor knew that she needed to corroborate Dr. Rizzo's testimony, so she called other experts who had reviewed the facts and had come to the same conclusion: that the injuries to Lance were so severe that death would have occurred within minutes.

Eleanor knew that Gail's testimony was pivotal to the case. Although Eleanor knew that Gail would like to tell the jury about her long and hard crusade to seek justice for Lance, the prosecution only needed her to explain her son's violent past. It was important to keep her on track as to how many times she saw bruises on Lance after he had spent time at his dad's. Eleanor was able to keep her focused on how Lance's happy attitude changed once he was forced to live with his father.

There was no question that Gail's testimony had emotional moments, especially when she told the jury about her diary, which listed the dates and times when she saw injuries on her grandson. The Defense wanted to paint Gail with a broad brush as a resentful relative who lost custody of a grandson. However, the Defense had to be careful, since all the photos she had taken of the bruises to Lance's face and body supported her position that Lance had been abused. The jurors had to be outraged when they saw the bruises on Lance. The Defense wanted the jurors to suspect that it was Eve who had caused those injuries.

Eleanor had a few aces up her sleeves that she dealt during the trial. She called numerous witnesses who lived in the Van Nuys apartment building where David lived. One after another told of incidents in which they saw David strike Lance on various occasions. One of the witnesses saw David hit Lance so hard that the blow knocked Lance out of his stroller and he landed on the ground. All these witnesses confirmed that it was David who was hitting and beating Lance and not the girlfriend. None of these witnesses had any axe to grind against David, so their credibility wasn't an issue that the jurors were going to have to consider.

The prosecution called one of the officers to testify to David's behavior when they questioned him as to what had happened. What was surprising to the officer was how David didn't say anything or show any emotion like one would expect if he had discovered that his girlfriend had just beaten to death his son. Although there are no scientific studies that have determined how a father would react to such a situation, undoubtedly the jurors had to wonder how strange his behavior was for one who had nothing to do with the death of his son.

Eleanor called one of the detectives to testify to statements that David had made about what Lance was doing when Eve had left to go to the pawnshop. David went on to say that he had given Lance water to drink twice after Eve had left. Eleanor coupled this with all the medical experts who indicated that no way could Lance have drunk any water after the beating. His stomach had been so severely injured that there was no way he was capable of drinking anything. In other words, David was outright lying when he tried to infer that it was Eve who had beaten Lance earlier.

Eventually, after two weeks the trial came to the end and it was time for both sides to argue the case. Eleanor had given considerable attention to how to convince the jurors that it was David and not Eve who administered the beating that killed Lance. Days earlier, Eleanor had sketched out a drawing showing that all the evidence pointed to David and not Eve. She gave the sketch to the DA's Trial Support to have them make it into a larger, poster-size visual that she used as the backdrop to her Argument. *This visual is shown on the next graphic page.*

The prosecutor sketched out this chart w2hich she wanted prepared for trial

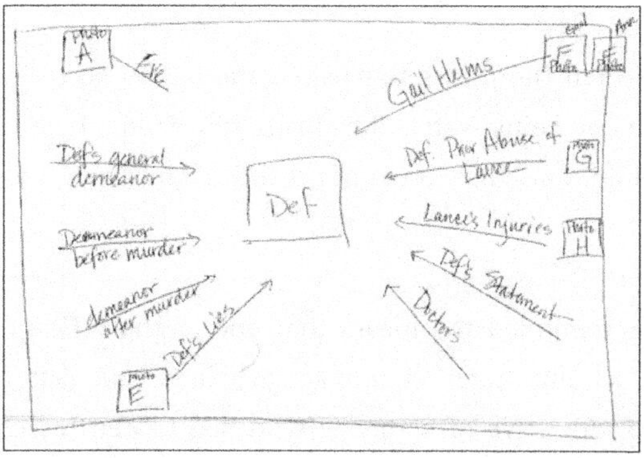

The DA's Trial Support prepared this chart that was used in Argument

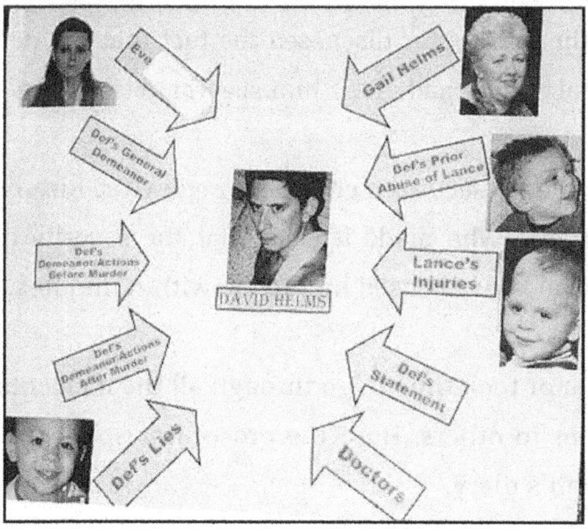

Eleanor used this large visual aid to be her notes that she used to describe all the pieces of evidence that pointed directly to the defendant, David Helms. She started with the first arrow:

Eve Wright (girlfriend)

She was able to tell the jurors that when she left to go to the pawnshop Lance was in good health and being watched by his father, David. When she returned to the apartment, she found that Lance was not breathing and David was the only person in the apartment.

Def's Demeanor After Murder

The prosecutor reminded the jurors that one of the officers indicated that the defendant didn't act like a father whose girlfriend had just killed his son. His conduct was more indicative of someone who had beaten his child and wanted to keep his mouth shut so he wouldn't appear to be a suspect.

Def's Lies

This was when the prosecutor discussed the fact that the defendant claimed that Lance seemed normal and he had given him several glasses of water to drink.

Doctors

This arrow gave the prosecutor a chance to review Dr. Rizzo's testimony and that of other medical experts who made it clear that the severity of the injuries to the victim's abdomen would have caused him to die within minutes.

Gail Helms

At this point Eleanor took time to go through all the incidents where David, Gail's son, had been violent to others. Here the prosecutor spent time going over all the incidents listed in Gail's diary.

Lance's Injuries

When Eleanor mentioned Lance's prior injuries, she pointed to photos taken by Gail that had been made a part of the big Argument chart. The jurors could graphically see that this two-year-old child had suffered at the hands of someone.

Def's Prior Abuse of Lance

When the neighbors and others testified in court that they had seen the defendant on various occasions strike Lance, this clearly pointed to David's guilt. Eleanor was able to summarize her Argument by showing how all the pieces of evidence pointed to the defendant and not to his girlfriend, Eve.

Then David's Defense attorney had his opportunity to put forth his Argument. He pointed the finger at Eve and characterized her as a chronic liar who also had a history of hitting the boy. He cited Defense experts who suggested that Lance could have lived for at least an hour after suffering the fatal blows. The Defense claimed that since there were contradictory medical opinions as to the time of death that in and of itself that constituted reasonable doubt and that they the jurors should acquit the defendant.

After both sides had argued, the judge read the final jury instructions, and the jury consisting of 10 men and two women went out to start their deliberation. Within short order the jury reached a verdict and they returned to the courtroom. To an anxious courtroom filled with news reporters, the clerk read the words that David Helms was found guilty of three counts, including second-degree murder. David seemed to be stunned by the guilty verdict and continued to stare into space.

When one of the reporters interviewed the jury foreman, he stated the following: "I think justice has been served for the first time in three years. The most emotional part of it was having to look at the pictures of Lance. That was very hard to look at . . . that little innocent face." One of the other jurors added, "There were so many mistakes . . . that boy didn't have to die."

Several weeks later, the sentencing hearing occurred, in which Gail was able to show the court a video she had created that illustrated the happier days of her grandson's short life. She told the judge, "I realize I will be losing another family member when David is sentenced, but it's the right thing to do. David has never taken responsibility for his actions. He robbed Lance of the only thing he ever wanted in this world, which was to be with the people who loved him, kept him safe, and made him laugh."

When it was time for sentencing, the judge said, "Hopefully, this is an end to this very tragic saga . . . a great tragedy. We always teach our children that life is not fair. I guess in Lance's case that was proven at a very early age." With that said, the judge gave David Helms a sentence of 21 years to life in state prison.

Shortly thereafter, a prison bus transported David to one of the state prisons. This was a case where there were no winners but only losers. As to Gail Helms, she definitely was a loser in that she lost her son and grandson. How many mothers would have the courage and fortitude to fight to have their son convicted of murder and sentenced to prison? She was a mother who recognized that maternal instincts have to give way to doing the right thing. However, when a reporter asked her how she felt seeing her son sent to state prison for murder she replied, "It's nothing to celebrate, because it's my son. All I kept thinking in court was, 'David, look what you did David.' This is finally justice for Lance."

The biggest winners of this case were hundreds of young children who will never realize that they are saved from being forced to go through the meat grinder of the Dependency Courts, whose policy was to reunite families even at the expense of the safety of the child. Gail's crusade paid off and the legislature passed a law that the Dependency Court can consider the safety and welfare of the child even if it conflicts with reunification of parent with child.

The prosecutor, Eleanor Hunter, felt that justice had finally been served, albeit it took three years. After all the hard work she had done, it had paid off; however, she seemed disappointed. When asked about the case by a reporter she stated, "It spoke volumes when the defendant didn't appear grief-stricken after his son's slaying and let the blame for the crime fall on his then 22-year-old girlfriend." Eleanor went on to say, "You always hope there will be some type of remorse or anguish and in this case the defendant showed nothing."

Eleanor may not have become as cynical as most of the veteran prosecutors in the Major Crimes Division. In trying this case, she had demonstrated the Division's 'Can-do attitude.' Eleanor had disproved the old expression, 'You can't make a silk purse out of a sow's ear,' since she had made something truly good out of something really bad. She had proved to everyone that she had earned a place with the BIG DOGS in the infamous Major Crimes Division.

PEOPLE VS. KATHLEEN SOLIAH

Symbionese Liberation Army

CHAPTER 4 SOLIAH-FACTS OF CASE

It was August 22, 1975, a typical Saturday night for two LAPD officers who were assigned to patrol duty in and around Sunset and Hollywood Boulevards. The Hollywood detail for LAPD officers wouldn't be considered a dangerous assignment involving gun violence. Their main duty was to handle the weirdos who seem to come out at night and somehow congregate in the Hollywood area.

On this night around 8:30 p.m. the radio calls had subsided and officers John Hall and James Bryan decided to take a break for dinner. Since they had been cruising along on Sunset Boulevard, they noted that they were near the IHOP restaurant. Both officers agreed that they could get a quick meal, since the tourist crowd wouldn't be frequenting a pancake house on a Saturday night. There was an open parking space near the back entrance of the restaurant, and they pulled in. The officers exited (Cop Talk— police officers never get out of a vehicle, they only **exit** a vehicle) their black-and-white.

They sat at an empty booth and gave the waitress their order. While waiting, they noticed a man constantly looking in their direction. They didn't know what to make of his behavior but they hurriedly started eating their dinner. After about fifteen minutes, the officers received a radio call over their portable radio, which they had set on the table. The dispatcher told them to respond to a certain address to check out a possible robbery.

The officers took one more quick bite of their meals and took one last gulp from their half-full glasses of coke. They didn't have time to ask for a bowser bag but merely put down the money for their meals. Rushing out of the back door of the IHOP, they hurriedly climbed into their police unit. Officer Bryan was the driver, and he took the steering wheel and abruptly yanked it all the way to the right as he backed out of the parking space. This allowed them to speed out of the parking lot and headed to the place listed in the radio call.

To the officers' surprise, there were no people at the address that was given as the site of the robbery. In short order, the officers were able to assess the situation and determine that no robbery had occurred. They felt a great relief that they weren't going to have to chase some robber through the streets and byways of Hollywood. As the officers' adrenaline fell back to normal, the dispatcher started asking a number of questions about where they had gone for dinner and what they were doing there. Initially, the officers felt they were being interrogated by the dispatcher. They wondered what they might have done wrong. Maybe they didn't tip the waitress enough, or was someone in the restaurant parking lot complaining how abruptly they pulled out of the parking space?

The next thing they knew was that they were told to report to the Hollywood Station for a debriefing as to a pipe bomb found in the IHOP parking lot. Soon they became aware that they were now considered victims of an attempted car bombing. They learned that a person walking through the restaurant parking lot discovered a large 3-inch pipe bomb where their police car had been parked.

Shortly thereafter, the bomb squad was called to the scene and they deactivated the pipe bomb. The experts, in examining the bomb, discovered that it was filled with a large amount of powder and hundreds of tiny, sharp nails. With that amount of gunpowder, if the bomb had detonated, the officers' police car would have been blown to pieces. The bomb had been placed directly under where the officers were seated. The officers' bodies would have been riddled with the nail projectiles and they would have met a painful and tragic death.

The LAPD had been keenly aware of the pipe bombs that had been detonated at police stations in the San Francisco Bay Area. When this bomb was discovered to have been planted under one of their LAPD police cars, the entire police department went on tactical alert. The LAPD administration put out an immediate order for all LAPD police cars to be checked out to make sure there were no other bombs that had been planted.

All the dispatchers urgently radioed all the LAPD officers to look under all police vehicles for anything that might look suspicious. Within a short time, one of the LAPD civilian employees working at the Hollenbeck Division in East LA grabbed a flashlight and started inspecting the police vehicles parked in the station's parking lot. Nothing suspicious was located. The personnel thought that maybe the administration was overreacting. What was the likelihood that more than one bomb had been placed under a police car? In order to examine the undercarriage of the police vehicles, the employees had to get on their hands and knees and shine their flashlight all the way under the front and back of the police cars.

There was a detective car parked down the street next to the police station. The various police personnel looked at each, wondering if it was necessary to check out that vehicle. The car was a 'Plain Jane' detective unit. It certainly wouldn't have been mistaken as a black-and-white unit. One of the employees said he would walk down the street and look under it just to be extra cautious.

The staff member went to the driver's side and leaned down in the dirty street and directed his flashlight beam to the pavement below the front seat. The beam of light reflected back from what appeared to be a large red camping light battery attached to a long silver object. With his head leaning down sideways it was hard to see what it was. His initial reaction was to take the flashlight and somehow move the item into a better position to see it. However, the item seemed too far to reach. He moved his head further under the car to get a better look. This time his eyeballs focused on the silver object, and now he could clearly see that it was 3-inch piece of pipe. He froze in his tracks as he noticed that there were wires connecting the camping battery to the large capped pipe.

He became transfixed on this item that he had seconds before been trying to move with his flashlight. Now he didn't want to make any type of move that might detonate this pipe bomb. Gradually, he slid himself from out under the detective car and immediately notified the watch commander as to what he had found. Within minutes, a Bomb Squad team converged on Hollenbeck Division.

It took considerable time to remove the bomb, since it was connected to the detective car and if they moved the car it would have exploded. When it was made safe, the bomb experts indicated if the LAPD person had hit it with his flashlight the device would have blown him to pieces.

The bottom line for LAPD was that the night of August 22, 1975, was a lucky day for the department. Literally and figuratively, their officers had dodged the proverbial bullet. In this case, the bullet was a massive 3-inch bomb packed with nails that could have killed anyone within a half a block. The next question was, Who did this and could they be caught before causing so much possible harm? It would take 30 years before that question could be answered.

In June of 1999, the Major Crimes Division was enjoying a lull in litigation, since the summer vacation season had started. This was the time when judges scheduled their vacations, and this meant less publicity cases were set for trial. The Major Crimes deputies knew this was the time of the year to take advantage of the slowdown in the courts' calendars. Many of the prosecutors planned their vacations to correspond with the judges' time off. In other words, the stress level in the Major Crimes Division was noticeably reduced since there was less 'barking of orders' to the lowly law clerks. Most of the year, the elite prosecutors in the Major Crimes Division are having the law clerks run around doing legal research. When the prosecutors are in trial they are unusually high-strung, and the tension in this Division can reach a fever pitch.

One day out of the blue the DA's Office received a phone call from LAPD with the news that one of the SLA members had been arrested somewhere in the Midwest. No one in Major Crimes seemed to get excited with this new information. The first reaction was, "What the hell is the SLA?" Most of the Major Crimes deputies were under ten years of age when the SLA was a household name. In 1975, these prosecutors were humming along with Glen Campbell's *Rhinestone Cowboy* for the guys and gals were mesmerized by Captain & Tennille's *Love Will Keep Us Together.* Everyone can admit that was a long time ago.

One of the LAPD detectives was nice enough to go down 'Memory Lane' to explain that the letters 'SLA' meant 'Symbionese Liberation Army,' and that it was an urban terrorist group from 1973 to 1975 that operated in the San Francisco Bay area. The group's 'claim to fame' was the kidnapping of Patty Hearst, as well as the infamous Los Angeles SLA shootout. That latter involved the LAPD SWAT team surrounding a house in South Central LA containing a bunch of radicals who refused to come out. The entire group ended up burned to death. What made it so noteworthy was that it was broadcast live on television, thereby being seen by practically everyone in the country.

However, none of those events were part of the charges in this case the LAPD detective was calling about. The detective patiently explained this case involved the

SLA members placing powerful 3-inch-diameter pipe bombs, filled with nails, underneath LAPD police cars on August 22, 1975. As a result, the DA's Office years ago obtained a Grand Jury indictment against Kathleen Soliah, along with fellow SLA co-conspirators James Kilgore and Bill Harris for attempted murder of LAPD officers and personnel. The two men were convicted of the charges; however, Kathleen Soliah wasn't apprehended, since she seemed to have disappeared into thin air.

In 1999, a TV program was aired about the 25th anniversary of the SLA activities, and the program mentioned that several of the members were still fugitives from justice. A photo was shown of the fugitive Kathleen Soliah circa 1975. The likelihood of any one recognizing her was remote to none, since people's appearances change drastically over 25 years. What were the odds that a person in Minnesota would be able to make a connection? Most fugitives will have plastic surgery or at least in some way change their appearance in order not to be identified.

Ironically, this TV program did create a viable tip that Kathleen Soliah might be living in the St. Paul area. It must have been a slow day for law enforcement, since the local police immediately decided to follow up on the tip. They tracked down the woman who had been tentatively described as being Kathleen Soliah. The police devised a plan to have a traffic officer pull the woman over for a traffic violation when she left her house. On June 21, 1999, a woman drove away from the suspected house and a patrol officer made a typical traffic stop. The officer asked her for identification and she handed him identification in the name of Sara Jane Olson. The officer asked her if she was Kathleen Ann Soliah, which she adamantly denied. That was a pivotal moment for law enforcement. Should they take her word or check her out? Fortunately, the police decided to transport her to the station and roll her prints to determine if she was telling the truth. If they were wrong, this could escalate into a major embarrassment for the police department if this person was a law-abiding pillar of the community.

Although this woman had a slight resemblance to the old photo of Kathleen Soliah, she definitely didn't fit the mold of a wide-eyed radical that wanted to destroy the Establishment. This woman personified the Establishment, in that she was a mother of three daughters and married to a prominent emergency room doctor. The police quickly learned that this woman was very active in the community and even performed as an actress in various local stage productions.

Thankfully, the police stuck their neck out, because it resulted in the culmination of one of the longest manhunts for a fugitive. When the police compared Sara Jane Olson's fingerprints to those of Kathleen Ann Soliah, it was a PERFECT MATCH. She was immediately arrested on the California Arrest Warrant. In short order, she was extradited to Los Angeles, and this is how the case ended up in the Los Angeles DA's Office, Major Crimes Division.

CHAPTER 5 SOLIAH-SLA ACTIVITIES

Even before Soliah made her first appearance in one of the Los Angeles Superior Courts, the news media seemed to be delighted over this intriguing story of a woman fugitive. For some reason, the public has always had a fascination regarding fugitives on the run. This may be a result of the old TV ***Fugitive*** series starring David Janssen, who was on the run for a crime he didn't commit. Then, in1984, a movie version of the ***Fugitive*** starring Harrison Ford was a huge hit. Somehow, the public likes to romanticize anyone who is running from the law.

This is particularly true for women fugitives. An example was how the media idealized Bonnie Parker in the dynamic duo of 'Bonnie and Clyde.' In reality, Bonnie was a despicable character although the newspapers of that time painted her as a poor damsel being persecuted by greedy bank barons.

In the Sara Jane Olson case, the news media interviewed her neighbors and associates in Minnesota, who praised her as an exemplary member of their community. The news slant was that law enforcement had the wrong person and it was just a matter of time before this mistake would be rectified. When the FBI made it clear that the fingerprints were a solid match, the media took another slant. At that point the story changed to emphasize that she had lived a model life, therefore what she had done 25 years earlier should be overlooked or forgiven. In other words, her 20-plus years of living a good life should be able to erase a mistake she may have made when she was an adolescent and a wide-eyed do-gooder.

When Kathleen Soliah arrived in Los Angeles, it was as though she was riding a wave of popularity. However, her arrival could best be described as a giant tsunami suddenly striking Los Angeles. The DA's Office recognized that the Soliah case was going to be a big controversial case that would create a great deal of attention. The stinging loss in the O.J. Simpson case had created a degree of paranoia within the Los Angeles DA's Office. As a result of that loss, the Office had implemented many changes to prevent a reoccurrence of such a disaster. However, the Office recognized that this new publicity case had to be prosecuted in such a way that there would be only a positive outcome.

That was when the DA's Office realized that they needed to assign prosecutors to the case who could navigate the stormy headwinds that accompanied the Soliah case. Eleanor Hunter and Michael Latin were both well-respected prosecutors in the Major Crimes Division. What was most noticeable about this prosecution team was their appearance in court. Eleanor Hunter was tall and Michael would best be described as shorter. At first, there was a comparison to 'Mutt and Jeff,' but that soon faded away as these prosecutors went to work on the case.

When Eleanor Hunter walked into a courtroom, she created a stir. What catches everyone's attention is her imposing presence. Being tall and thin with honey-blond hair sets her apart from most other attorneys. Her radiant smile could be misinterpreted by those who met her as one of a naïve woman to be taken advantage of. At first, Eleanor may give the illusion of being Nicole Kidman dressed up as an attorney, but she is a woman with a mission.

Eleanor's disarming pleasantness doesn't reveal her true nature. It is only a thin veneer covering a heart that is tough as nails. As she moves through the swing doors of the courtroom, she exudes confidence and shows no hesitation to do battle. Her attire is formal but stylish, giving the impression that she had merely stepped out of one of the L.A. Laws top law firms. Her high heels allow her to tower over her opposing counsel, who has to tilt his or her head back when talking to her. She seems to relish the fact that her opponent is forced to look up to her.

Being in control of the courtroom and what is going on around her is nothing new for Eleanor Hunter. When she started out in the DA's Office, she was willing to try any and all cases, even those that had 'Reasonable Doubt' spelled out all over them. Nothing frightened her, or at least she didn't let others know the trepidation she might truly feel. Each trial she took on was a learning experience. Whether it was a gang case or a domestic violence situation, she took on the challenges of those cases, giving them her all. In the process, she gained a reputation for being able to win the unwinnable cases. This impressed her supervisors as well as the police investigators, who started to believe that she was a reincarnation of Wonder Woman (played by Linda Carter), who seemed able to do the impossible.

During her early career, Eleanor was churning out and winning cases in the Torrance Courthouse, far from the Los Angeles DA's Office downtown headquarters. For several years, she went unnoticed by the head administrators. Then one of her cases was transferred to the downtown Criminal Courts Building and she needed office space to use while trying the case. I, the author, at that time was in charge of the Prosecution Support Division which included the Statistics Unit. My DA statistician had a large office next to the top administrators' offices. I permitted Eleanor to utilize space in my Statistics Unit while she was trying the Torrance case downtown.

The end result was that she became very familiar with my statisticians, which led to them getting married. However, what was most important for her legal career was that the top administrators noticed her as a very capable upstart. After a long trial, she won this problematic publicity case and the downtown administrators were impressed. From that moment on, her career was on the Fast Track, and eventually when the Major Crimes Division had an opening for a hard charging prosecutor, she got the nod.

She settled into Major Crimes Division and earned her stripes by taking on several difficult cases, only to 'bring home the bacon' by solid convictions. Eleanor was a rising star who had proven that she was ready for 'Primetime.' The other prosecutor assigned to the Soliah case was Michael Latin, who was a steady, heavy hitter in Major Crimes.

Although Michael Latin would certainly be described as short in stature, he hadn't been shorted in the intellectual department. Anyone who encountered Michael in court would be awestruck by the intensity he exhibited in prosecuting his cases. He was always dead serious and never cracked a smile. When he addressed the court, the words he used were concise, as though he were reading from a written brief. He didn't waste time using words that didn't precisely describe the legal concept he was explaining.

Whenever he spoke, he would focus on the person he was addressing and totally look them in the eyes. He believed in what he was saying and conveyed his belief in the truth of his position. He projected the image of being prepared for battle on every single issue of the case. There was no misunderstanding whose side he was on. No matter what was thrown at him he never vacillated in his resolve. He wrapped himself in righteous indignation and he always stood with the guys wearing the 'White Hats.'

Some might have looked upon Eleanor and Michael as a strange dynamic duo. Both definitely were Type A- personalities who wanted to be the leader of the pack. How could such strong personalities work side by side without an implosion when they differed in approaches? Neither attorney was accustomed to being the second fiddle. Both wanted to be out front leading the attack. The DA Administrators were rolling the dice in hopes that Eleanor and Michael would be sharp enough to recognize that they had come together as a team. Could they contain their strong egos in order to build a compelling case against this defendant, who by then had become a popular radical icon that the news media and some groups had elevated to sainthood status?

As the song goes, this wasn't the 'first rodeo' for either Eleanor or Michael. They recognized that they had to work together even when they might disagree. At first, they both were entirely consumed by the fact that they had been assigned to a high-publicity case which they knew little about. They contacted the LAPD detectives on the Soliah case and arranged a time when they all could get together. In short order, they were hunkered down at a table in the DA's Office asking the detectives all sorts of questions. The attorneys were more interested in hearing about witnesses who were still alive and what physical incriminating evidence could be still located. However, the detectives were more interested in stressing the fact that this could have been a murder case except for the distance of 1/16th of an inch. For the entire police department, this was a case in which extremists had targeted their police officers for the mere fact that they represented the so-called 'Establishment.' The detectives were more than convinced of the evil intentions of these SLA members, especially Kathleen Soliah. In the detectives' minds she was guilty of attempted murder not merely beyond a reasonable doubt but they honestly felt she was guilty beyond any possible doubt.

These prosecutors had tried their share of difficult cases and they knew that jurors always want more evidence in order to convict, especially in a publicity case. No matter how they approached this Soliah case, they recognized that there was no witness who personally saw Kathleen Soliah in Los Angeles planting the bombs under the police cars. There was no smoking gun.

Michael and Eleanor continued to have countless sit-down meetings with the detectives and tried to find evidence that the prosecutors could use in court to prove Soliah's involvement. The best that the detectives came up with was that Patty Hearst could testify that several days later Soliah had told her how she and the other two members drove to LA and placed the bombs under the LAPD police cars. The prosecutors both told the detectives that Miss Hearst's testimony was fraught with problems. For one thing, she would be testifying after she had been convicted of committing the Hibernia Bank Robbery. The jury would be instructed by the judge that the testimony of a felon could be questioned. Secondly, she could be considered as a co-conspirator, which meant that her testimony had to be corroborated by other witnesses or evidence.

After extensive discussions, Eleanor and Michael decided that the only way that Kathleen Soliah could be successfully prosecuted was if the prosecution could present to the jury the **complete picture of the SLA, its purpose, its activities, and its members**. At that point, the two prosecutors had a game plan to transform an exceedingly weak case into a strong one. However, what had to be done was first to get law enforcement on board to be willing to do all the heavy lifting that was needed. The prosecutors would then have to convince a judge to be willing to allow them the opportunity to present extensive evidence about the SLA and its members in the actual trial. The big issue was to convince the judge that the history and background of the SLA was RELEVANT EVIDENCE. *A graphic was prepared to make it easier to understand the organization of the SLA since the membership changed over time. The illustration is on the next graphic page.*

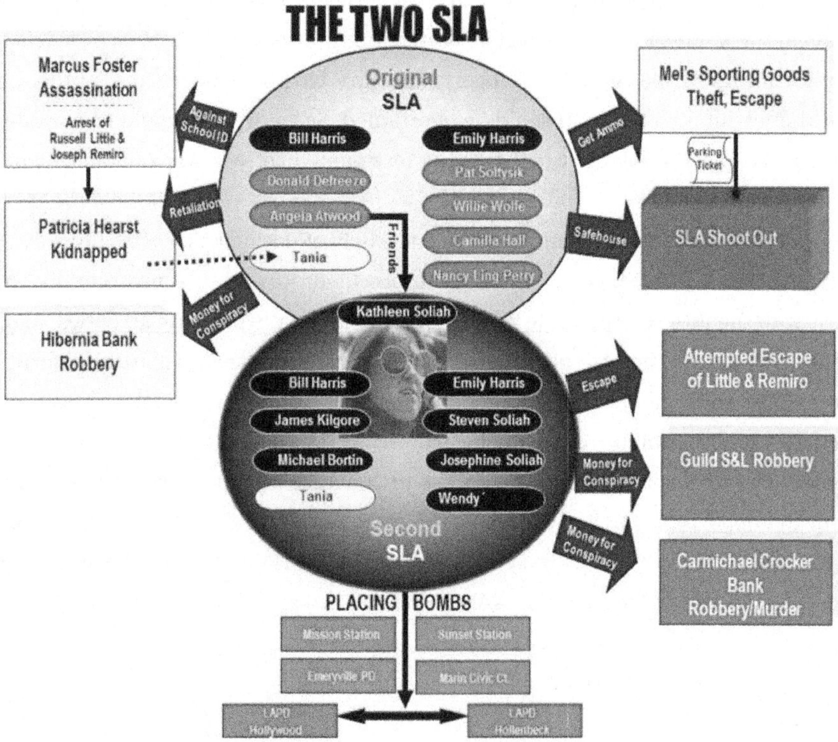

Chart showing how the original group overlapped with 2nd group.

CHAPTER 6 SOLIAH- EARLY SLA HISTORY

Eleanor and Michael had to distill thousands of pages of reports about the SLA into a package that the jurors would be able to comprehend. They reviewed everything they could get their hands on and weighed whether that should be made a part of the background material for the jurors.

The SLA organization was active between 1973 to 1975, and its role was to wage Guerrilla Warfare against the fascist Establishment. The group had prepared a Declaration of War stating:

"The purpose was to Mobilize the people in order to reach the state of people's war, we must first engage in urban guerrilla warfare."

"The strategy of the Symbionese Liberation Army is to carry out urban guerrilla warfare in the U.S.A. as a mobilization state leading to all out revolutionary war and the total annihilation of the capitalist ruling class . . ."

The leader of the SLA was Donald Defreeze, who went by the name 'Cinque.' Even though the SLA became a well-known group, it was never very large in size, only consisting of some 18 to 20 members. The original members were as follows:

Donald Defreeze

William Harris

Emily Harris

Angela Atwood

Nancy Ling Perry

William Wolfe

Camilla Hall

Patricia Soltysik

The SLA didn't want to just talk about revolution but wanted to actively carry out the attack on the Establishment. On Election Day, November 6, 1973, Dr. Marcus Foster, Superintendent of Oakland Schools, and his Assistant Superintendent, Robert

Blackburn, were walking together from their offices at the Board of Education building in Oakland to Mr. Blackburn's car in the parking lot. Mr. Blackburn went to unlock the passenger side door for Dr. Foster when he was shot in the back by a shotgun. The attackers then shot Dr. Foster eight times. Each of the shotgun shells was dipped in cyanide to make it extra deadly. The fatal shot punctured Dr. Foster's heart. Mr. Blackburn miraculously survived the attack.

It was important to the SLA that they receive the publicity and credit for this malicious act. In order to assure that they received the recognition for the killing, they issued a public announcement which they called a 'Communique.' These Communiques were delivered to designated spots near news or radio stations. Anonymous callers informed the news outlet where they could find a message at a designated location. These tapes were then played on the radio and television so the entire country would be aware of their accomplishments.

Their first communique was titled "WARRANT ORDER: Execution by Cyanide Bullets" and stated the following:

"This attack is also to serve notice on the Board of Education and its Fascist supporters that the court of the People have issued a Death Warrant on all members and supporters of the internal warfare identification computer system. This "SHOOT ON SIGHT" order will stay in effect until such time as all political police are removed from our school and all photo and other forms of identification are stopped."

The SLA clearly was more militant than other radical groups, who used peaceful demonstrations and protest to bring about social change. The SLA was made up of a small group of self-described revolutionaries who had joined together with the common purpose of effecting change by terrorizing, kidnapping, and even murdering innocent people based on their employment, socioeconomic status, or political positions. The murder of Dr. Foster was a defining event for the SLA. With that action, and the issuance of their communique, they in essence declared revolutionary war upon the government and the so-called 'enemy, the rich ruling class.' They believed that the assassination was the beginning of guerilla warfare to achieve change. They believed that true change could only occur through violent means. The SLA clearly departed from the more common non-violent methods used by other radical groups.

It wasn't until January 2, 1974, that two of their members, Rogers Little and Joseph Remiro, were arrested for their participation in Dr. Foster's assassination. During a traffic stop, they engaged in a shootout with police and ultimately they were taken into custody. The SLA viewed their arrests not as the apprehension of murder suspects but as the government taking of Political Prisoners. As a result, the SLA decided to respond by taking a prisoner from the 'rich ruling class.' That was when the SLA decided to kidnap Patricia Hearst, daughter of Randolph Hearst, whom they had labeled as a corporate enemy of the people.

One month after their cohorts had been arrested, three members of the SLA carefully executed the violent kidnapping of nineteen-year-old Patty Hearst from her Berkeley apartment, which she shared with her boyfriend, Steven Weed. It was carried out by Donald Defreeze and Bill Harris with the help of Angela Atwood, who knocked on the apartment door asking to use their telephone. When the door was opened the three SLA members forced their way inside, where they tied, bound, gagged, and beat Hearst. Also, during this incident Hearst's boyfriend was severely beaten. Afterwards, the kidnappers carried her out and loaded her into the trunk of their car. While trying to get away, the members shot at the concerned neighbors who had heard the noise of the attack. The kidnappers drove Hearst to a safehouse in Daly City (located south of San Francisco) where she was held captive and locked up in small closet for 47 days.

The SLA tried to coordinate an exchange of Patty Hearst for their members who were in custody for the murder of Dr. Foster. Over many weeks of negotiations, there was no swapping of parties, although the Hearst family was forced to give food to the poor in the Bay area. When it was clear that their kidnap victim was not going to be released, they decided to indoctrinate her into their cause. Within weeks, they had convinced the young impressionable Patty Hearst that her wealthy family was part of the problem causing poverty in society. Eventually she became convinced of the merits of their cause, and she herself became one of the revolutionary SLA members.

In order to acquire funds to support the SLA and the mission of their organization, they decided to commit several bank robberies. Their first target was the Hibernia Bank in San Francisco, in which Patricia Hearst, their newly recruited member, was one of the full-fledged robbers. The bank surveillance cameras captured the images of Hearst, now called "Tania," dressed as an SLA soldier holding an automatic weapon.

The Hibernia Bank robbery was highly successful for the SLA. First, the robbery was lucrative in that they came away with a substantial amount of cash for their radical efforts. The vivid images from the bank surveillance cameras showed how easily they had pulled off such a brazen robbery. With the massive media coverage of the robbery, the establishment was going to have to take the group's demands more seriously.

The SLA felt greatly empowered by the easy success of the bank robbery. As a result, they were proud of their crime. Even though these bank robbers shot two innocent bystanders during the robbery, there was no remorse for those injured. In a Communique, the SLA explained the necessity of shooting the civilians as follows:

Subject One, male. Subject was ordered to lay on the floor face down. Subject refused the order and jumped out the front door of the bank. Therefore, the subject was shot.

Subject Two, male. Subject failed or did not hear warning to clear the street. Subject was running down the street toward the bank and combat forces accordingly assumed subject was an armed enemy force element. Therefore the subject was shot.

The SLA group truly believed the end justifies the means. They believed that everyone has a choice either to join and support their cause or become their enemy.

However, the bank surveillance photos were of amazingly good quality, which made those SLA robbers highly recognizable by the public in the San Francisco area. For that reason, the SLA decided to move their base of operation from the Bay area to Los Angeles, where they would be less likely to be identified. The SLA members divided into groups of three.

By May, the group was in Los Angeles moving from one safehouse to another. Then on May16, 1974, fate would forever change the SLA as an urban terrorist organization. Bill and Emily Harris went into Mel's Sporting Goods store in Inglewood, California, possibly to purchase some ammunition. While looking at the merchandise in the store, they noticed some wool socks on sale. After inspecting the socks, Bill and Emily looked at each other and nodded their approval to steal them. The socks weren't expensive, and they certainly had sufficient funds to purchase them. Both Bill and Emily hid the socks from view and proceeded past the check stand, headed for the front door of the store.

The security personnel inside Mel's Sporting Goods had fixated on the husband-wife duo because of their suspicious actions. One of the security guards notified another guard, and they converged on Bill and Emily by blocking them from leaving the store. At that moment in time, four individuals were confronted with a situation that changed many lives forever. The security guards had to think that this was a pathetic attempt to steal items from the sports store. In the guards' minds this feeble attempt to steal wool socks would be over in a few minutes, after they retrieved the socks and obtained some form of identification from both thieves.

However, Bill and Emily Harris were petrified and knew that they couldn't show any ID without compromising the safety of the SLA group, which had decided to hide in the Los Angeles area. Complete and utter desperation filled the Harris's minds as to what to do. They knew that they couldn't be taken into custody. To them, the only option was trying to escape the store. The security guards attempted to restrain them, which resulted in a noisy pushing and shoving between Billy and Emily and the guards.

This entire ruckus inside the store came to the attention of Patty Hearst, who was outside sitting in a parked VW van. Only three months before, she was attending the University of California in Berkeley when she was kidnapped from her apartment by members of the SLA. During this time, she was locked in a small closet for 47 days, which ultimately converted her to their way of thinking. The old Patty Hearst was now named Tania, who was faced with a critical decision. Should she drive off in the VW van, leaving her new friends Bill and Emily Harris stranded? Or should she attempt to help them by coming to their aid? For some unknown reason, she grabbed a shotgun that was concealed in the van and started firing rounds into the Mel's Sporting Goods store. Needless to say, this more than surprised the security guards, who turned their attention from taking the shoplifters into custody to seeking cover from the shotgun blasts blowing out the store's front windows.

The Harries had to feel that their trust in Tania was well placed, because this distraction was all they needed to run out of the store and jump in the van, and they sped away. As much as the three terrorists would have liked to 'high five' each other, they knew their immediate problem was to get rid of the VW van. They knew in short order that law enforcement would figure out that the SLA group had resettled in Los

Angeles. They notified the other SLA members that they needed to relocate to another safehouse.

By the next day, May 17, 1974, the other SLA members had quickly moved to a small house at 1466 East 54th Street, in South Central Los Angeles. Since the security guards could identify the Harrises, it was decided that they, with Tania, would travel to Orange County to find a separate place to stay. That evening, the Harrises and Tania were comfortably staying in a motel near Disneyland. They felt secure as they sat around in the motel room eating some take-out food and watching TV. Suddenly the TV was filled with images of a live shoot-out taking place in South Central LA involving the LAPD. The TV news anchor announced that the people in the wood frame house were members of the notorious Symbionese Liberation Army.

For hours, the TV camera focused on the small house as shots could be seen fired from inside. In the background, the police used a bull horn to notify the occupants of the house to come out. As time passed, no one came out of the house, and the police had the area completely surrounded by SWAT sharpshooters. After several hours, it was becoming darker and the police had made over 18 requests for the parties to come out. When there was no response, the police shot several teargas canisters into the house in hopes of forcing the occupants to exit the house.

The only thing coming out of the house were some of the teargas canisters being tossed back by the SLA members. However, the police were able to lob in more canisters than the members could toss out. Then there was a change in the situation. In several rooms, the curtains and furniture inside were starting to ignite. Since the old house was built of wood, within minutes the interior of the house was totally consumed with fire.

When the police realized that the teargas may have triggered the fire, they stopped the shooting of the teargas. At the same time, the firefighters approached in order to attempt to extinguish the flames. When the fire trucks were in front of the house, a volley of shots were fired at the firefighters. Immediately, the fire equipment was pulled back out of range of the gunfire.

It only took minutes for the entire house to become an inferno. The police held their fire in hopes that the members would flee the blaze to save their lives. As millions watched on live television, the SLA safehouse burned to the ground. By the next morning when it was light, the police and coroner recovered six bodies. Several of the bodies were retrieved from the crawl space under the floor of the house.

Eventually, it was determined that the bodies were of the SLA leader Donald Defreeze, William Wolfe, Nancy Ling Perry, Camilla Hall, Patricia Soltysik, and finally, **Angela Atwood**. The Harrises and Patty Hearst were shocked and horrified to see their comrades being killed before their eyes.

However, the person who was most affected by this shoot-out was Kathleen Soliah, who had become a close friend to Angela Atwood. Kathleen was so moved by this tragic loss of her companion that this changed her life forever. From that point on, she would avenge the untimely death of her good friend Angela Atwood.

CHAPTER 7 SOLIAH - SHE JOINS SLA

After the shoot-out, Kathleen Soliah's life would forever be linked to the violent radical SLA group. The unexplainable question always had been, how could a young Midwestern girl end up involved in one of the most violent urban terrorist groups? Her life started on January 16, 1947, when she was born in Fargo, North Dakota, a place not known as a hotbed for wild-eyed hippies trying to save the world. When one hears the word 'FARGO' one conjures up in one's mind the 1996 movie by that name, in which a pregnant police chief tried to solve a bizarre homicide case. What made the killing so graphic was the fact that one of the victims ended up being fed through a wood chipper. In other words, the city of Fargo gives most people the chills and most people born there can't wait to escape from the forlorn town.

That is exactly what the Soliah family did in that they moved to neighboring Minnesota. By the late 1950s, the family had had enough of the frigid weather and headed for the scorching hot Mojave Desert, settling down in Palmdale, California. There her Norwegian father accepted a job as a teacher and coach at the local high school. Kathleen blended into this desert community and grew up as an ardent Beatles fan. Besides excelling academically in her classes, she was active in sports and did well on the track team. In high school, she became the captain of the Cheerleading Squad and starred in one of the school's theatrical productions.

In 1965, she graduated from high school, earning the Spirit and Service Award. At that time in her life, she made a prediction about her future. Kathleen stated, "I'm going to be a famous actress and everyone will know me." Interesting how accurate her prediction was, in that by the year 2000 her name was well known to anyone who read the newspapers or watched TV news. She at that time had become the nation's most wanted fugitive.

Everyone wondered how the wholesome Kathleen Soliah crossed over to the radical world of urban terrorists. Most believe it occurred when Kathleen attended Antelope Valley College. There she fell under the spell of a young philosophy teacher who introduced her to more-radical views. She developed a romantic involvement with him and became hooked on his Marxist teachings.

After two years of exploring more critical thought-provoking views, she moved on to the University of California at Santa Barbara, where she majored in theater arts. Her views of the Establishment were molded by the times of the late 1960s, which were dominated by the tension caused by the Vietnam War. After graduation, all males were faced with the fact that they could be drafted into military service, where they most likely would end up being listed in the weekly Vietnam War body count. In 1970, there were a series of war demonstrations in which the police clashed with the student protestors. Kathleen was greatly influenced by the violent clashes, in which she identified with her college friends who opposed the war effort.

During this turbulent time, she was living with her boyfriend, Jim Kilgore, in the Isla Vista community next to the University. After receiving a degree in English, she and her boyfriend headed to Northern California. Eventually they settled down in Berkeley, California, which was the home of the Free Speech movement and a hotbed for radical groups. Kathleen mingled in easily with the fervent crowd. Then in September of 1972, she auditioned for an acting part in the production of Henrik Ibsen's ***Hedda Gabler***. It was a play about a strong-willed woman, and Kathleen won the leading role. During the production of this play, Kathleen came into contact with **Angela Atwood**, who was the other leading lady in the play.

The two of them became inseparable friends and remained in contact with each other. Shortly thereafter, Angela became one of the founding members of a group known as the Symbionese Liberation Army (SLA). As a result, Kathleen became acquainted with the various members of this group and grew familiar with their cause. However, Kathleen didn't become involved in group activities as did her friend Angela.

It wasn't until months later that Kathleen's views about the revolutionary group changed. The tragic death of Angela Atwood seemed to ignite a fire within her. Only two weeks after Angela's death, Kathleen delivered an impassioned eulogy for her in

Ho Chi Minh Park in Berkeley. She exhorted the SLA to continue its fight. She said, "I am with you."

Shortly thereafter, SLA member Emily Harris contacted Kathleen and recruited her and her boyfriend Jim Kilgore to join a new SLA group. After the fateful SLA shoot-out in Los Angeles, the SLA organization had been decimated. At that point, it consisted of Bill Harris (Tero) as the new leader, with his wife Emily and Tania (Patty Hearst) as the only existing members. When Kathleen joined, she brought with her, as new SLA members, her brother, Steven Soliah, and her boyfriend Jim Kilgore, as well as Michael Bortin and Wendy Yee.

The members of this newly constituted SLA realized law enforcement was looking for them in the Bay area. In order not to be captured, the group left the San Francisco area during the summer of 1974. It wasn't until October that the members reassembled as a new group, this time in Sacramento. Their first order of business was to devise a plan for the escape of their fellow comrades Little and Remiro. These assassins had requested a change of venue and won this motion. As a result, the case was transferred from Oakland to Sacramento. Kathleen Soliah was the contact person to set up the escape. The plan was to rescue Little and Remiro as they were being transported to the Sacramento courthouse.

However, after extensive planning and practice, the group decided that it was too risky, and they abandoned any further rescue attempts. The next effort of their activities was finding ways to fund the activities of the SLA. It was agreed that committing bank robberies would be the fastest and easiest way to gain the resources they needed to buy firearms and explosives that they needed for their revolution.

On February 25, 1975, they committed the robbery of the Guild Savings and Loan in Sacramento. Kathleen's role was to be a lookout and arrange for the getaway car, which was to be later picked up by a tow company. Although the robbery could be declared a success, it only netted $3,000. The group immediately started working on plans to rob another bank. These plans were more sophisticated, with attention paid to the details, including the employees' shift patterns, the layout of the bank, escape routes, descriptions of the employees, traffic patterns, and the response times of the local police.

The next bank they selected for a heist was in Carmichael, a suburb just outside of Sacramento. This time Kathleen's role was to steal identification from a patron of a local health club. Then Kathleen used the stolen identification to rent one of the getaway cars. They used a total of four cars to carry out the robbery. On April 21, 1975, at 9:00 a.m. they converged on the Crocker National Bank in Carmichael. The members who entered the bank were Kathleen Soliah, James Kilgore, Emily Harris, and Michael Bortin. As these members went into the bank, they pulled down ski masks to cover their faces.

Inside the bank, Myrna Opsahl, a doctor's wife and mother of four children, was in the process of depositing the collection money from her church's service. Then Mrs. Opsahl, the bank employees, and other customers were ordered by the four masked robbers to lie on the floor. Emily Harris, who appeared to be in charge, ordered the customers to hurry up and comply with the robber's requests. Emily used her sawed-off 12-gauge shotgun to nudge the customers to lie on the floor. Then there was a loud blast from the shotgun. This round entered Mrs. Opsahl's abdomen at close range and she sank to the floor. At that time, Kathleen, armed with a Browning 9mm semi-automatic handgun, along with the other robbers, began collecting cash from the bank tellers' drawers. Kathleen didn't assist the fallen victim, but as she collected the bank money she kicked a compliant teller who was pregnant, which later caused the teller to go into premature labor.

Emily Harris, who appeared to be the kingpin of the group, yelled out instructions to the bank robbers and continually counted down the amount of time before they had to leave. After the money was collected, Emily ordered the other robbers to exit the bank as they ran to a stolen Firebird vehicle for their escape. As they sped away, Patty Hearst followed in a seperate van. Several blocks away, the Firebird was abandoned. All the robbers jumped into the van driven by Hearst.

As they drove away, there was a conversation among the robbers as to a shooting incident. Hearst asked who did the shooting, and at that point Emily Harris replied, "I did." Later in the day, when all the women were present, Emily Harris said that she had heard that the woman who was shot had died. Her remark was, "Oh well. She (Mrs. Opsahl) was a bourgeois pig anyway. Her husband is a doctor." Eventually, everyone returned to their safehouses in Sacramento. The money was counted, and this time they netted $15,000.

The shooting made the group consider whether it was safe for them to remain in Sacramento. After further reflection, it was agreed that it would be better for them to return to the San Francisco area. They purchased an old 1967 Ford Galaxy for $400 and packed up their belongings and headed for the Bay area. There they rented three new safehouses. They took their newly acquired proceeds from the bank robbery and purchased additional firearms and accumulated the parts to build high-powered pipe bombs.

Between August 7th through 22nd , 1975, the group planned and carried out five attacks using explosives at selected police and civic center offices in the Bay area. One was planted near the Mission Police Station and the other at the Sunset (Taraval) Police Station. However, neither bomb detonated. Six days later they tried again, this time at the Emeryville Police Department, and this bomb went off and destroyed a police car.

The next bomb sites were in Marin County at two locations in the Civic Center. One was planned to explode under a police car in the lower parking lot and a second one to detonate under a Sheriff's vehicle ten minutes later when deputies would be present. However, because of a malfunction of the timing mechanism, the second device went off first. As a result, no police personnel or civilians had gathered, so there were no injuries. The SLA group was pleased that the devices activated, causing extensive damage to the vehicles. However, there was some disappointment that no police or civilian personnel were injured or killed.

CHAPTER 8 SOLIAH-DEMISE OF SLA

Kathleen Soliah and the other SLA members wanted the Establishment to take their rag-tag group more seriously. Their main activities had been in the Bay area and Sacramento. They wanted the police and public to think of them as a massive statewide movement. In order to give the impression that they were larger than they were, the group decided to plant some bombs in the Los Angeles area. In late August 1975, Kathleen Soliah, Bill Harris, and Jim Kilgore drove from San Francisco to Los Angeles in the old car they had purchased from the proceeds of the Crocker Bank robbery. When they arrived in LA, they purchased a .38 caliber handgun using a fraudulent identification.

Originally, the three SLA members took a **two**-inch pipe bomb and placed it in a briefcase. The idea was to leave it in a Veterans of Foreign Wars convention, where it could inflict major injuries to American veterans. As the three wandered around the Veterans' convention they realized that they stood out and they agreed that this wasn't such a suitable venue. They got cold feet and returned to their car and placed in the trunk the briefcase with the bomb in it. This **two**-inch bomb was never detonated and was later found in one of the safehouses in the Bay area.

Their main mission to Los Angeles was to plant two large bombs under parked LAPD vehicles. They purposely made a couple of **three**-inch bombs, which had the capacity to place more explosive powder in the interior, causing a more powerful explosion. Since it was LAPD who had killed Kathleen's good friend Angela Atwood, the SLA members wanted to do as much harm as possible to the LAPD and their officers. Kathleen wanted to use the much more powerful **three**-inch pipe bombs, since these could be filled with more than 100 ¾-inch concrete nails. The force from a three-inch bomb would send each nail out of the bomb at a velocity several times that of a bullet from a high-powered army rifle.

These bombs were built to maximize their destructive effect, and the placement of the bomb was crucial. That was why the bombs were placed under the seating area of the officers. They were set to detonate only when the officers were in the car with the engine running and when the gas lines would be full.

The bomb was designed so the circuitry was wired to a wooden clothespin with brass wood screws installed into the front portion. The screw heads were drilled into the inside tips of the clothespin with the threads sticking out on the top and bottom. The bombs' wires were attached to the screw threads. The screw heads made contact only when the clothespin was snapped closed.

A wooden shim was placed between the screw heads to prevent the circuit from closing and the bomb from exploding. Fishing line was used to connect the wooden shim at one end to a small horseshoe magnet at the other end. The horseshoe magnet was attached to the undercarriages of the car. The bombs themselves were placed on the ground underneath the vehicle, positioned under the front seats of the police vehicles.

Basically, the bombs were set to explode as the officers pulled out, causing the wooden shim to pull out of the clothespin attached to the bomb, thereby making contact between the two screws and detonating the bomb. On August 22, 1975, the SLA placed one bomb under a detective's car used by a civilian LAPD employee just down the street from the Hollenbeck station. The other was placed under a black-and-white police car parked in the parking lot at the rear of the International House of Pancakes at the intersection of Sunset Boulevard and Orange Street in Hollywood.

Since none of the pipe bombs exploded, the three members of the SLA returned to the San Francisco feeling a sense of disappointment. Their hopes had been dampened by the fact that Officer Bryan—by turning the steering wheel so abruptly to the right when backing out the wooden shim pulled the top screw sideways, just enough so when the clothespin snapped closed the two screws didn't make contact thereby inadvertently disrupted their plan.

The minuscule space between the screws was 1/16th of an inch, which made the difference between life and death, not only for the officers but probably for several other innocent customers just feet away inside the restaurant. When the call went out about finding the pipe bomb in the parking lot, the officers looked under their police car and noticed a magnet with a wooden shim attached to it stuck to the undercarriage of the police car.

For all their effort, these three SLA members hadn't received any recognition. Now there was concern that they might be tracked down by the FBI and the police. That was when they leased an apartment at 288 Precita Street in San Francisco. That would be used by Kathleen as her residence with several of the others. Several days later, another apartment was rented at 625 Morse Street, also in San Francisco. This became the home for Jim Kilgore, Patricia Hearst, Wendy Yee (Pseudonym), and Steven Soliah.

With these two new safehouses, the men moved out of an apartment at 401 Irvington in Daly City. They hired another man to help in the moving. While boxing things up, that man came across a completed **2-inch** pipe bomb as part of the material to be moved. Since he wasn't into the revolutionary cause, he immediately contacted the police. When the police arrived, they called on their bomb squad to make it safe. The bomb experts noticed that it was similar to the other pipe bombs that had exploded at various police stations.

When they dusted the pipe bomb for prints, they were able to compare it to James Kilgore's fingerprints. At that point, they had an idea they were on the trail of the SLA. As Kathleen and the Harrises settled into the Precita safehouse, they felt that they had outsmarted law enforcement. However, what they didn't know was that the FBI had placed the Precita address under surveillance. On September 17, 1975, the FBI agents observed Kathleen enter the safehouse. The next day, Steve Soliah came by and picked up his sisters Kathleen and Josephine Soliah.

The agents permitted the Soliahs to leave the premise. A short time later, the agents saw Bill and Emily Harris leave the Precita safehouse. Just as the Harrises started jogging, the agents surrounded them. Several of the agents returned to the Precita house and went inside looking for Patricia Hearst. As they went from room to room, they did not find her. At that point, they secured the location while other law enforcement officials went to obtain a search warrant for the Precita apartment.

Steve, Kathleen, and Josephine Soliah had driven to a location in the Bay area, where they were working as house painters. This was one way the group made money for their cause. While working at the location they had brought along a radio, which they were listening to as they did the house painting. All of a sudden there was a news flash that the notorious Bill and Emily Harris had been captured and taken into custody.

All of the members of the Soliah family froze in their tracks. Panic spread over their faces. What should they do? Where was it safe to go? Had anybody followed them to this painting job? Without washing out their paint brushes and putting the lids on the paint cans, they slithered out the back window to get away. Steven was concerned that Patty and Wendy were unaware of the Harrises' arrests. Steven drove over to the Morse address to warn them, and as he approached the building he was surrounded by agents and taken into custody. He later learned that both Patty and Wendy had already been arrested and been taken into custody. By nightfall, most of the SLA members were in custody and no longer able to continue their guerilla warfare. However, Kathleen Soliah had evaded detection and ultimately was able to escape to the Midwest.

After law enforcement had taken most of the SLA members into custody, the FBI agents obtained a search warrant for both the Precita and Morse safehouses. The agents conducted meticulous searches of the locations. What they recovered would be vital to the various cases filed against the SLA members.

The first case that went to court was the robbery of the Hibernia Bank. In that case, Patty Hearst was one of the defendants prosecuted. She was represented by the infamous Defense attorney F. Lee Bailey. It was one of the most controversial cases of all times. The Defense was using the Stockholm Syndrome to explain why Patty Hearst joined with her kidnappers to commit the bank robbery. Most legal experts believed that her Defense would excuse her behavior. As Miss Hearst tells it, her attorney was distracted in representing her. Possibly alcohol, or the fact that at the same time he was conducting a legal seminar, may have contributed to the fact that the jury found his client Patty Hearst guilty of bank robbery.

She blamed Bailey for losing the case. Hearst was sentenced to seven years in prison, and she served 21 months of that sentence before President Jimmy Carter commuted her sentence. It wasn't until 1999 that President Bill Clinton granted Hearst a full pardon, which would erase the bank robbery conviction from her record.

In another proceeding, Bill and Emily Harris were tried and convicted for the kidnapping of Patty Hearst in the Bay area. Later, Bill Harris was transferred to Los Angeles, where he was tried and convicted for planting the bombs under the LAPD cars.

CHAPTER 9 SOLIAH- CASE PREPARATION

When law enforcement arrested most of the SLA members in September1975, they conducted thorough searches of the two safehouses where the members had been living. The Precita apartment consisted of two bedrooms, which uniquely had a walk-in closet situated between them. This closet had padlocks installed on both doors. When the police were able to get inside, they found a virtual guerilla warfare supply cabinet. It consisted of hundreds of rounds of ammunition, automatic and semiautomatic rifles, shotguns, handguns, bomb-making supplies, explosive powder and gel. Accompanying these items was bomb-making literature that provided instructions on how to make bombs.

Also, recovered was a .38 Caliber Smith and Wesson revolver that had been purchased in Los Angeles the week the bombs were planted in LA. This weapon was found in a desk drawer in the front bedroom, which Kathleen Soliah had occupied. In addition to that weapon, a Browning 9mm automatic pistol was also found.

In the closet was a briefcase containing a fully assembled 2-inch by 12-inch pipe bomb. Several other pieces of 2-inch diameter pipe and compatible 2-inch end caps were located in the closet. The treasure trove of bomb-making items included the following:

Wooden clothespins

Wires

Blasting caps

Alligator clips

Copper wood screws (both flat head and round head screws)

Switching devices

Black powder

Fishing line

6-Volt batteries

The searching of the apartment produced a stolen Identification of a person named Brian Bach. This identification was used to purchase the .38 Caliber Smith and Wesson, as well as to rent a getaway vehicle during the Carmichael Bank robbery. There was other identification in the name of Michal Ann Mora, who was an infant born in 1946 and died before her first birthday. This individual's identification was used by Kathleen Soliah to obtain a driver's license in the name of Michal Ann Mora.

The day before the arrests, a wallet was found within one block of the Precita apartment address. Inside the wallet was a California Driver's License in the name of Michal Ann Mora with a photograph of Kathleen Soliah wearing a short wig as well as Kathleen's fingerprint. The other connecting item was a list of encoded combinations of numbers and letters. The significance of the encoded numbers and letters was that they were identical to lists found in Patricia Hearst's and Wendy Yee's purses and also in Bill Harris' wallet. It was determined that these represented phone numbers in a network of 'safe pay phones' to be used for secret conversations.

As to the Morse Street apartment where Patty and Wendy were living, the FBI agents recovered additional wigs, gas masks, firearms, and ammunition. What was most interesting was the fact that the SLA members had kept the 'bait bill' (this is money that has serial numbers that are recorded by the bank either by making a copy or by listing in a log book) taken in the Carmichael bank-robbery/murder. It was found in the strangest place: hidden in a jar in the refrigerator. The question was, Why would any professional bank robber keep in their apartment a 'bait bill' that would connect them to a robbery?

Fast-forward to 1999: the LAPD detectives had spent several hours explaining the Soliah case to Deputy District Attorneys Eleanor Hunter and Michael Latin. After considerable questioning by both prosecutors, they felt they had a basic understanding of Kathleen Soliah and the SLA. By then the prosecutors recognized that the entire case would have to be based on circumstantial evidence. The prosecutors had to rely on the strength of Patricia Hearst's testimony. That was quite iffy, since she had been involved in the Hibernia Bank robbery and many people looked upon her as a spoiled rich kid who would say anything to earn herself a pardon from the president.

The prosecutors could read the newspapers and watch the TV news to realize that Kathleen Soliah's public relations machine was painting her as the victim. The Defense argued to the courts that the defendant was in reality Sara Jane Olson, a much beloved housewife from St. Paul. Even though her fingerprints were the same as Kathleen Soliah's, this Sara Jane Olson was an entirely different person. Her supporters from Minnesota were of the belief that she shouldn't be prosecuted since she was a changed person who wasn't like the urban terrorist that the DA's Office claimed.

Sara Jane's hometown community had come together in their support of her. Eventually a group of supporters came out with a Cookbook to raise money for her Defense Team. Prosecutors could read the 'tea leaves' in the tea cup and recognized that they had an uphill fight ahead of them. When Judge James Ideman set bail at one million dollars, the prosecutors initially believed that would speed up the case because very few defendants are able to raise such high bail. Again her supporters stepped forward, and somehow they were able to raise the amount to get her bailed out. As soon as the defendant was out on custody, the case seemed to go into slow motion. The defendant had no reason to rush the case to trial.

Originally, attorney Stuart Hanlon represented Kathleen in her case. He was a legendary San Francisco attorney who had become involved with the radical politics of the 1960s. He had represented other SLA members over the years. Hanlon was joined with Defense attorneys Henry Hall and Susan Jordon. They challenged the fact that the defendant in court was referred to as Kathleen Soliah. They claimed that her true name was Sara Jane Olson and that was what she had gone by for the past 20 years. Eventually, the court agreed to change the complaint to the name of Sara Jane Olson, and from that point on that was the name she was referred to in court.

The prosecutors claimed that it would be devastating for their key witness Patricia Hearst to testify on live TV. Judge Ideman agreed by saying, "To make her go through all that again on live television would be like raping her all over again." He said, "I am not going to allow her to take the stand with the whole country hanging on everything that comes from her lips." As a matter of fact, the prosecution asked for a 'gag order' to be issued to prevent the defendant, her attorneys, or Defense witnesses from discussing the facts of the case with the news media.

Then a young attorney named Shawn Carpenter (Pseudonym) joined the parade of Defense attorneys. After a year of pretrial motions, the prosecution convinced Judge Ideman to allow them to use SLA kidnap victim Patricia Hearst to present a history lesson on the SLA and 22 crimes, including the bank robberies and murders. The judge permitted the DA to include the violent history of the SLA even before Kathleen Soliah became a member. Carpenter and the other attorneys took the judge's ruling up on appeal, which was eventually denied by the appellate court.

Attorney Carpenter vigorously claimed that she needed LAPD to turn over to the Defense all the records pertaining to the SLA shoot-out. The judge denied the Defense's motion, stating that those documents were irrelevant to the present case against Sara Jane Olson. The Defense was losing most of the legal motions, and the case was set for trial on August 16, 2000. The prosecution was ready for trial and out of the blue came attorney J. Tony Santos (Pseudonym), who stepped forward claiming to be the new trial attorney replacing Stuart Hanlon and Susan Jordan. Santos complained that he need to read and analyze 15,000 pages of FBI and Police reports and prepare for 150 potential prosecution witnesses and build a solid Defense for Sara Jane.

Attorney Santos made a dashing appearance with his tall stature. His long flowing silver-gray hair cascading down his shoulders set him apart from the other attorneys in the courtroom. His shiny gold tooth made him noticeable in a crowd. However, his 'used suits' he proudly bought at thrift stores gave him the appearance of a poor soul in need of a handout. Few would think of him as an accomplished football player at Stanford University graduating with a major in epistemological philosophy and a minor in 19th century English poetry. He extended his graduate education by crossing the Bay Bridge of San Francisco and attended law school at Berkeley's Boalt Hall.

His main claim to fame was that he was a colorful, flamboyant civil rights lawyer. Describing Santos, his co-counsel Shawn Carpenter said, "Olson can expect a vigorous operatic performance by a self-described courtroom warrior and racial true believer." Attorney Stuart Hanlon said, "He is the most unique and probably best trial lawyer in the United States and there is no one like him."

Santos was a showman who worked well with the news media. The prosecutors recognized that Tony Santos was about to turn the Sara Jane case into a Soap Opera. However, with the 'gag order' in place the prosecutors wondered how Santos would deal with not being able to talk to the news media.

The immediate issue was what Judge Ideman was going to do about further delay of the trial after he told them to be ready for trial that August. This type of delay tactic of the Defense bringing in a new attorney just before the trial date was nothing new for Judge Ideman. If the judge doesn't grant the additional time for the new attorney to prepare the case, then the Defense has a built-in ground for the reversal of any conviction. With great reluctance, the judge continued the case to January 2001 for the trial. Judge Ideman was merely handling the case while on special assignment with the Superior Court, and the case was permanently assigned to Judge Lawrence Fidler.

Needless to say, when January arrived the Defense had filed certain motions and the case was continued to May 2001 for trial. Then Defense attorneys Santos and Carpenter told the judge that they weren't ready for trial since they didn't have sufficient funds to mount a Defense. What was strange about the case was the fact that the defendant was married to a doctor and had enjoyed a well-to-do lifestyle. She wouldn't be considered an indigent by the usual definition. However, the Defense claimed that since the court was permitting the prosecution to present extensive evidence about the SLA terrorist organization, this required considerably more resources on the part of the Defense in order to be prepared.

The judge was about to hold both Defense attorneys in contempt of court for not being able to be ready for trial. Santos and Carpenter had brought back Stuart Hanlon to represent them in a contempt proceeding. Hanlon told the court, "If the court is going to decide to try the entire history of SLA, then somebody has to pay to defend her." The County had already paid over $200,000 to Miss Carpenter, who was a court-appointed attorney for Soliah. She was claiming that amount wasn't enough and wanted more money in order to be ready for trial.

The Defense team already consisted of Carpenter, Santos, two paralegals, three investigators, and two discovery attorneys. Judge Fidler felt that he had been more than fair in permitting the Defense the same resources that the court provides for a defendant facing the Death Penalty. Judge Fidler stated from the bench that the defendant Olson was entitled to have a reasonably funded Defense. He went on to say, "She is not entitled to the same level of Defense as O.J. Simpson received, who was responsible for his own legal bills. We're not cutting Ms. Olson off. You are not entitled to a DREAM TEAM."

The judge wouldn't give a blank check to the Defense and told the Defense they could take the matter up on appeal. The appellate court considered the matter, and as a result the case was put over to September for trial. The case now had been continued for trial by the Defense for the fifth time. The prosecutors were furious about the delays.

The prosecutors asked the judge to hold a Conditional Witness hearing allowing them to obtain the testimony of several elderly witnesses before they passed away. The prosecution had seen the case continued for two years since the arrest of the defendant. They wanted the witnesses who were present at the Carmichael Crocker Bank robbery to testify as to the defendant's actions during the robbery. Since the appellate court had taken up the Olson case, Judge Fidler refused to consider such hearings.

During all these delays, the case took on a new turn of events. These delays gave Law Enforcement the opportunity to follow up on some of the old evidence. Then at one of the continuances, the prosecutors provided the Defense with new evidence that the prosecution had just recently uncovered. The DA claimed they would be presenting evidence to show that the defendant had ordered 'fuse cord' two weeks before the 1975 attempted bombing of two LAPD squad cars. At the time of the SLA arrests and search of their residences, the FBI was led to a post office box that contained 200 feet of fuse, which can be used either with firecrackers or bombs. Later the FBI was able to track down a letter that had been sent to the manufacturer of the fuse cord to place that order.

The FBI had a handwriting expert examine that letter, and the expert formed the opinion that the handwriting on the letter was made by Kathleen Soliah. This new piece of evidence boxed the Defense in. Their original Defense was that Kathleen Soliah may have lived with several SLA members but she wasn't actively involved in their bomb-making efforts. If this handwriting expert's testimony was admissible, the Defense would have to change their approach.

The Defense's attorneys had to fight any admission of the handwriting evidence coming before the jurors during the trail. Attorney Hanlon stated, "If the People could make Sara Jane Olson ordering fuses for a bomb two weeks before the bombing, the nature of the Defense critically changes and I think that's self-evident." When the Defense realized that the court was going to permit the handwriting testimony, they didn't know what to do. The Defense immediately added this as another matter they wanted the appellate court to review. As a result, the entire case went on hold until September 2001.

CHAPTER 10 SOLIAH- FACTUAL BASIS FOR PLEA

All of the Defense delay tactics seemed to be detrimental for the prosecutors. However, these postponements turned out to be beneficial to the prosecutors in that they had the time to fine-tune their case. The prosecutors, Eleanor Hunter and Michael Latin, took advantage of the delays by working very diligently with the two LAPD detectives, Jay Moberly and Vic Pietrantoni, to dig up more witnesses, to track down witnesses, and to locate evidence, as well as to analyze the evidence.

What the prosecutors quickly learned was that LAPD had all their ducks in a row and the case was well investigated. But when it came to the SLA history, the prosecutors soon realized that the other law enforcement agencies hadn't followed up on some of the evidence. The reasoning for the limited investigation was that every agency had their priorities. At the time, the FBI agents seemed fixated on thoroughly investigating the kidnap case of Patty Hearst, as well as the prosecution of Patty Hearst in the Hibernia Bank robbery.

Another side benefit that occurred was that when the prosecutors were assembling the pieces to the story of the SLA history they had to delve into the facts of the Carmichael bank robbery. Generally, the FBI handles bank robberies as federal crimes, since the banks are insured by the Federal Deposit Insurance Corporation. Back in 1976, the U.S Attorney's Office prosecuted Steve Soliah in federal court for his part in the Carmichael bank robbery. After a lengthy trial, the jury found him **not guilty**. As a result of his acquittal, the U.S. Attorney's Office declined to try any of the other SLA members for the bank-robbery charge. Eventually, the statute of limitations had run on the bank robbery charge, so the SLA members who took part in it could no longer be prosecuted for the crime of bank robbery.

The Sacramento District Attorney's Office considered the entire bank robbery case a federal matter and left it up to the U.S. Attorney to decide whether to prosecute. As Eleanor and Michael dug into the evidence regarding the bank robbery they discovered that there was substantial evidence that proved that Kathleen Soliah had taken part in that bank robbery. This all could be proven by forensic evidence, which included ballistics, latent prints, and handwriting.

The LA prosecutors had spent the time connecting the dots, and they were going to show this to their Los Angeles jury on their present case regarding the planting of bombs under the two LAPD police cars. Obviously, the statute of limitations had run on the bank robbery, so she couldn't be prosecuted for the ROBBERY in Sacramento County. However, the LA prosecutors knew there was no statute of limitations on MURDER. Since Mrs. Myrna Opsahl was shot and killed during that robbery, anyone who took part in that bank robbery still could be prosecuted for FELONY MURDER.

One of the problems the LA prosecutors learned about the investigation of the Carmichael bank robbery was that it had NOT received a thorough investigation. The FBI looked at the murder during the bank robbery as something to be handled by the Sacramento Sheriff's Department. At the same time, the Sheriff's homicide detectives thought that since it was a bank robbery the feds would handle it. For whatever reason, the Carmichael murder case fell through the cracks.

Kathleen Soliah's attorneys thought they were doing the right thing in delaying the Los Angeles trial. However, what they had done was provide the LA prosecutors with enough time to develop a solid MURDER case involving the Carmichael bank robbery.

The other advantage these delays gave the prosecutors was that they had the time to take every factual and legal issue and thoroughly figure out the best way to explain it to the jury. The prosecutors had worked with the DA's Trial Support Division on prior cases. After one of the lengthy continuances, the prosecutors walked by the door of the Trial Support facility. For whatever reason, they both turned around and entered into Trial Support and came over to talk to me, the author. Eleanor was livid that the judge had granted another continuance. She was ranting and raving how the defendant's attorneys were manipulating the judicial system.

Michael, on the other hand, started asking me several questions as to how much time it would take to create a poster of the various parts that made up both of the LA bombs. I asked them if they had photos of the various bomb parts. Eleanor spoke up that Bill from the bomb squad had all those photos. I asked Eleanor if she could set up a meeting with the bomb expert. Within minutes, Eleanor had calmed down and was on the phone arranging the meeting.

The next morning, right on time, Bill, the Bomb Squad expert, was in my office with a folder of dozens of photos of the various parts of the pipe bomb. Bill was one of the senior bomb detectives. I had worked with or come in contact with all types of law enforcement personnel. However, I had never had a case involving the Bomb Squad officials or worked on any of their cases.

For some reason I had always pictured the Bomb Squad as made up of daredevil types like Evel Knievel who were willing to accept risky assignments. However, working with Bill for several days I was surprised that he was a soft-spoken individual who methodically went about his job. In a calm, almost placid, voice he explained how the SLA made their bombs. Without showing any expression, he described the proper order in assembling the various parts for the bomb.

He stressed that if the bomb maker followed the instructions there would be a good outcome. However, if the person took shortcuts or rushed there might not be a good result. He never used the term that the bomb maker would be blown to bits. Bill never uttered the word 'Death' when describing bomb making. Apparently, the Bomb Squad is made up of people who approach their task in a slow mechanical manner.

After obtaining the photos and diagrams from Bill, the visuals were laid out for Michael to review. When he saw how all the parts fit together, Michael suggested that he wanted to see how well a PowerPoint presentation could be used to quickly and effectively explain the makings of the bombs. Eleanor mentioned that they were doing a Focus Group (where various arguments are tested before different groups) in two weeks. They agreed that a Slide Show would be the fastest way to explain the facts of the case to the Focus Group jury. With one of my paralegals, we prepared a 40-slide presentation that showed all the evidence and how it all fit together.

The Defense had been able to delay the case all the way into September of 2001, which was over two years from the time the defendant was arrested. Such long delays benefit the Defense and weaken the DA's case. However, the Defense didn't realize that such delays were going to be devastating for their Defense. The game changer happened on September 11, 2001, when terrorists attacked the Twin Towers in New York and the Pentagon in Washington, D.C. At that instant, no one in the USA had any sympathy for anyone who was connected to terrorism. True, those were foreign terrorists and the SLA were domestic urban terrorists. However, potential jurors weren't going to make some type of distinction between 'foreign' and 'domestic' terrorists.

All those months that the Defense delayed the Soliah trial now were coming back to haunt them. All of sudden, the Defense attorneys wanted to discuss a possible plea bargain. The prosecution had been announcing for over two years that they were ready for trial. They didn't feel obligated to give up much in any type of case settlement. The DA's Office took a hard position in that Soliah would have to plead GUILTY and not merely plead 'No Contest.' That meant that the defendant would have to admit to her role in preparing and planting the bombs under the police cars.

Then on October 31, 2001, the Defense attorneys asked to meet in the judge's chambers with the prosecutors. The Defense said that the defendant was willing to plead guilty but wanted some type of commitment as to what sentence she would receive. At first, both sides had to agree as to what charges she would be pleading guilty to. The original indictment was for the crime of Conspiracy to Commit Murder and two charges of Possession of Destructive Device. After considerable discussion, the prosecution agreed that the defendant could plead guilty to two counts of Attempting to Explode a Destructive Device with the Intent to Commit Murder.

Next, they discussed what the sentence should be for such a crime. The problem with determining the number of years in state prison was that the sentencing law had changed two years after the actual crime had occurred. Neither side knew for certain whether the old or the new statute would apply. The prosecution indicated that the maximum sentence could be 20 years to Life in Prison. However, the Defense attorneys believed that the maximum would be five years since it was highly unlikely that the parole board would find Sara Jane Olson the housewife and mother to be a threat to the public.

The judge wasn't certain what the maximum could be, so he wanted the defendant to understand that the maximum sentence could be Life in Prison. The negotiation continued, with the Defense attorneys wanting Sara Jane to serve her time in Minnesota to be near her family. The prosecution was more concerned about the maximum sentence, so they were willing to go along with her serving her time back in Minnesota.

Eventually, all the details had been hammered out, and the Defense had spent the noon hour explaining the specifics to the defendant. At 2:00 p.m. Judge Fidler took the bench and immediately called the case of Sara Jane Olson. The courtroom was packed. The audience section was crammed with news reporters with their spiral notebooks flipped open. In the front row was Sara Jane's husband, Dr. Fred Peterson, seated next to their daughter who had tears streaming down her pale freckled face. Next to her was Sara Jane's, mother who was trying to comfort her granddaughter while she sternly shook her head in disapproval.

Sara Jane was accompanied at counsel table by her attorneys Tony Santos on one side and Shawn Carpenter on the other side. The defendant stood sandwiched between her tall counsels. At that moment in time, Sara looked more like a lanky 'Plain Jane' redhead than a ferocious guerilla revolutionary fighter. The judge asked her if she was ready to plead guilty, to which she stated, "Yes, your Honor." Then the judge asked prosecutor Eleanor to take the waivers and the plea.

Eleanor, at the end of the counsel table, stood ramrod straight and looked directly at the defendant. She spent five minutes explaining to the defendant her rights that she would be giving up if she plead guilty. She finished off by asking the defendant, "Are you pleading guilty freely and voluntarily?" Sara Jane responded with a stern reply, "Yes, I am." Then the judge announced that the sentencing would be put over to December 7, 2001.

In less than 15 minutes, it was all over as the judge stepped down from the bench and everyone exited the courtroom. As prosecutor Michael Latin left the courtroom, he was interviewed by a news reporter and said, "After 27 years, she has finally been held accountable." Then District Attorney Steve Cooley gave a press release which stated, "Today's plea of guilty by Sara Jane Olson ... closes a chapter in the book of terrorism conducted by the SLA members and associates."

As far as the DA's Office was concerned, it was over. They had waited 2 1/2 years and had been frustrated as the case had been continued eight times by the Defense. The DA's Office was high-fiving each other for finally being finished with this nightmare of a case. However, the DA's Office was about to learn a lesson that "It is never truly over until the Fat Lady (to be politically correct, the heavy-set Lady) has sung."

After Sara Jane walked out of the courtroom, she was cornered by reporters who asked her why she pleaded guilty. Sara Jane without any hesitation stated, "I pleaded to something of which I am not guilty. It became clear to me after 9/11 it was going to have a remarkable effect on the outcome of this trial." She continued to explain to the reporters that she hadn't built any bombs or placed any bombs under the police cars.

Sara Jane denied being guilty of any crime only moments after she had said in open court that she was in fact guilty of the charges. When Judge Fidler heard how she was reneging on her plea, he was furious and set a hearing a week later regarding the statements she had made to the news media.

At that hearing, the tension in Judge Fidler's courtroom could be described as being highly charged. It seemed that the courtroom was a ticking 'time bomb' about to explode. Judge Fidler was a jurist who didn't like to be lied to. When he came out of chambers and took the bench, everyone in the courtroom could see from the expression on his face that he was DEAD SERIOUS.

Both prosecutors were standing at counsel table and looked to be spring-loaded to pounce on the so called 'Lying defendant' who was standing only ten feet away wedged between her two attorneys. Sara Jane had a frightened look on her face, as though she would like to be anywhere in the world except standing before Judge Fidler.

In the audience were her family and friends, who had a dazed expression as if they didn't know whom to believe. It was if some big bully had told them for the first time that there is no Santa Claus. For 2 ½ years this vulnerable Sara Jane Olson had repeatedly told them she was NOT GUILTY. The most she had admitted to was the fact that she had associated with some radicals 27 years ago when she was living the hippy life in San Francisco.

Sitting next to Sara Jane's supporters were numerous reporters who had told their editors that the 'Heavy Set Lady' had sung. They had been so certain that it was over that some of the reporters had moved on to cover new stories.

It is fair to say no one was happy to be in Judge Fidler's courtroom. With a stern voice, the judge directed his remarks to the Defense attorneys, asking if the defendant wanted to plead guilty or go to trial. Defense Attorney Tony Santos started rambling about how the defendant still wanted to plead guilty because she thought it was in her best interest. He explained that she entered the plea because of fears she would not receive a fair trial as a result of the September 11th terrorist attacks.

Judge Fidler fired back, saying he didn't buy Olson's reasoning because potential jurors had not yet been questioned about their views on terrorism. Santos in a contrite voice stated that his client, Sara Jane, wanted to maintain her plea and that her comments after last week's court session were in line with what she had said all along. Some of the news reporters had an inquisitive look on their face, like she is either Guilty or Not Guilty. Just like the old expression 'either you are Pregnant or you are Not Pregnant, but you can't be a little Pregnant.'

Judge Fidler took the tack that if she still wanted to plead Guilty, then let's get a 'Bullet Proof Guilty Plea' from her. He started out by explaining the law to her so she couldn't later say she didn't understand the law involved. The following is exactly what was stated in open court between the judge and Sara Jane:

Judge Fidler: ***Based on the law as I explained it to you and your consultation with your attorneys, at this time based on that law, are you indeed guilty of the charges you entered a plea to the other day.***

Sara Jane Olson*: **I want to make it clear. Your Honor, that I did not make that bomb, and I did not plant that bomb, I did not possess that bomb, and I did not plant that bomb. But under the concept of aiding and abetting, I plead guilty.***

Judge Fidler: ***Because you are in fact guilty?***

Sara Jane Olson: ***Yes***

Judge Fidler: ***All right. Thank you very much.***

By that time, the judge was convinced that he had a thorough plea of guilty until the discussion turned to the sentencing. In order that the defendant couldn't later complain that she had relied on the representation by her attorneys that her sentence would not be more than five years and four months the judge wanted her to plead guilty with the understanding that the state Board of Prison Terms could order her to serve a life term.

Judge Fidler: ***You understand the sentence you could face?***

Sara Jane Olson: ***You know, I don't want to answer that.***

Judge Fidler: ***Well, you have to, Ms. Olson. Do you understand what I just explained to you?***

Sara Jane Olson: ***Yes, Your Honor, I understand.***

Judge Fidler: ***All right. You wish your plea to stand?***

Sara Jane Olson: ***All right.***

Judge Fidler: ***Is that a "yes?"***

Sara Jane Olson***: yes***

Judge Fidler: ***Thank you.***

By the end of this court hearing, the judge and prosecutors were confident that this was now the most solid plea of guilty that had ever been taken in the Criminal Courts Building. This time when Sara Jane exited the courtroom her attorneys made sure she didn't talk to any of the reporters who were waiting outside.

The prosecutors gleefully went down to their offices and started contacting witnesses and told them the defendant had reassured the court that she wanted to plead guilty. This time the prosecutors told the witnesses that they could go on vacations or travel out of state since they would not have to stay around Los Angeles to testify at the trial. This time there was no doubt that the 'Fat Lady' had truly sung loud and clear and it was finally over forever.

CHAPTER 11 SOLIAH-ENDLESS CASE

Then one week later Sara Jane's supporters announced that their hero had filed with the court a motion to Withdraw her Plea of Guilty. For the prosecutors, the LAPD, and the court it seemed that this Kathleen Soliah aka Sara Jane Olson was right out of the script of the movie ***Groundhog Day*** from 1993 in which the Bill Murray character is trapped in the endless repeating loop of waking up in the exact same day to the same song on his alarm clock radio playing ***I've Got You Babe*** by Sonny and Cher. The prosecutors in the Soliah case had to believe the whole thing was nothing but a bad dream that had been transformed into a NIGHTMARE.

The court set December 3rd as the date to consider the Defense motion to Withdraw the Plea of Guilty. If the prior hearing was extremely tense, this hearing was even more hectic, and there were no smiles on anyone's faces. Everyone was talking in hushed voices so as not to set off the time bomb that could explode at any moment. J Tony Santos the infamous fighter for the oppressed was nowhere to be seen. Shawn Carpenter indicated that Mr. Santos was flying in from San Francisco and there were some problems with him missing his flight, but that he would be there soon.

As everyone waited, the question was, how long would the judge's patience last before his razor-sharp tongue would become unleashed on anyone appearing in front of him? The judge requested an update, and attorney Carpenter had a stressed look on her face as she addressed the judge. She indicated that she didn't want to go on with the motion without attorney Santos present to assist her. The judge had a harsh expression on his face. His bald head looked like a balloon stretched to the breaking point.

When it was clear that no one knew when Mr. Santos would be present, the judge indicated that they might as well get started. The judge looked at Miss Carpenter and said that it was the Defense's motion so she could start. Miss Carpenter slowly stood up at the end of the counsel table. She was dressed in a dark women's suit with a turtleneck blouse. Her dark hair was pulled behind her ear and draped over her shoulder. Her face was ashen gray, looking more like a scared deer gazing into the headlights of an oncoming car. She was grasping for words to say. At first she said that her client didn't want to plead guilty because she didn't think she was guilty.

But the judge snapped back, saying that Miss Olson had pleaded guilty twice and there had been a lengthy hearing explaining the consequences of her plea of guilty. Miss Carpenter admitted that Ms. Olson had plead guilty to the charges. Since everyone in the court had heard her plea of guilty and admission of guilt, everyone had a perplexed look as to what was her attorney trying to say.

At that moment, Miss Carpenter seemed to recoil; looking to both sides and not seeing her co-counsel Santos, she started 'trashing' him by saying that he had bullied her client into pleading guilty against her wishes. She stressed that Miss Olson was reluctant to plead guilty but was overwhelmed by Santos's power of persuasion.

Attorney Carpenter said, "He yelled and screamed and demanded that she accept the deal. Without pointing a gun to her head, he made her come in here and say what she said. She didn't want to." Among other things, Carpenter indicated that attorney Santos had told Olson, "You would be a *fucking idiot* if you don't take the plea agreement in the bomb conspiracy case." Carpenter's choice of words may have not coincided with Judge Fidler's idea of the proper decorum for his courtroom.

Judge Fidler listened to Miss Carpenter's explanation, which sounded more like a child's argument—'the dog ate my homework.' Then the judge fired back saying, "Are you claiming that Mr. Santos is some sort of Svengali that could somehow overpower a very intelligent woman's free will? I thought we were out of the Dark Ages." At that moment, Miss Carpenter looked over to the defendant, who had the palms of her hands covering her face. Both looked like they would rather have been any other place but facing the wrath of the judge.

The judge reminded the Defense attorney that in a Withdrawl of a Plea motion, the burden of proof was on the Defense to show that the defendant was innocent or that the evidence was somehow erroneous. The judge explained that the defendant, Ms. Olson, would have to take the witness stand to explain her innocence. Again, Miss Carpenter looked down at the defendant, indicating she wanted her to take the witness stand and testify under oath. Olson's face became so pale that it appeared devoid of blood.

The judge could see that criticizing Carpenter wasn't getting anywhere so he turned to the subject of Defense attorney, J Tony Santos, who had still not arrived. Since the Defense was using him as the scapegoat, the judge stated in open court that the absence of Mr. Santos was "absurd, unprofessional, and inexcusable." Fortunately, the judge had not received a fax message from attorney Santos explaining his absence. That fax message stated that he had missed his flight from Oakland to Los Angeles and thought there wouldn't be a seat on the next plane. Santos wrote, "Therefore, in a state of mind of dank frustration, I went home and went back to bed."

For all concerned, it was best that Judge Fidler didn't know that Mr. Santos was going to evoke the old 'Bad Karma' excuse. During the rest of this morning's hearing, Miss Carpenter blamed the prosecutors for changing their position about whether they would be arguing before the State Board of Prison Terms for Olson to serve Life in Prison. Just before the lunch break, the judge addressed both sides and said the first thing he wanted both the Defense and the prosecution to do in the afternoon was to give a summation of their evidence. The Defense needed to show how she was Innocent and the prosecution needed to show a Factual Basis for the Plea. That ended what was described by several journalists as one of the most contentious hearings to occur in the Criminal Courts Building.

I, the author, was having a busy morning with three homicide cases, which were in their argument stage. It was shortly before noon and I was working in my Trial Support facility, when Michael Latin abruptly came in. I was unaware of all the fireworks that had just taken place in Judge Fidler's court. Michael looked like a man on a mission when he said, "I need you to be in Judge Fidler's courtroom first thing this afternoon, since Eleanor and I have to give the Soliah PowerPoint slide presentation to the judge."

I thought that was an unusual request, since I didn't have time to spend sitting around in courtrooms. I inquired why they were doing a slide show in court even though the jury hadn't been selected. Michael quickly responded that the judge just asked him to present a Factual Basis for the Plea on the Soliah case and he thought the best and fastest way to do it was by showing the PowerPoint presentation that we had been working on for the trial's Opening Statement.

I could see from Michael's expression that he was dead serious, but somehow I laughed, saying, "Michael you know that was merely a draft. It's not ready for 'prime time.'" Michael looked at his watch and said, "Fidler wants the presentation shown at 1:30!"

I said, "We don't have time to redo it." I could see the panicked look on Michael's face and sighed. "OK, let's see if we can use the draft." I motioned to him to come over to one of the computers, where I sat down and turned on the unit. Immediately I opened the file listed as "Soliah Opening Statement Draft."

Over the next hour, while Michael was seated next to me, I was cutting and pasting from the files that we had on the Soliah case. I got the gist of how Michael wanted to tell the story about the Soliah case by constantly referring to the background history of the SLA and the various activities of its members. Several times while we were working on the presentation, Eleanor came in and stood behind Michael and me. She kept throwing out ideas, and I would try to incorporate them. I kept looking at my watch and saw that it was 12:45 p.m. I knew that we had approached the 'point of no return.'

I needed some time to do the finishing touches, such as the animation and transitions. Eleanor was eating something like a granola bar, so I told both of them to get something for lunch and I would see them in Fidler's courtroom at 1:15 p.m. Thankfully, they took the hint and left. I quickly did some magic to smooth out some of the rough transitions in the slide show and burned a CD of the PowerPoint presentation. I then grabbed a laptop and found a cart with an LCD projector and lined them up to be taken to Fidler's court. My watch indicated that there wasn't sufficient time to go get some food at the snack bar on the 9th floor, so I found my half-empty cup of ice coffee from Starbucks and gulped it down pretending it was lunch.

Since it was approaching 1:15 p.m., I started pushing the cart with the equipment to Fidler's courtroom. With some luck, I got an elevator to the 9th floor and squeezed in listening to the complaints from those packed inside. When we got to the 9th floor

I tried to get out, but others were blocking me from leaving. After a little pushing and shoving, I maneuvered my cart and equipment out the elevator door.

After missing lunch and having to fight my way out of the elevator, I wasn't in the best of moods. However, I thought nothing else could go wrong as I pushed the cart into Fidler's courtroom. I set everything in place and double-checked to make sure the equipment worked properly. While reviewing the PowerPoint presentation on the laptop, I noticed a TV cameraman pointing his camera lens straight at my laptop screen. I leaned over to Michael and said, "You didn't tell me this was being televised." Michael sort of giggled and said, "Of course, this is on live TV." I glanced at Michael and didn't dare say in open court the obscenity that was on my mind.

If I had known this was going to be on live TV, I would have double-checked the spelling of the titles, since 'spellcheck' doesn't correct the titles. I was a little on edge, showing a draft of our Opening Statement on live TV, but it soon became apparent that the defendant and Defense attorney had more serious problems facing them. When the judge took the bench, the tension in the courtroom could be described as electric, or maybe more correctly, the air seemed TOXIC. Since I hadn't been present in the morning, I wasn't aware of the hostility between all the parties.

The Judge came out and took the bench, and asked both sides if they were ready. Seeing that the prosecution seemed to be ready, he asked them to go first. Eleanor addressed the court and briefly started talking about the facts of the case and how the defendant got involved with the SLA. Eleanor alluded to the defendant as Miss S-o-l-i-a-h. All of a sudden from the other side of counsel table the defendant roared in a loud, defiant voice, "It is S-o-lee-ah not S-o-l-i-a-h." I heard the judge in a stern tone say, "Miss Olson curb your tongue, or I will send you to the slammer pronto." As Judge Fidler looked daggers at the defendant, she contritely stared at the counsel table and didn't utter another word.

From that point on I wondered, "How the hell did I get in the middle of this snake pit?" I could see that the judge wasn't in a good mood, and I didn't want to screw up and end up in the slammer with Kathleen Soliah (or however she pronounced her old name). Next, the judge looked over to Eleanor and asked her to start the Factual Basis for the Plea. She indicated to the judge that the fastest way to do that was by showing the court a PowerPoint presentation of the case. Initially the judge seemed a little reluctant, but when he heard the words 'Speed Up' the hearing he said, “OK, if it doesn’t take too long.” The prosecutors assured him it wouldn’t take more than 15 minutes.

Eleanor looked at me and nodded, and I projected the title slide, which showed a photo of the defendant. All of a sudden, the Defense attorney was complaining that the light from the projector was shining in the defendant’s eyes. The judge looked at me and asked me to raise the projector’s light. I went over to the projector to slightly raise it, but the only way to use the projector was to shine the light over the defendant’s head so it illuminated the screen attached to the courtroom wall behind her.

I told the judge that was the best I could do, and he accepted my representation. He told the defendant if it bothered her then she could move to another seat. After that was resolved, the show went on. Eleanor and Michael divided up the presentation. I had asked them to use a clicker so they could have complete control over the transition between slides. For some reason they weren't comfortable in doing the presentation on their own. They wanted me to advance the slides, so I had to guess when they were ready to move on to the next slide.

The following pages show the various slides of their presentation

This was the Title slide of the PowerPoint presentation.

This slide was used to show the Locations of the Bombs in Los Angeles.

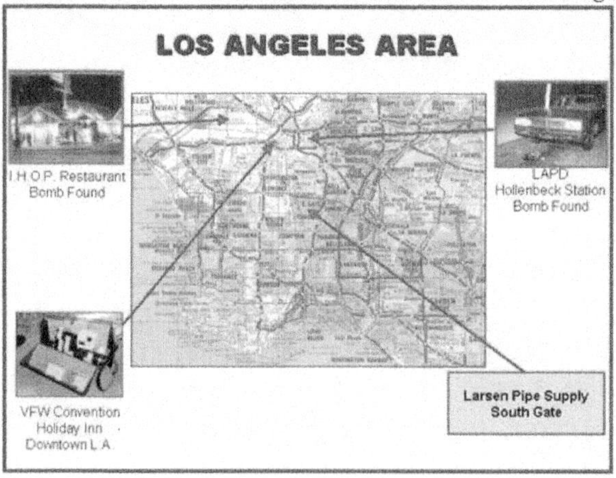

The following pages show the various slides of their presentation

This slide showed how similar the two bombs were found in LA.

This slide showed the similarity of the components of each of the bombs

The following pages show the various slides of their presentation

This slide compared the clothespins found in safehouse & those on the bombs

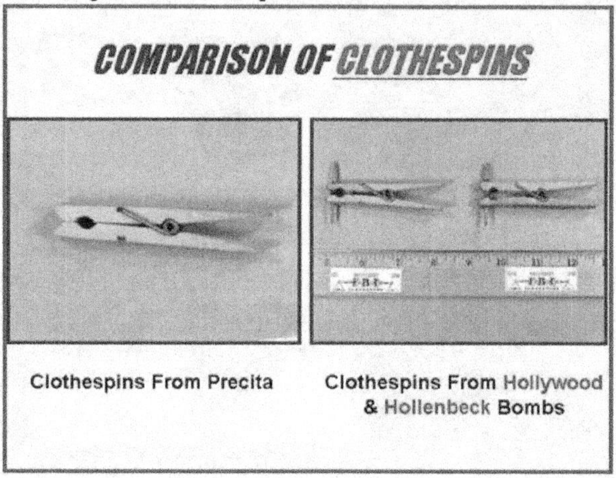

This slide compared the screws found in safehouse & those in the bombs

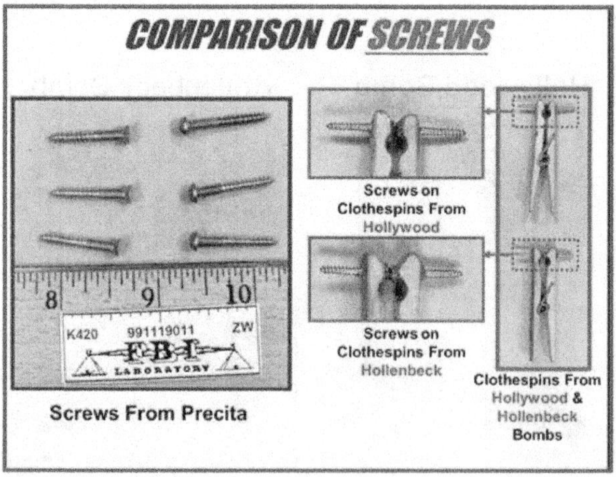

The following pages show the various slides of their presentation

This slide compared the types of nails at safehouse & used in each bomb.

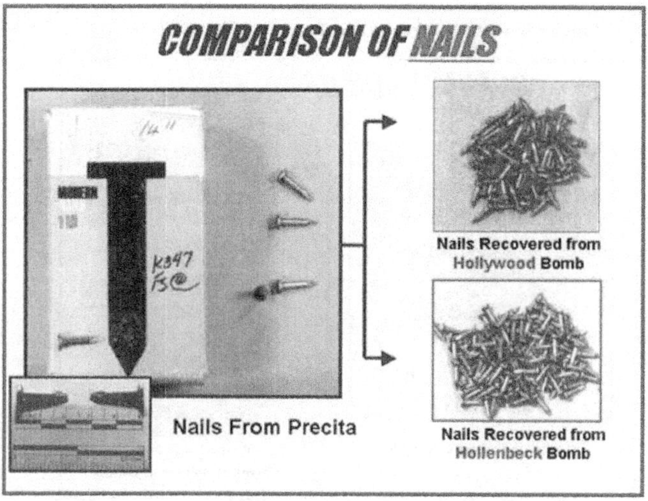

This slide illustrated the similarity of the types of wires used.

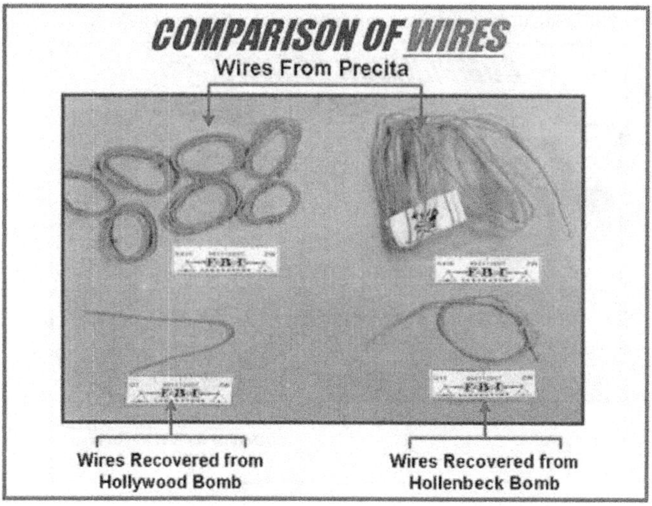

The following pages show the various slides of their presentation

This slide compared the various types of batteries.

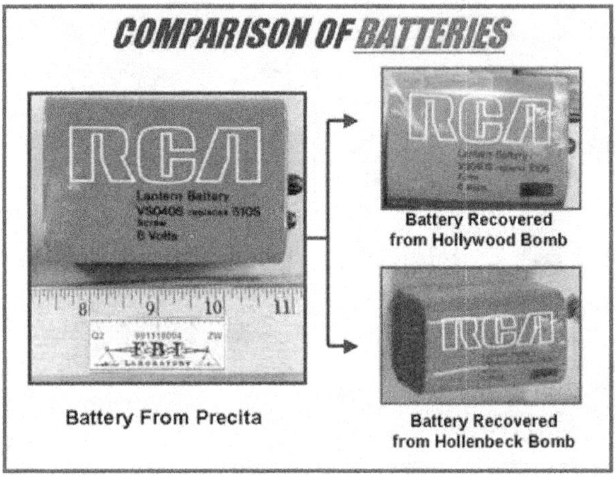

This slide illustrates the similarities of the bomb switches.

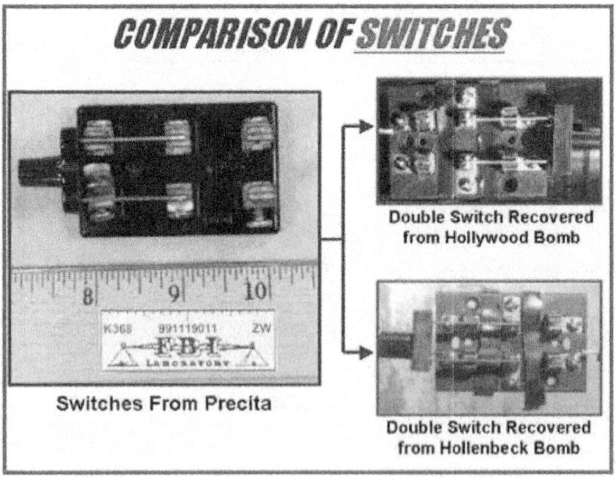

The following pages show the various slides of their presentation

This slide showed the floor plan of the Safehouse where evidence was found.

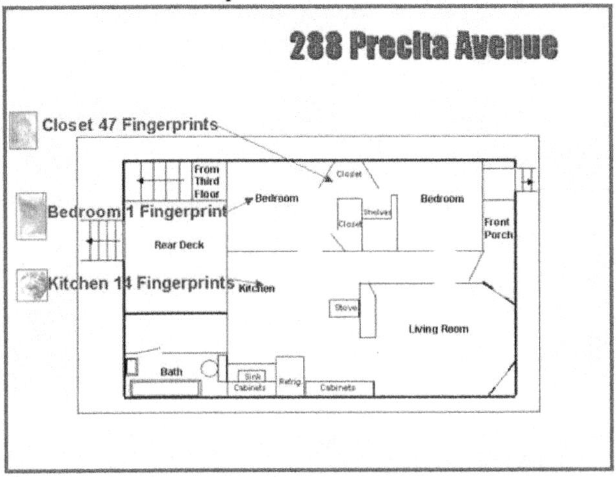

This slide shows all three members of the Soliah family leaving the house.

The following pages show the various slides of their presentation

This slide showed jurors the stated purpose of the SLA.

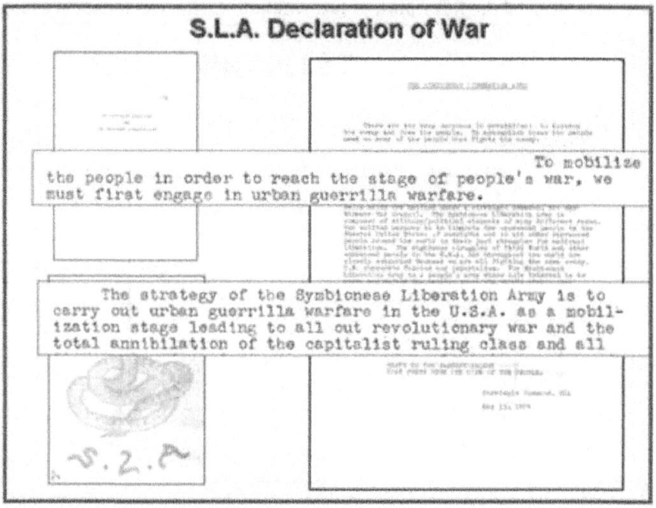

This slide was used to explain the various SLA activities.

The following pages show the various slides of their presentation

This slide was to help the jurors understand who were the new members.

This slide showed how Soliah was able to acquire false ID.

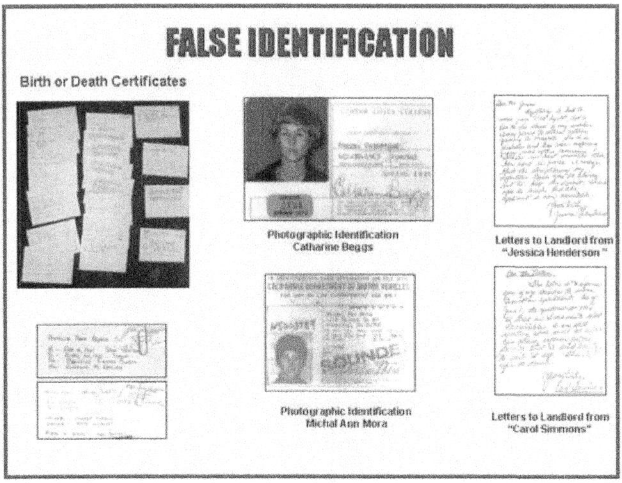

CHAPTER 12 SOLIAH-SENTENCING & BEYOND

Finally, we got to the last slide. The so-called 15 minute presentation had taken over an hour. The judge was leaning back in his oversized judge's chair with his eyes fixated on the screen. Many of the reporters were franticly writing down everything popping up on the large silver screen. The judge seemed a little disappointed that the slide show was over. Shifting his attention from the screen, the judge looked at the prosecutors and said, "Thank you, now let's here from the Defense, Miss Carpenter." He turned to direct his attention to her and asked her to present her evidence showing that the defendant was Innocent.

Ms. Carpenter told the judge that she would be calling her client, Ms. Olson, to testify that she helped the SLA by giving them money and renting cars for them, but that she did not take part in the bombing attempts in LA. Carpenter also said that she would be calling several of the former SLA members to say that Olson never joined the organization and they would say that she was not in Los Angeles at the time of the planting of the bombs. She went on trying to say that her client had associated with some radicals but was innocent of the charges. Ms. Carpenter was trying to put a different spin on everything that had been flashed on the screen over the past hour by the prosecutors.

Attorney Carpenter painted a picture of her client, Ms. Olson—or Kathleen Soliah—as an innocent party who had succumbed to the pressure from her attorney, J Tony Santos, to plead guilty to something she was completely innocent of. Her attorney, Carpenter, struggled to find words to explain exactly how her client was INNOCENT. She glanced at the judge for some indication as to what to say. Judge Fidler glared at her with a stoic gaze with his chin resting on his left hand. After giving the Defense plenty of time to explain how she could call witnesses to show the defendant's INNOCENCE, however at no time did the Defense attempt to call any witnesses to testify.

People in the courtroom had bewildered looks on their faces, as though they couldn't follow the Defense's reasoning. Ms. Carpenter struggled to find words to say that didn't sound like circular reasoning. Judge Fidler sat patiently on the bench, like a fisherman who had a fish on a line while it floundered around; he just waited patiently before reeling it in. In other words, Ms. Carpenter could go on talking, but she wasn't presenting any evidence to prove the defendant's INNOCENCE.

Finally, the Defense attorney recognized that there wasn't any more she could say. Just like the exhausted fish on the line, she turned and slowly sat down in her counsel chair as though the 'Good Fight' was over. That ended a long and contentious hearing in which the judge stated that no evidence had been presented to convince him of the defendant's INNOCENCE. He told the Defense that they had used ploys to drag out the case, and he called Olson's effort to withdraw her guilty plea, which she had twice entered, as completely 'absurd.' Fidler expressed his feelings by sarcastically saying, "I often wonder if the Defense thinks I drive a car to work on a turnip truck." The judge went on to say, "I believe she has a tremendously difficult time admitting to what she did, not just to herself, but also to her family and her many supporters in her adopted home, St Paul."

The judge finished by saying, "I couldn't for a minute accept a guilty plea from a person who I believed was innocent." The judge went on to say, "I couldn't sleep. But I intend to sleep well tonight." At that point the judge uttered the words "Motion denied" and pushed his large chair back and swiveled to the side and left the courtroom. He dashed off to his judge's chambers as though he had had enough for one day.

I stood up and turned toward the public gallery. There, leaning against the back wall of the courtroom, was the District Attorney, Steve Cooley. I couldn't remember ever seeing the actual DA in the courtroom watching trial proceedings. I wondered how many misspellings he caught in my PowerPoint presentation. What went through my head was that all those watching on live TV would never know that this was all done on the fly. This was like ***Saturday Night Live***, in that you had to get it right on the first attempt since there was no second chance. I had to take my hat off to Eleanor and Michael, who did a superb job handling this acrimonious hearing.

I thought to myself how professional both prosecutors had been. They never lost focus and were able to think on their feet when the judge asked pointed questions. What a great tag team. Each could stand up and dish it out. Even though none of this was rehearsed, they were well prepared and had the intellect to articulate how the facts and the law pertained to this case.

Judge Fidler had set the sentencing in the Soliah case for January 18, 2002. What more could happen in this case which was already one of the strangest cases ever to have weaved its way through the Los Angeles Criminal Justice System. Several days before this sentencing hearing, the defendant granted a 2 ½ hours interview with an LA Times reporter. Apparently, Sara Jane Olson felt compelled to tell the world that she really wasn't such a bad person. During the interview, she admitted that she did give money to the SLA and rented cars and apartments on their behalf, and helped them flee from the police. She felt morally obligated to help the SLA after six members, including her close friend Angela Atwood, died in a shootout with LAPD.

She went on to tell the reporter, "I thought I was doing society a favor by preventing more deaths, and it was in honor of my friend . . . There were just not bad intentions." She adamantly denied any participation in any plot to bomb two LAPD cruisers in an attempt to kill officers. "I didn't blow anything up, or even try to."

The reporter asked about some of the evidence that the prosecution said they had against her, such as the letter that appeared to be her handwriting ordering fuses before the bombing attempt. Her response was that the handwriting looked like hers but she just didn't remember any such letter. This seems to be a curious response if she was telling the truth that she had nothing to do with the bombing or making explosives.

Further, she said that she did help the group off and on for a few months, but she never knew exactly what they were doing. Then she stressed, "I never participated in any bank robberies."

What was interesting was that Kathleen Soliah, with her attorney, Carpenter, had told the LA Times reporter that they were going to be totally truthful with the reporter. However, she wasn't telling the truth about the bank robberies since in several months she would be pleading guilty to the Carmichael Bank robbery killing of Myra Opsahl. As Soliah was trying to paint a 'poor me' image she was enjoying Christmas in 2001 with her family.

What Kathleen Soliah didn't realize was that her 2 ½ years of continuances of her case only gave unlimited amount of time to the prosecutors. Soliah's delaying of her case was a big mistake for her and her old comrades in the SLA. The prosecutors, Michael and Eleanor, had time to review all the evidence regarding the Carmichael robbery murder. After conducting new forensic tests and tracking down witnesses, there was no doubt in their minds that a case could be successfully prosecuted against all the remaining SLA Members. Michael and Eleanor had mentioned to the victim's husband, Dr. Opsahl, and his son, Jon Opsahl, that they should now contact the Sacramento Sheriff's Department and ask them to take a new look at the old bank robbery case that had resulted in the death of their family member.

As a result, Jon, the son, did contact those in Sacramento to take another look at the bank robbery murder case. The authorities in Sacramento weren't aware of all the new evidence that the LA DA's Office had developed. Sometime around the early spring of 2001, Michael contacted me, the author, and asked me to create a PowerPoint slide show presentation about the Carmichael bank robbery. I had assembled several maps showing where the various getaway cars were parked in relation to the bank. Also, I had assigned one of my paralegals to create slides pertaining to the ownership of the cars.

Later, we did a slide referring to the ballistic evidence found in the bank connecting the bullet and shell casings to evidence later found in Bill Harris' apartment in San Francisco. We put all the slides together in a presentation and made a CD of it. Michael sent it to the personnel in the DA's Office in Sacramento. The next thing I knew, Michael was back asking me for another CD for a presentation he and Eleanor were going to give to the Sacramento DA's Office. I quickly pulled up the file on the computer and made a few additions and corrections and burned him a CD copy. I thought that would be an interesting meeting and wished I could be a fly on the wall to see if the 'Welcome Mat' was out in Sacramento for us from LA.

For almost a week, I didn't hear back from Michael and wondered what the outcome of the meeting was. Then one day I saw Michael walking down the hallway outside his office. I approached and asked him, "How did the Sacramento meeting go?" Michael was deep in thought with a legal motion he was reading in his hand. He glanced up at me and gave me a smile that lit up his face. I didn't know how to interpret his reaction. Then Michael chuckled and waved me to come into his office.

I stepped in, and in a muffled voice he said that he and Eleanor gave their 'Dog and Pony Show' to the Sacramento DA's staff. At first they received an icy reception which was like, "Who the hell do you think you are, telling us how to run our DA's Office?" The Sacramento staff seemed to dwell on the fact that the bank robbery case had once been tried and the jury didn't buy the argument and Soliah's brother was acquitted. Michael said that as he and Eleanor showed them the slide show laying out all the new evidence that had been developed since that acquittal 27 years ago, the tone of the meeting changed.

Michael said he showed them the slide illustrating the forensics experts' opinion linking the live shells found in the bank and shotgun projectiles in the victim's body with ammunition found in the Harrises' San Francisco apartment. Also found in that apartment were documents including the escape routes, layouts of the plans of the bank, surveillance notes, and typewritten strategy outlines. Also, he said that the DA's staff seemed impressed when he showed them the Kathleen Soliah's palm print that was found in a Sacramento garage where the SLA members stored the getaway car from the robbery. *Some of the slides shown to the Sacramento DA's Office are illustrated on the next graphic page.*

Graphic Page

This slide was used to explain which bank was robbed & where victim shot.

This slide showed the inside of the bank & who went inside during robbery.

Graphic Page

This slide summarized the use of the various vehicles for bank robbery.

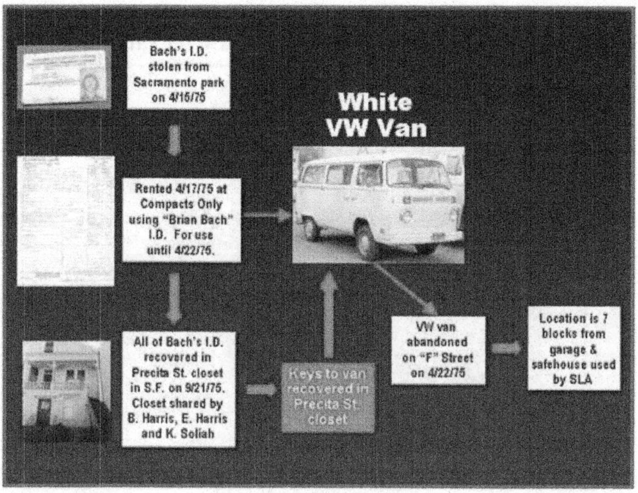

This slide was used to illustrate where the Bait Money was found.

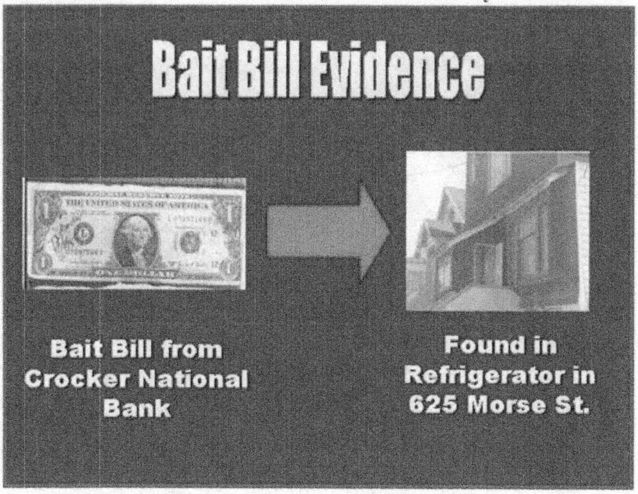

Graphic Page

This slide showed the arsenal of weapons in the various safehouses.

This slide showed where various handguns were found.

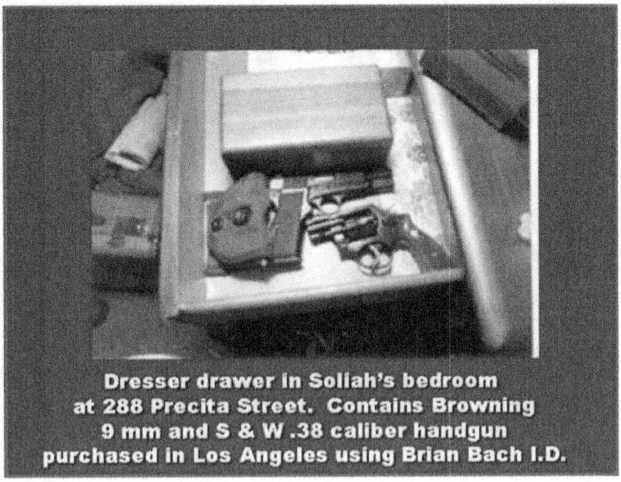

Graphic Page

This slide showed how false names were used.

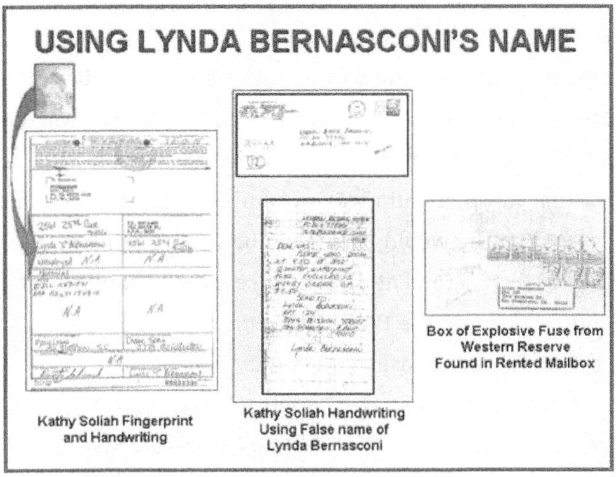

This slide was used so jurors could better understand the locations.

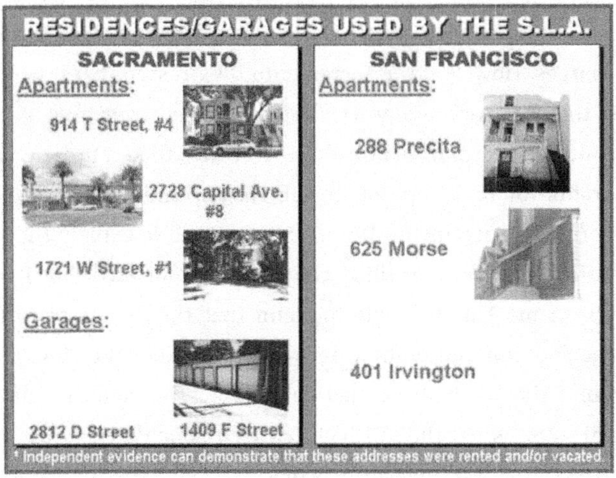

It was like a 'Got You' moment, but there wasn't any thawing of the frigid reception. Those present still seemed to have the impression that Michael and Eleanor were acting like 'Hot shots from the big city of LA trying to show off.'

Later, Michael and Eleanor had a meeting with the victim's family, explaining the new evidence that was now available to the Sacramento prosecutors. Somehow, the news media received the word that the Los Angeles DA's Office thought that the SLA members could be successfully prosecuted.

The news media contacted the Sacramento DA's Office about the new approach. Apparently, the Sacramento DA was told by the media that Michael had said that there was more than enough evidence to convict all the SLA bank robbery suspects. The media said that Michael Latin was so confident in a conviction that he had told the victim's family that he would personally be willing to prosecute the case for the Sacramento DA. As the Sacramento DA's Office showed no interest in reconsidering filing bank/robbery charges, the DA of LA County, Steve Cooley, was asking his staff to find a way to prosecute the case in LA County.

The Sacramento DA response was to tell the Los Angeles DA to stay out of her business. Needless to say, very hard feelings were created, and the news media through the victim's family was putting pressure on the Sacramento DA to do something. Eventually, the pressure became so intense on the Sacramento DA that she indicated that she was creating a joint task force to look into the possibility of bringing charges. However, the Sacramento DA stressed that it would be at their own speed after they had thoroughly reviewed all the new evidence.

The result was that the Sacramento DA's Office filed murder charges and received arrest warrants for Kathleen Soliah, Bill Harris, Emily Harris, Michael Bortin, and James Kilgore. The Sacramento DA, Jan Scully, tried to explain the 27-year delay that her DA's Office had taken in filing charges. She indicated that it wasn't until 2000 that the FBI Crime Lab was able to claim that the pellets from the victim's body matched the shotgun ammunition recovered in one of the SLA safehouses. Further, the FBI found that both items had come from the same manufacturing plant. It wasn't until 1999, when the FBI had Kathleen Soliah's exemplar fingerprints taken after her arrest, that the fingerprints could be used to be compared to the palm print found on the garage door in Sacramento where one of the two getaway cars was stored. Finally, DA Scully pointed to the fact that Soliah, in October 2001, had pled guilty to attempting to blow up the LAPD police cars.

On January 16, 2002, in swift succession three of the SLA members were arrested. It all started when Emily Harris was pulled over as she drove away from her house in Altadena, located just to the northeast of Los Angeles. An officer pulled behind her and turned on his red lights to make a traffic stop. Little did she know that it was all about an arrest warrant for the bank robbery/murder that had occurred 26 years earlier.

Needless to say, she was surprised. Her ex-husband, William Harris, was also being pulled over in the Oakland area as he was driving his two young sons to school. Within a short period of the time of the arrests of Emily and William Harris, Michael Bortin in Portland, Oregon, was hearing a knock on his door. He opened it and looked out on a sea of police officers with their guns drawn. Based on the fact that James Kilgore had vanished years earlier, the Sacramento Sheriff had no idea where to find him and merely obtained an arrest warrant for him wherever he might be found.

As to Kathleen Soliah, the Sacramento Sheriff knew that she was going to appear on January 19, 2002, in two days before Judge Fidler's court. Michael Bortin was married to Kathleen's sister Josephine Soliah, so as soon as he was arrested in Oregon, Kathleen became aware that all the dominoes were falling and she would be next. Kathleen's attorney Carpenter called Sacramento Sheriff's Department and indicated that if there was an arrest warrant for Kathleen that she could turn herself in at the sentencing hearing in Judge Fidler's court. Somehow, the Sacramento Sheriff didn't want to wait, and attorney Carpenter arranged for Kathleen to be in her Beverly Hills office where they could come and arrest her.

By late afternoon, four of five charged bank robbers were in jail on no bail warrants. It was worked out that Kathleen would remain in Los Angeles to make her appearance for her pending sentencing. Then on January 18, 2002, Judge Fidler conducted the sentencing hearing, which was reminiscent of the old Ralph Edwards TV program ***This is Your Life.*** The defendant told the judge and those who were affected by the actions of the SLA, "Forgive me for the pain I've brought to you." This was followed by her mother, Elsie Soliah, saying, "I want to say again that my daughter was never a member of the SLA. We have been harassed for 26 years. Our mail has been tampered with, telephone tapped . . . our daughter is a good person."

Next, Kathleen's daughter addressed the court by saying, "She is the best mother anyone would ever want. I'll be always at your side no matter what." She sobbed and embraced her mother. Then a parade of her supporters proclaimed, "Ms. Olson is a good woman who has devoted her life to public service and to raising her three daughters."

The sympathy was overwhelming and was heartfelt. The prosecution, however, didn't want the court to forget about the lives of the LAPD officers who came within a $1/16^{th}$ of an inch of being blown to pieces. Officer John Hall's message to the court was that he hoped that Olson's sentence would "send a message that terrorism of any kind will not be tolerated in this nation."

After both sides had had their say, Judge Fidler imposed sentence by giving Soliah 20 years to life for the two charges she had pleaded guilty to. Then she was arraigned on the bank robbery extradition warrant. It seemed that Los Angeles was finished with the likes of Kathleen Soliah. As in tennis, the ball was all of a sudden in the Sacramento court. All the old-time SLA members, through their attorneys, claimed that they were innocent of the bank robbery incident. Their attack was on Patricia Hearst. They vehemently attacked Miss Hearst as a witness. They claimed she was a felon who had been convicted of robbing the Hibernia Bank. They painted a picture that Miss Hearst would say anything to get a Pardon from the President of the United States.

Years ago, after her arrest, Miss Hearst had talked to the FBI about the involvement of each of the SLA members in the bank robbery. Later she wrote a detailed book called ***Every Secret Thing***, listing everyone's role in the bank robbery. She admitted that she drove a getaway car and was parked outside the bank while Emily Harris, Kathleen Soliah, Kilgore, and Bortin went inside. She described that they all wore disguises, including ski masks and wigs. She said that Bortin stood on the teller's counter and waved his gun around while Kathleen Soliah emptied the tellers' cash drawers and Emily Harris shot the female customer.

Patty Hearst went on to explain that the Harrises were extremely dedicated revolutionaries. And she explained that Kathleen was a forceful personality who dragged her siblings and friends into the SLA in the 1970s.

CHAPTER 13. SOLIAH-SLA FINAL CHAPTER

The bank robbery case in Sacramento with the four SLA members seemed to drag on forever. Since the defendants were in custody, there was some pressure to find a way to resolve this case. The defendants were charged with first degree murder, for which they could be sentenced to 25 years to Life. The situation was that the Sacramento DA's Office wasn't fond of having to file this case to begin with, and the SLA robbers didn't want to spend the rest of their lives behind bars, so the case was ripe for some type of case settlement. In short order, the defendants were willing to plead guilty **to second degree murder** with various sentences depending on their involvement in the killing of the victim.

The question became what should be the appropriate sentence for each of the participants in the Carmichael robbery murder. When looking at the actual facts of the robbery, one would have to agree it was a sophisticated and well-planned robbery with multiple robbers, multiple getaway vehicles, and every detail well thought out. This has to be considered one of the most deliberate and premeditated bank robberies. Its purpose was to obtain a large amount of money to be used to finance the further illegal activities of the radical group. Patty Hearst stated, "This wasn't a mere robbery but it was an expropriation. It was a combat operation. It really was their own little jihad that they had going."

The SLA members liked to say that their only intent was to commit a robbery and there was no intent to kill anyone. They like to claim that the shooting was a mere accident. However, the point that they seemed to overlook was the fact that they carried into the bank real guns that were loaded with live ammunition. Their rationalization of the shooting was that Emily Harris was trying to get the women to lie down on the floor. Since the victim, Myra, was slow to get down, Emily took the sawed-off shotgun and pushed it into her side when all of sudden the shotgun went off. Emily claimed it wasn't her fault since the shotgun had a 'hair trigger' that didn't require much pressure to fire the weapon.

However, this SLA version of the shooting doesn't take into account the fact that everyone in the group knew that the shotgun had a 'hair trigger' and anyone who used it had been warned to be careful when using it. The other point that makes the shooting seem more heinous was the fact that the bank robbers wouldn't let any of the other people in the bank go to the victim's aid as she was starting to bleed to death from the shotgun wound.

The callousness of the robbers was illustrated when Patty Hearst asked what happened during the robbery and Emily replied, "Don't be concerned about the victim, since she was a bourgeois pig anyway." That would seem to elevate the shooting to an even more malicious cold-hearted killing rather than a mere accidental shooting.

So when considering the appropriate punishment for the bank robbers, there is a strong argument that the actions of the robbers would certainly be considered aggravating in nature. However, when one looks at the other side of the coin, each of the defendants had compelling mitigating facts to their credit. For the past 30 years they each had lived a law-abiding life, which could certainly be argued by the Defense as a mitigating factor. What was so fascinating was how this extremely violent group of revolutionaries had changed over time. They were like chameleons that could totally blend into the Establishment that they had so vehemently despised. They all became highly responsible, hardworking citizens who were stable members of society.

As to **William Harris,** he paid his price for his involvement of kidnapping Patty Hearst by serving eight years at San Quentin. Upon his released, he worked as a private investigator, and at one time he worked for the San Francisco District Attorney's Office. After he divorced Emily, he remarried and had two sons. He was well respected as a hard-working private investigator, a good husband, and a caring father.

Emily Harris had a transformation after serving seven years in prison for her crimes involving the SLA. She learned computer skills in prison that she was able to build into a successful career as a computer consultant for the entertainment industry. She developed a long-time commitment with her significant other, Nancy (pseudonym), and they maintain a lovely home in Altadena, a community just above Pasadena. She is hardworking and well-liked by her neighbors.

Michael Bortin has lived quietly in Portland, Oregon, for two decades. He has worked as an installer of hardwood floors and made a good living at that occupation. He married Kathleen's sister, Josephine Soliah, and they have four children. He is also well respected in his community.

As to **James Kilgore,** he left the country and took up a new life under another name in Cape Town, South Africa. He was employed as a professor at one of the universities, and is married and has children.

Of course, we are aware of **Kathleen Soliah,** who assumed another identity under the name of Sara Jane Olson. She married an emergency room doctor and they have three children. She has been active in her community, especially in the local theater productions. To show how well liked she was in her community, she was easily able to get her friends and neighbors to put up sufficient money to raise her one-million-dollar bail.

The big question was, what considerations should go into the sentencing? Is it the actions of a young rebel or what the person has done with their life over the last couple of decades? Is sentencing to be punishment for what one did or what one has become and their contribution to society? Is the sentence to act as a deterrent to the defendant or to others?

The sentencing was put over to February 14, 2003, and the Sacramento judge gave the longest sentence to Emily Harris which was eight years in state prison. Emily admitted she was the one who shot Myrna Opsahl with a sawed-off shotgun. She claimed that she was pushing the barrel of the shotgun against the victim's side when the shotgun went off accidentally. It is hard to know if that is true or whether it was an accident, since the SLA members knew that the sawed-off shotgun had a 'hair-trigger.' While in tears, she was able to tell the victim's family in the front row of the courtroom, "I feel a deep sense of remorse and will be sorry for the rest of my life."

As to her ex-husband, Bill Harris, he received seven years in state prison for his part in the robbery murder. He turned around and looked directly at Jon Opsahl, the victim's son, and delivered a rambling nine-minute monologue. "Your mother was never an abstraction to me. It's absolutely unacceptable that this happened . . . I feel horrible . . ." Then he digressed and started lamenting how his family would be devastated without him. Then he caught himself and realized what he was saying. He then switched by saying, "But I concede that my absence will not begin to approach the devastation caused by the murder of your mother."

Michael Bortin received a six-year term in state prison. All he could say to the victim's family was, "I can offer nothing but my apologies." As though recognizing how words couldn't erase the damage that had been done, he looked at the victim's son and slowly said the word "I'm sorry" and sat down.

Then it was time for Kathleen Soliah to make her peace with the victim's family. For all the years she denied being involved in the bank robbery murder, what could she say that anyone would believe? The judge gave her a sentence of six years and she didn't stand to utter one word to the victim's family. She had merely submitted a letter, which the judge read into the record. She wrote, "If we had foreseen her killing, we would never have robbed the bank. We were young and foolish . . . In the end we stole someone's life."

A short time later the fifth SLA member involved in the bank robbery, James Kilgore, was arrested in South Africa. On his return, he received a sentence of six years in prison. Also, he had received a 4 ½ year sentence for federal explosives and passport fraud convictions in San Francisco.

An interesting point was what the victim's son, Jon Opsahl, thought should be the appropriate sentence. Even with all his efforts he had spent trying to find justice for his mother, he couldn't ignore the fact that all of the bank robbery suspects had lived a law-abiding, productive life. The question that had no answer was, what did it mean when each of the old SLA members told Jon and his family that they were sorry for what they had done?

How sincere were their words, "I am truly sorry for loss of your mother?" Each one of the suspects had their own way to express how sincere they were when they said the words 'I AM SORRY.' But Jon found that no matter how they said it, it still didn't bring his mother back. All the heartache of losing such a devoted, wonderful mom couldn't be made right by any words that the defendants tried to convey.

By the time James Kilgore's case was completed, everyone gave a sigh of relief that the Soliah-Olson SLA cases were finally over after five years. As we have seen, sometimes we don't always know when the 'heavy set lady is going to sing.' Kathleen Soliah's sentence in Los Angeles became an issue since the Board of Prison Terms determined that her appropriate sentence should be longer than 14 years because the crime had a high potential for great violence and targeting multiple victims. A judge in Sacramento ruled that the Board had not done any analysis in deciding to increase her sentence. That judge reduced Soliah's sentence back to five years and four months.

Eventually an appellate court reversed the Sacramento judge and set the sentence at 14 years in state prison, as the Board had originally set. That seemed to finalize the sentence and she continued in state prison until she was eligible for parole. Then, in March of 2008, she was granted parole and was thrilled to be slamming the prison door behind her to end this dark period of her life. However, the Los Angeles DA's Office checked their records and noticed that she wasn't set to be released for another year. The DA's Office contacted the prison to check their calculation of the release date. To the embarrassment of the state prison, it was determined that Kathleen had been released one year too early. Five days later a dejected Kathleen Soliah was rearrested and transported back to prison. There she remained until March 17, 2009, when she was again released, and she was allowed to serve her parole in Minnesota. Even her parole wasn't without controversy. There were those who protested her getting to serve her parole where her family lived.

What was strange was that Kathleen Soliah—or as she liked to be called Sara Jane Olson—seemed to be one of those hot topics that people have strong feelings about. On one side there are those who oppose urban terrorists. On the other side are people who say Sara Jane Olson didn't hurt a living soul since the pipe bombs didn't actually go off. They say 26 years living a model life should cancel out a foolish act she may have done when she was young.

This case is a perfect example of how the judicial system is often faced with conflicting points of view. What should determine a fair and just punishment for an impetuous act done a quarter of a century earlier? A mere 1/16th of an inch was the difference between life or death. If the screws on the clothespin had made contact, the pipe bomb would have detonated and hundreds of hardened nails would have gone flying through the two officers' bodies, causing them to die a terrible death.

Not to mention the dozens of customers in the IHOP restaurant who would have been killed or maimed by the blast.

One can debate forever as to what should be the appropriate punishment in such a case. However, the purpose for including the Soliah case in this book, *DA Delta Force*, was to illustrate what an incredible job Eleanor Hunter and Michael Latin of Major Crimes Division did in this case. If it hadn't been for their stellar preparation, Kathleen Soliah would have gotten away with planting the bombs to blow up LAPD officers. However, these prosecutors' tenacity in putting pressure on the Sacramento DA's Office finally got justice for Myrna Opsahl's family. Needless to say, Sacramento District Attorney Jan Scully told the news media that she had refused to be bullied by the Los Angeles prosecutors. It would be safe to say that Michael Latin and Eleanor Hunter will never be invite to do LUNCH with the Sacramento DA. But without these persistent prosecutors, five criminals would literally have gotten away with MURDER.

These prosecutors from Major Crimes had once again met the challenge. The public and the news media had no idea what extraordinary people make up the DA's Major Crimes Division. Eleanor and Michael didn't receive a bonus or any award for doing such a remarkable job. They are merely county civil servants who do an amazing job not for the money, but to see that JUSTICE IS DONE even if it takes 26 years.

However, not everyone was pleased with these prosecutors' tenacity. Michael Latin had spent 15 years of his career as a prosecutor. In order to further his legal career, he decided to apply for a judgeship through the governor's office. What was interesting was that his tenacity in seeking JUSTICE was held against him. Some of Soliah's Defense attorneys tried to derail his judgeship by contacting the governor's office and claiming that he was unqualified to be appointed as a judge. Again, the Sacramento DA wasn't supportive of Michael to be a judge. That DA said that it was the height of arrogance for the Los Angeles prosecutors to say they would come to Sacramento to pursue the murder case against Soliah if she didn't do it herself.

Even after all the badmouthing Michael received, he was still appointed to a judgeship in 2003. Two years later when Eleanor was applying for a judgeship, she received much the same attacks from the same sources. Her tenacious approach was used against her; however, she still received a judgeship from the governor.

The moral to this story could be that 'No Good Act Goes Unpunished.' As dedicated as both prosecutors were, it always seems perplexing that there are still those who think that vigorous prosecution is looked upon as being too zealous. These critics take a position that the prosecutors should be more forgiving of others' transgressions. One gets a feeling that these objectors would like to see everyone in a circle holding hands and singing 'Kumbaya my lord' with Peter, Paul, and Mary.

PEOPLE VS. BRUCE KOKLICH

Is Wife a Missing Person or a Victim of a Homicide?

CHAPTER 14 KOKLICH-FACTS OF CASE

Bruce Koklich was accused of murdering his wife, Jana Koklich, whose body was never found. He didn't confess to killing her, and he denied having anything to do with her disappearance. The Koklich case involved a middle-aged couple who had been married for eleven years. They gave the appearance of being happily married. Bruce Koklich was a successful businessman who had made an enormous impact in the real estate market in the Long Beach, California, area.

Jana Koklich was the daughter of former California State Senator Paul Carpenter, who was a well-known politician in Orange County. Her family had always been in the news, and she indirectly benefited from all of these connections. Jana was very close to her family even after her parents separated. She was especially close to her mother, who lived nearby. As her father grew older, he left the stress of politics in California and moved to San Antonio, Texas. Even with this considerable distance, Jana stayed in constant contact with him.

When Bruce and Jana married, they were like the ultimate "power couple." In northern Long Beach, they operated the Remax Park real estate office, which was immensely successful and a big money maker for both of them. Bruce had the business acumen to know how to make and close a deal. Jana possessed the organizational skills to run an efficient business office. Jana used the office computer system to calendar and keep track of all the important business dates. She even used the office computer system as her personal calendar. Jana projected a softer and gentler approach to Bruce's brasher more direct attitude. In the fiscal year for 2000/2001, their real estate business jointly earned them $273,000. Over the years of their marriage, they had acquired 21 properties, which gave them a significant equity interest in those properties amounting to more than $3.6 million.

It was clear that Bruce and Jana Koklich were doing well financially. Bruce Koklich was certainly not fond of the idea of sharing half of their acquired assets with his wife in case of a divorce.

In addition to their real estate business, they had launched a new venture involving a computer software company they named "Amos Software Development." They had a partner, Chris Brooks (Pseudonym), who was doing most of the computer development for this little startup company. Since the couple's expertise wasn't in computers, they left Mr. Brooks in charge of their new adventure.

Jana and Bruce didn't have any children to bind them together. Over time, they developed their own personal interests and groups of friends. Bruce liked to associate with a faster-moving group than his wife. As a result, Jana Koklich recognized that she enjoyed spending more of her time with her female friends and family.

On Friday, August 17, 2001, Jana was looking forward to attending an Eric Clapton concert at the Staples Center in downtown Los Angeles. She and her dear friend Nini Andres (Pseudonym), who operated a skin-care business, were excited to have this night out together. Jana left work at 4:00 p.m. and drove to the family home in the city of Lakewood, a bedroom community north of Long Beach. Nini came by at 4:45 p.m. and picked Jana up, and they headed to the Staples Center, first stopping at Frenchie Restaurant for a quick bite to eat. That gave them enough time to travel against the downtown traffic that was attempting to escape the big city for the weekend.

Their journey didn't take long before they found a convenient parking place near the arena. They traversed the street in front of the steel and glass Staples Center and headed for the entrance. The crowd seemed to be wired in anticipation of the big event. The atmosphere oozed excitement. After going through the doors, they were faced with a wall of people selling programs and CDs. The decibel level of the crowd was so high that the only way to communicate with another was by shouting.

It was sensory overload from the frenzy of the people milling around to the wave of noise, including the PA system shouting out directions. The two women tried to get oriented to the location of the tunnel they needed to find their seats. As they inched their way through the mass of humanity they couldn't help but get a whiff from the concession stands of the smell of sizzling hot dogs and greasy French fries.

Since the women had already had eaten, they weren't tempted to buy a ten-dollar hot dog with raw onions and pickled relish.

They slowly moved toward their tunnel entrance, and when they turned into this concrete tunnel they had a momentary feeling of what it was like for a herd of cattle being led to slaughter. As they advanced through the tunnel, their ears were filled with the loud echoing noises while their lungs inhaled the stale air of spilled drinks. Finally, they made it to the end of the tunnel and were awestruck by the view of the enormous arena.

As an usher pointed out the location of their seats, they turned to walk up the stairs. They were wearing high heels, and it was challenging to maneuver up the numerous steps to their row. Of course, their row of seats was filled with people who had settled in. Jana politely asked those seated to let her and Nini through to their seats. Those who were seated gave them a look as if to say 'you should have gotten here earlier so you wouldn't have to disturb us.' Jana used her most pleasant voice in saying "Sorry" to each one who let her pass.

Finally, they reached their two seats and plunked down. They looked at what time it was and realized that they had arrived in plenty of time. They stretched out and got comfortable. However, neither of them dared to get up and attempt to go for drinks. Jana glanced over the program and it wasn't long before the music roared, announcing the beginning of the concert. Within moments, Jana was totally absorbed into the familiar Clapton songs. To his fans, Eric Clapton is considered one of the Greatest Guitarist of all times. He is so talented that he can play a whole range of guitars. At the same time, he is a singer and songwriter with a list of more hits than most performers. It was enjoyable to listen to Clapton walk his audience down memory lane during his two-hour performance. At the end, the audience kept applauding in hopes that Clapton would continue his encores forever. Finally, his fans realized that the endless clapping wasn't going to bring him back on stage for more. It was over, but Jana and Nini still wanted to savor every last moment in hopes that they didn't have to return to the real world with all its knotty problems.

After a few moments, they snapped back into reality. Jana knew she had to get home to get some sleep because she had an early workout with her trainer at 7:00 a.m. Nini didn't waste any time driving back since she knew that she was going to have a full day working at her skincare business. Saturday was her busiest day, and as a matter of fact Jana was scheduled to come in for a facial at 2:00 p.m.

When the two women got back to the Koklich house in Lakewood it was after 11:30 p.m. When Jana stepped out of the car, she could see that all the interior lights were off in her house. Jana and Nini had a special routine they went through to assure each other's safety. When Jana went inside, she immediately turned the lights on and closed the door. Then she waited a moment and flipped the lights off and then back on, signaling that everything was all right inside. When Jana did that, Nini knew her good friend was safe and it was okay for her to drive to her home.

What Nini couldn't have known was, at that very moment it was the last time anyone would see Jana alive except for Jana's husband. Bruce later claimed that he and his wife spent a pleasurable weekend together at their house.

However, Bruce was telling a bold-faced lie that his wife was still alive when in fact he knew she was dead since he had killed her. Bruce would try to find ways to make it appear that Jana was still alive when she was dead. Bruce Koklich wanted people to believe that his wife was alive at home with him on Saturday, Sunday, and Monday morning. He wanted to make it appear that his wife was still alive at the house when he left to go to the office on Monday morning.

The inference by Bruce was that on Monday morning she either was kidnapped from the house or she was carjacked as she was driving to work at their real estate office. Unfortunately, Bruce Koklich wasn't as careful in handling his wife's body, and a small amount of her blood dripped or was transferred onto the back carpet of her SUV. It may have been nighttime when he disposed of her body and he didn't notice the blood. When the car was recovered about a week after his wife's disappearance, the detectives thoroughly searched it, and at that time they noticed a small amount of blood in the rear interior of her car.

Bruce still could claim that his wife was merely a missing person; however, the small amount of blood suggested that the matter was more likely a homicide. Bruce's carjacking theory still had viability in that the carjacker could have taken the car with Jana in it. At a later time and place, the carjacker could have killed Jana and that was when Jana's blood was transferred onto the carpet in the rear of her car. What made this a harder sell was the fact that no one reported seeing a woman in a SUV being carjacked, especially along the usual route Jana drove to go to work.

Killers often trip themselves up in the most unsuspecting ways. So many perfect murders are fouled by the so-called unseen people who work for the killer, such as gardeners, handymen, or even housekeepers. In the Koklich case, it was the housekeeper who supplied the most damning evidence against the killer. It was the housekeeper who remembered that she had placed clean patterned fitted sheets on the master bed on Tuesday. She had worked for the Koklichs for nine years. It was her routine to change the sheets on Tuesday and wash them on Friday. When the housekeeper returned on the following Tuesday, the day after Jana was reported missing, she noticed that the patterned fitted sheets she had placed on the master bed the previous Tuesday were missing. Someone had replaced them with a small-size sheet that didn't fit the bed. The housekeeper had never seen either of the Koklichs change sheets on their own. She thoroughly searched all the cabinets in the house, the washing machine, and even the trash, and nowhere could the sheets be found.

The most logical inference was that Jana was killed on the master bed and the sheets may have gotten covered by blood or bodily fluids. Or the other inference was that Jana's body may have been wrapped in those sheets in order to dispose of her body.

However, Bruce Koklich wasn't quite as discreet in his immediate urge to get back in the dating game. Days after Jana's disappearance, Bruce hit on one of the women who worked in his local bank by saying, "I think your blouse would probably look even better if it were off of you." A few days later, he sat on her lap while she was seated in the bank manager's office. None of that was getting him a date, so finally he asked her out to a Britney Spears concert. Her answer was a resounding "No."

He appeared to be striking out at his rebound into the dating game. Bruce wasn't deterred, and he looked for someone new to approach. He started hitting on his travel agent, offering to take her to the Arrowhead Pond for a concert. When that didn't get a favorable reaction, he proceeded by saying he would include dinner. Even that didn't result in an acceptance.

Bruce Koklich was a salesman who knew the art of selling. He knew how important it was not to be discouraged by continual rejections. He considered it an opportunity to better refine his salesmanship skills. He continued to vigilantly watch for pretty young women. He noticed that one of his elderly neighbors had an attractive granddaughter who came by to visit her grandmother. Bruce went to the trouble of putting a note on her car with his photo, indicating that he was interested in meeting her. The young woman wasn't moved by his offer, and she never made the call to meet him.

Bruce wasn't having any success meeting other women in his neighborhood. He thought about heading north to visit his 18-year-old niece, Jessica (Pseudonym), who was Bruce's stepbrother's daughter. Jessica was having some adjustment problems with her family and wanted to live away from home. Bruce wanted to be helpful, so he indicated that he needed someone to look after him since his wife's disappearance. Bruce was nice enough to offer her money and a car if she came down to Long Beach to help him while she lived rent-free in his house. Bruce made it clear that she wasn't to tell her father about the arrangement if she decided to take advantage of the offer.

Jessica indicated she needed some time to think it over, so Bruce returned to his home in Lakewood. After a week of numerous phone calls, Bruce was able to talk Jessica into trying out the arrangements. Bruce went barreling up Interstate 5 like a stallion in heat to pick up Jessica in the Bay area. He didn't want to contact her at his stepbrother's house so he met her at a local church several blocks from her house. Bruce quickly piled all of Jessica's belongings in the trunk of his car and headed straight down the Interstate to his place as if he were a man on a vital mission. There may have been a slight misunderstanding in the role-playing of the two. Bruce continued to try to persuade Jessica to have sex with him. Jessica, on the other hand, wasn't interested in having sex with her uncle. Bruce tried to put her mind at ease by indicating that since they weren't blood relatives but only step relatives that there was nothing wrong with them having sex. She wasn't persuaded or impressed with his reasoning. Her main interest was to enjoy the freedom of being away from her restrictive parents.

When she moved into Bruce's house, the so-called "grieving husband" told Jessica she could wear any of his missing wife's clothing, including her bras and swimsuits. When Jessica wanted to take a shower, she had to use the shower in the master bathroom, which unfortunately had a broken shower door that couldn't be closed. The result was that Jessica had no privacy and Bruce got a free show. At night, Bruce insisted on Jessica watching TV in the master bed with him. When it came time to go to sleep, he required her to sleep with him in the master bed since he felt so alone without his missing wife.

Bruce tried to pursue Jessica by taking her to the Arrowhead Pond for a hockey game. On a following day, he took her to lunch. The air conditioning at the restaurant had been turned up too high, so Bruce, being the gentleman he was, took his coat off and placed it around her. Jessica noticed that Bruce had a handgun in one of the pockets of the coat. This had a chilling effect on her thoughts of trying to leave him. On another night, they went to the Pond for another event, and when it was over she asked if they could stop at Walmart to buy some tampons and nail polish remover. While in the store, Bruce purchased a box of condoms. Apparently, Jessica was having her period and had a need for tampons. It was unclear why Bruce needed the condoms, since he was supposedly grieving the loss of his wife!

It was late September, and it was still very hot during the days. Jessica took up Bruce's offer to spend time out by the pool while he went to work. After sunning herself, she wanted something cool to drink. Bruce had earlier made some special drinks that he told her were called "Blow Jobs." She hadn't tried them, but he told her that they were a cool and refreshing drink when it was hot. She drank one and it made her feel relaxed. She had some more and she felt no pain. As a matter of fact, she didn't feel anything and passed out from the drinks. The next thing she remembered was that she was in an upstairs bedroom with her bathing suit pulled up. She was in a haze and was trying to figure out where she was and what she was doing there. She glanced to the side and could see Bruce in the other room talking to someone on the phone. What caught her attention was the fact that he only had on his boxer shorts with what she described as a "Hard On." As Jessica was sizing up the situation, Bruce hung up the phone and returned to Jessica, who was lying flat on her back in this bed. He told her that he was in the middle of giving her a massage. Jessica was starting to come to her senses and realized that a lot more had taken place when she was passed out. First off, she could feel that the tampon had been removed. She started to accuse him of removing her tampon. Bruce denied knowing anything about where her tampon might be. She was getting the picture that she had been raped after seeing his erect penis and the fact that she had no tampon. By this time, she had recovered enough from the effects of the drinks to be able to stand up on her own. She went to the other bedroom by herself and closed the door.

Jessica didn't know for sure what Bruce had done to her. However, what she did know was that she didn't want to be alone with him in the house any longer. She talked Bruce into taking her out for the evening. They went to Sharkeez, a sports bar, where she felt safer with so many other people around. Jessica hoped he would find some other woman at the bar whom he could direct his attention to. It was getting late, so they left the bar and he drove her over to a condo in Huntington Beach to show her where a friend lived who was often out of town. The friend had let Bruce use the condo to entertain women when his friend wasn't around. Bruce said, "In my time of grieving, my friend is letting me stay here. Like I'm really grieving." After which Bruce chuckled, making a joke of it.

They returned to the Koklich house and prepared for bed. Bruce decided to make a reasonable compromise. He told Jessica that if she didn't want to have sex with him during her period, at least she could give him a "cute little blow job." Jessica wouldn't agree to any form of sexual activity with Bruce. Jessica had been staying at Bruce's for only five days, and it was clear that Bruce had been wasting his time with all his salesmanship abilities, Bruce wasn't able to consummate the deal in making his 18-year-old step-niece into his own sex kitten. The very next morning Bruce explained to Jessica that their arrangement wasn't working out and he was going to take her back home to the Bay Area.

CHAPTER 15 KOKLICH-PERFECT CASE CRUMBLES

Bruce zoomed up Interstate 5 to the Bay area. Neither Bruce nor Jessica was pleased with the situation. Bruce didn't obtain what he expected and Jessica received more than she had anticipated. What Bruce couldn't have foreseen was that Jessica would immediately report that Bruce had raped her at his house. This information was conveyed to the Mountain Women's Resource Center. Jessica claimed that she had been raped or sexually assaulted when she had passed out by the pool in her swimsuit. The local law enforcement agency was contacted by the Center.

The reports and information were forwarded to the Los Angeles County Sheriff, since it was their jurisdiction in which the sexual acts occurred. This information percolated up to the Sheriff's homicide detectives, who within days executed a search warrant on the Koklich residence. The search revealed the box of condoms and the box of tampons under the sink where Jessica saw them placed. This corroborated what Jessica had said. If Bruce didn't have enough suspicion on him, his five-day venturesome lust with Jessica had focused considerable law enforcement attention on him. He no longer appeared to be the grieving husband but more like a husband who wanted to get rid of his wife so he could have younger, sexier companions who would satisfy his sensuous desires.

At that point, the Sheriff's Department detectives had some salacious tidbits, but what did it prove? When Jana's SUV was found with her blood in the back, the detectives were convinced that this was a homicide and not a mere missing persons case. The big question was, who was the killer? The more the detectives looked at that last weekend Bruce and Jana spent together, the more things didn't add up. Everyone who knew Jana said that there were two things that Jana always did. First, she never missed an appointment. She was so well organized. She had everything planned out so well that she knew when and where she had to be at all times. The other thing that her friends and business associate indicated was one of her hallmarks was the fact that she immediately returned voice mail phone calls. This may have come from her experience in the real estate business, since any message left could be a potential sale. The other factor could be a result of her upbringing by her family, in which she was taught the values of being responsible and respectful of other people. Jana was one of the most predicable persons one could ever meet. Some might say that was a boring trait, but to others who worked with her and depended on her, they appreciated her trait of keeping her word and always being punctual.

Jana was the epitome of reliability, responsibility, and dependability. The detectives in the Koklich cases analyzed everything that Jana was to do that weekend. On Saturday morning at 7:00 a.m., she didn't show up for her physical workout. Dean Costales, her trainer, called her cellphone at 7:03 a.m. and later her house phone to see why she wasn't there. She had never been late before. Jana didn't answer any of the calls, and the trainer left a message on her cellphone. He was concerned, as this was out of character for Jana.

At 2:00 p.m. that Saturday, Jana had an appointment for a facial massage with her good friend Nini, with whom she had gone to the Staples Center the night before. When she didn't show up, Nini figured something had to be wrong because Jana never missed an appointment. The night before, Jana had been talking about how much she was looking forward to the massage. Nini made phone calls to Jana's cellphone, house phone, and even her business phone. There was no answer, so Nini left a message for Jana. She went so far as to call Jana's husband Bruce to find out if he knew where she could be. She waited and waited and there was no contact from Jana or Bruce.

Jana's mother had been expecting to hear from her regarding getting together on Sunday to go out to see a movie. She wanted to hear from her on Saturday because she didn't know what time she would have to be ready. Her mother called her and left messages. When she didn't hear back from her, she called Bruce's cellphone and left a message. By Sunday, her mother was becoming concerned, since Jana hadn't called back and completely missed coming by to take her out to the movies.

Even Jana's father was disappointed that she hadn't contacted him as she said she would. She was planning to fly to Texas to visit him, and he needed to discuss what day she would be arriving.

It wasn't until Monday morning that everything seemed to get sorted out. Jana's mother had called the house three times Monday morning and left messages. Finally, around 9:30 a.m., Bruce called Jana's mother back and said that Jana had left for work and she should be arriving at the office in a few minutes. Jana's mother was much relieved to hear this information but was shocked to hear from Bruce, since he seldom had any contact with Jana's side of the family.

Another strange thing happened about the same time. Nini got a message from Bruce saying that he got Nini's message about where Jana was and wanted to let her know that Jana could be reached later at home. Nini was likewise shocked that Bruce would call her. Bruce went on to say that he was going to a funeral but afterwards would be in the office.

On Monday morning, Bruce went to the office early and was there before anyone else had arrived for work. He did some work on the computer and later he met with the local bank representative and the two of them left to attend a funeral.

It was after 11:00 a.m. when Bruce returned to the office. He was met by the staff asking where Jana was. Bruce indicated that something must have come up and that she was still at home. Bruce asked Chris Brooks (the computer guy) to accompany him home to see if they could figure out where Jana was. It seemed strange that Bruce would need someone to go with him the short distance to check out the house.

By 11:30 a.m., Bruce called Jana's mother and told her that Jana was missing but he was going to make some more calls to see if he could track her down. Bruce called Jana's physical trainer to see if he knew anything about her whereabouts. This proved to be unfruitful so Bruce called Detective Molean, who he knew worked for the Long Beach Police Department. He explained to him that his wife seemed to be missing and asked advice as to what to do in that type of situation. The Koklich house was located in Sheriff's territory, but the real estate office was located in the City of Long Beach. If Jana was carjacked on her way to the office, it could have occurred in either jurisdiction. After some initial questioning, the Long Beach police decided to take a missing person report.

Jana's mother was beside herself and called Bruce to find out what he knew. He told her that he had officially reported her missing to the police. At that point, Jana's mother jumped in her car and rushed over to the Koklich's house, where she met Bruce. To Jana's mother's surprise, Bruce said to her, "I have loved your daughter since the day that I met her." Jana's mother wondered why he was saying that to her if Jana had only been reported missing for several hours. There was no sign of foul play and there had to be an explanation as to where she might have gone.

Another odd conversation occurred at 5:30 p.m. when Bruce called Mrs. Berton (Pseudonym), one of Jana's best friends. He told her that the last time he saw Jana was early that morning when he kissed her good-bye as he left for the office. He asked Mrs. Berton if she had any idea where Jana might be. Mrs. Berton thought it was a strange conversation, since he sounded as if he were crying while talking to her. She thought that was unusual for him to be crying under the circumstances. It was not until the next day when Mrs. Berton went to the Koklich house that she noticed Bruce giving the appearance of crying but there were no tears in his eyes. On the following day, which was Wednesday, Jana's mother was at a press conference with Bruce. He went before the cameras and asked the public to help find his wife. He gave the appearance of being a distraught husband. He appeared to be crying as he spoke to the TV cameras. But Jana's mother, who was standing a few feet away, noticed that there were no tears in Bruce's eyes.

There wasn't any direct evidence that Bruce was involved in Jana's disappearance. The detectives were receiving bad vibes that Bruce knew more than he was telling them. To support their gut feeling, the detectives encountered people who thought Bruce's behavior was quite unusual under the circumstances. There were a number of Jana's friends and office workers whom Bruce had approached trying to find out if any of them had known if Jana had missed appointments. He kept pressing them to say that it wasn't unusual for her to be late or to altogether miss appointments. To her friends, this was a bizarre inquiry for a husband to make when his wife had just recently disappeared. Many of Jana's friends were offended that Bruce would try to paint a picture of Jana being an irresponsible person. Every one of Jana's friends told Bruce that they couldn't think of a time when Jana was a "No Show."

Bruce had made contact with one of the neighbors. She was talking about Jana's disappearance and Bruce said to her, "You remember when we walked by and waved to you on Saturday or Sunday." The neighbor had a good memory and remembered distinctly that she didn't see Jana or Bruce walk by at any time during the weekend. She couldn't understand why Bruce was so insistent that she confirm the fact that she had seen the two of them walking together. The neighbor was shocked that Bruce continued to tell her that she must have seen them.

Bruce made another odd comment to Jeff Berton. He was the husband of one of Jana's best friends, and he was trying to console Bruce over his wife's disappearance. Bruce asked him, "How long does it take before a missing person can be declared legally dead?"

The detectives realized that none of these statements by themselves proved anything, but when they were put together they were providing a clearer picture of what might have happened to Jana.

Bruce Koklich was a very clever man who had a confident air, and he presented himself as though he were smarter than those around him. Bruce's 'diversion plan' was to have someone steal his wife's car, and that would corroborate the fact that she had been carjacked and most likely killed in the process. The plan was to make it appear that she was carjacked on her way to work Monday morning. This made it difficult for Bruce, since he had to be at a funeral at the time of the supposed carjacking. He had to set up the plan the night before so everything would be in place for Monday morning.

The Koklich's neighbor saw Jana's car in the driveway on Saturday and part of Sunday; however, she didn't see it any time after that. Late on Sunday night, some distance away in the city of Signal Hill, a woman saw a white male dressed in a white business shirt seated in an SUV parked in an alley. What caught the woman's attention was that this was a high-crime area where white people were seldom seen. When she drove slowly by, the man quickly started up the car and drove away.

The next morning, Monday, Ruthie Sims (Pseudonym) saw a white Nissan Pathfinder vehicle with no one inside, parked in front of her house in the low-income section of Long Beach. She walked by and glanced through the open window. She could see that there was a purse on the seat and the keys were in the ignition.

Ruthie laughingly told her sister that this looked like a setup job—it was too convenient. She and her sister went on their way down the street.

A short time later, her son and another kid from the area came walking by and likewise looked inside the car. They could see the purse on the seat with no one inside. The boys possessed less willpower to avoid this tempting situation. They looked around to see if anyone was watching and quickly reached in and snatched the purse. This seemed to be the kids' lucky day. When they looked inside the purse they found a cellphone, which they took, and money they found inside was split among themselves. When it came to the credit cards and the identification, they figured that they were too young to use them. Their reaction was to throw the purse with the credit cards and ID in it on the roof of the neighboring apartment house across the street. The car remained parked at the curb for some time, even though it had the keys in the ignition and the windows rolled down. It wasn't until 4:30 p.m. that a man who was described as a Mexican or Asian was daring enough to get in the car and drive it away.

Bruce had hoped that his diversion plan would cause someone to start joyriding the car around the streets of Long Beach. That didn't happen, since whoever took the car decided to store it in a small enclosed garage off an alley. Bruce had also hoped that someone would start using the credit cards, so the detectives would be diverted by chasing those users down as suspects in Jana's disappearance. He couldn't have anticipated that the kids would have thrown the credit cards in the purse on top of a roof where no one could see or use them.

Bruce also didn't anticipate that Ruthie would be watching the TV news, which showed a photo of Jana's car and asked the public that if they saw that car to call the Sheriff's Department. Ruthie thought to herself that the car looked familiar, but where had she seen it? Then the light went on in her head and she said to herself, "I told you so, I told you, it was a setup." That was the car she had seen parked outside her apartment with the purse inside. She said to herself, "Praise the Lord," that she had had the good sense not to take the purse. Ruthie was pleased that she had instilled the same values in her son and was very proud of him.

Then she noticed that her son had a new cellphone. She clearly understood that he couldn't afford one on his allowance. She asked him if someone had loaned it to him and what was the story on the cellphone. Ruthie may have taught her son too well. It wasn't long before he admitted that he and his friend had taken a purse from a car that had been parked out in front of their apartment. They found the cellphone in the purse. Her son acknowledged that they had thrown the purse up on the roof.

This was too much for Ruthie to bear. She knew that was the car that had been shown on the TV news as possibly being involved in a homicide investigation. She didn't want her son to be mixed up in a murder investigation just because he had taken a purse and a cellphone. She didn't feel comfortable going directly to the police. Ruthie's religion had helped her through many difficult times, and that was where she turned in this time of need. She knew that she could trust her pastor to know what was the best thing to do to protect her son from being arrested. After explaining everything to the pastor, he agreed to help out. He soon learned that someone else had found a handgun in the side of the driver's door. Some other guys from the neighborhood had taken the gun. The good pastor knew the first thing he needed to do was retrieve the handgun before it fell into the hands of the gangsters who could start using it to shoot up the neighborhood.

The pastor knew whom to contact in the neighborhood, and with a few phone calls he had gotten the gun off the street and had it in his possession. The pastor's next contact was with the law enforcement authorities. He explained that the gun and the cellphone and purse had been removed from the car after the car had been parked on the street. The homicide detectives were more interested in talking to Ruthie's son than prosecuting him for what he had done. The son showed the detectives where the purse was thrown. Within a short time, the police had retrieved the purse with all of Jana's identification in it. The next question was, where was Jana's car?

It wasn't until August 27, 2001, almost seven days later, that Jana's car was found parked in an old garage in an alley in the Signal Hill area. When it was recovered, it appeared to be wiped clean of any incriminating evidence. The only useable evidence was the fact that Jana's blood was found on the carpet in the rear of the Pathfinder vehicle. The detectives knew when the car had been recovered that they were dealing with a homicide, not a mere missing person situation. Was there enough evidence to criminally charge someone with a crime, in particular, Bruce Koklich?

CHAPTER 16 KOKLICH-FIRST TRIAL

The Koklich case made for a sensational murder trial for a number of reasons. First, it involved prominent people in the community and it had mystery and intrigue. Most of all, it had a little sex to spice up the story. The defendant had money and was therefore able to hire a prominent Defense attorney to defend him in court. The DA's Office seldom filed 'No Body' cases, for the simple reason that such cases have a built-in Defense that the victim is merely a missing person possibly by their own design. For many jurors, 'No Body' cases have Reasonable Doubt spelled out all over them.

With all these factors, it wasn't surprising that the Koklich case was assigned to the DA's Major Crimes Division. The bigger question was, who would be the prosecutor that would get stuck with this 'No Body' case? Apparently Eleanor Hunter had a full caseload, but she wasn't the type to shy away from controversial cases. She never complained to her boss that she was too busy. When her boss, Pat Dixon, was inquiring around who to assign the case to, Eleanor's reaction was a big smile and she said, "Why not?"

By 2003, Eleanor had learned there was no way to predict when a case would go to trial. Eleanor was confident enough to believe that she would be able to work out any scheduling problems. When she originally reviewed the facts of the Koklich case, it seemed simple enough. As she immersed herself deeper into the case, she soon realized that it was more than a usual Domestic Violence murder. In this case, it appeared that the husband, Bruce Koklich, wanted to get rid of his wife and replace her with a younger and more attractive female companion. Another reason to get rid of his wife could have been the fear that she would divorce him, which would result in his losing control of half of the couple's community property. However, Bruce didn't want to merely get rid of Jana; he wanted to make sure that he didn't get caught. In many domestic murders, the spouse is just reacting emotionally because the spouses are mad at each other. These killers don't always thoroughly plan how they are going to get away with murdering their spouses.

However, some spouses go to great lengths to cover their tracks. They might concoct some type of alibi or even try to claim the killing was a matter of self-defense. In most cases, these Defenses don't hold up in court. An alibi puts the Defense on the defensive by trying to convince the jury that the alibi is genuine. As to self-defense, it is hard to sell when the husband is twice the size of his dead wife.

What was challenging in the Koklich case was the fact that the husband/killer was smart and had the capability to stand up and make boldface lies without any hesitation. Bruce looked upon himself as being much more sophisticated and was confident that he could pull off the "Perfect Murder." He understood the weakness of using the alibi approach. For him the best approach was to dispose of his wife's body in such a way that it would never be found. If he kept his mouth shut, this would make it virtually impossible for the prosecution to convict him.

It was never clear how Bruce killed his wife or where he dumped or buried her body. Even though the exact details aren't known, Bruce Koklich most likely wrapped his wife's body in the bed sheets from the master bed. Maybe in the early morning darkness he placed her body in the back of her SUV car and drove her to some isolated area. There he disposed of her body so no one would ever be able to find it. The police and Sheriff detectives searched everywhere, especially in the Signal Hill area, after Jana's car was found parked in an old dilapidated garage in the very humble part of the city.

In that part of town there are hundreds of old abandoned oil wells where a body could be easily discarded. If a body was dumped in some of those wide mouth old wells, it would quickly deteriorate without any noticeable pungent odor and would remain there forever. The Koklichs also lived near the Pacific Ocean, which is a great dumping ground for bodies. Anyone who has access to a boat could go out several miles in the ocean and drop overboard a weighted body and it would never be found.

There was an endless supply of possible sites where one could get rid of a body within a short distance of the couple's home in the city of Lakewood. To add to this was the fact that Bruce was a real estate broker who was very familiar with almost every piece of property in the north Long Beach area. On top of that, he and Jana owned 21 parcels of property. Any one of those sites could be used as a clandestine gravesite.

The Sheriff's Department had conducted an extensive investigation to find Jana alive or locate her dead body. The detectives had spent hours talking to everyone in the neighborhood. They interviewed family and friends as to any ideas they might have regarding where Jana might have gone. They had police cadets and volunteers go door to door handing out fliers. The media was used for weeks showing photos of both Jana and her car. The public was asked to call the detectives if they had seen her or had information about her whereabouts.

The hospitals were contacted to see if they had any patients by the name of Jana Koklich or anyone who fit her description. An extension of that was that all the coroners' offices in Southern California were contacted as to any Jane Does fitting Jana's description. Just in case Jana wanted to get away from Bruce and a broken marriage, the detectives reviewed the divorce records of the courts and checked for any restraining order that may have been filed using her name.

Although it was highly unlikely, the detectives had to investigate the possibility that Jana left the area to start a new life without Bruce. They even contacted the Office of Social Security to see if there was any activity on her Social Security number or a new one issued in Jana's name. They checked with DMV to see if there was a new driver's license under Jana's name. The detectives followed up on that by checking to see if there were any traffic violations under her driver's license number and if she was in custody in any jail or prison. Just to cover all bases, they contacted the Voter's Registration to see if she had voted since her disappearance. They continued to monitor her personal and the business bank accounts to see if she had made any withdrawals. At the same time, they checked her credit cards to see if there was any new activity in her name.

When a 'No Body' case is prosecuted, the Defense has the distinct advantage. The prosecutor ends up on the defensive, having to continually combat the lingering doubt that the victim in fact was never murdered but had moved on with a new life somewhere else, possibly with someone else. On the other hand, the blood in the back of the Jana's SUV did make it more difficult to claim that there was no homicide.

As the investigation continued, more information was uncovered that portrayed a muddy picture of Bruce and Jana's personal life. Under a closer examination, the couple appeared to have some disharmony in the home even though they tried to perpetuate the image of being a loving and caring couple. Their eleven-year marriage had not yielded any children. The emphasis of the marriage was on a dynamic team working to acquire as much wealth as time would permit. Without children, there was no feeling of family to come home to. Most couples become so involved with their family that there isn't time to decide whether one had become bored with the marriage.

It didn't take much time for the detectives to determine that Bruce wasn't the devoted, enamored husband doting over his lovely wife. Bruce had a reputation of playing around with other women. He may have wanted the excitement that Jana couldn't provide him. Jana had worked long and hard at their business, which was the center of their lives. In the process, she may have not focused on her appearance. She put on pounds and didn't spend time primping herself to impress those around her.

As Jana and Bruce drifted apart, the question was what to do. Should she try to win back Bruce's roaming eyes by fixing herself up, or should she fix herself up to attract attention from others? She had the money to remake her image and she wanted to feel good about herself. When Jana put her mind to it, she could do anything. She worked with a physical trainer to force her to work out and lose the weight. She got the facials and started to take care of her appearance. The result was that there was a new Jana emerging from within the old stodgy Jana. If Bruce didn't want her, she would be able to get someone else on her own terms.

As helpful as the blood in the back of Jana's SUV was for the prosecution, the Defense was taking advantage of the evidence that Jana was making herself over. This gave the Defense the perfect argument that she had run away from a bad marriage and started a new life with another person. It didn't seem very likely that Jana would walk away from half of the couple's assets. The Defense wanted to make it appear that true love can be blind to money, or that she could have found a 'sugar daddy' who was going to take care of her. She may have wanted a quick exit in order to avoid a messy divorce and bickering with Bruce over every nickel the couple had earned.

The Defense wanted the jurors to believe there was no homicide and that in fact there was no victim. If there was a victim, it was the defendant husband who was the true victim. Poor Bruce had to defend himself against homicide charges that he wasn't guilty of.

The prosecutor, Eleanor, knew from the start that she had an uphill fight just trying to prove that there was in fact a murder. At the beginning of the trial, the prosecutor concentrated on proving a Motive for the murder. She tried to show that Bruce killed Jana because they were having financial problems with the two businesses they owned and operated. The prosecutor tried to show that Bruce killed his wife for the life insurance money in order to save the business.

The Defense attacked the prosecution's theory by showing that their Real Estate and Computer businesses were financially sound. The Defense was able to bring in witnesses to say the Koklich's real estate business was doing well and that it was worth over $5 million. The Defense was able to twist Bruce's infidelity issue into an example of how weak the prosecution's case was. The Defense claimed that the prosecution was trying to smear Bruce's reputation, since they didn't have any real evidence. Bruce was so confident of his salesman's skills that he took the witness stand and tried to explain that he had no Motive to kill his wife. He claimed that he and his wife were getting along well when she disappeared.

The Defense continued to fan the flames that the victim was still alive somewhere and that the defendant was being set up for a crime he didn't commit. The case went to the jury and they deliberated long and hard. Finally, they said that they were hopelessly deadlocked and any further deliberation would be of no benefit. The judge declared a mistrial, and it was determined that the jury was split seven for conviction and five for not guilty.

The defendant and the Defense attorney were ecstatic with the hung jury. Although Eleanor, the prosecutor, was disappointed with the results, she was more interested in learning what went wrong and how to be more convincing in the next jury trial. Eleanor knew that Bruce Koklich was as guilty as sin, but how could she prove it to a jury? She thought long and hard about what would be a better way to present the case to a jury. Her co-prosecutor in the Soliah case, Michael Latin, had just finished up a trial and didn't have anything upcoming for trial for several months. As a result, Eleanor and Michael joined together to work again as the dynamic duo. The two of them had many strategy sessions as to what would be the best way to present the evidence to convince the jury to convict the defendant.

Both Eleanor and Michael recognized that the Defense was able to attack her Motive evidence. They were able to create a Reasonable Doubt as to the condition of the businesses the couple owned. For the next trial, the prosecutors developed another strategy, one which would not rely on the issue of whether the defendant had a financial Motive to kill his wife.

The law doesn't require the prosecution to prove that the defendant possessed a Motive to kill. All the prosecution needed to do was to prove that the defendant had committed each of the elements of the crime of murder beyond a reasonable doubt. The evidence of Motive is helpful to the prosecution to explain the reasons why the defendant committed the crime, even if it isn't required by law to be proven. The reason the law doesn't require Motive to be proven is the fact that in many crimes it is impossible to know the real Motive that drove the defendant to commit the crime. Michael Latin liked to use the example, "If we were here on a rape case, would we be talking about motive? Of course not."

If the prosecutors could prove that the defendant was the only person who had the opportunity to kill the victim, that might be sufficient to convict the defendant. They decided to take a completely different approach in the case, one which would require them to spend considerable time explaining to the jury the facts of the case and what those facts meant when they were all considered in totality. The argument would be that there wasn't one thing that proved that the defendant murdered his wife Jana, but there was a series of many things that had to be considered collectively.

For the second trial, Eleanor realized that she had to educate the jurors regarding how important every piece of the circumstantial evidence was to prove that in fact Jana was dead and that her husband Bruce was the killer. Eleanor contacted the DA's Office's Trial Support Division for assistance. At the time, I was the Head Deputy of the Division, so it wasn't long before I was deeply involved in learning the facts of the case and determining what the specific issues were. As a result, I decided that a PowerPoint slide show would be the most effective way to present the story to the jury. In order to capture the jurors' attention I always incorporate four factors into every presentation. They included: Will it Inform? Will it Clarify? Will it be Persuasive? And ultimately will it be Memorable?

At that time, Eleanor was relying on her oral skills to get her message across to the jury. She and Michael had seen firsthand what a powerful effect PowerPoint had been in the Soliah case, but neither of them had mastered all the steps that are a prerequisite for creating a slide show. There was never any question as to what the prosecutors wanted to say, but they didn't know how to visually display it for a jury.

Since Eleanor was the one who was most familiar with the facts of the case, I worked with her and prepared a draft version of a slide show for her consideration. Eleanor by her very nature had her own ideas, and they had to be combined in any presentation that she would accept. I assigned one of the paralegals to work with her to reduce her lengthy text to bullet points that could be easily listed on a slide. Along the way, we tried to insert graphic images such as photos or documents to make the presentation less wordy and more memorable.

CHAPTER 17 KOKLICH-SECOND TRIAL

In the second trial, the Defense thought it was merely deja vu and they would have an easy job of hanging up the jury for a second time. What the Defense miscalculated was who they were up against. Eleanor wasn't born yesterday. She was the type who was willing to learn from her mistakes. In this second trial, she was going to present a more visual trial in order to assure that the jurors clearly understood the facts of the case.

Eleanor was given the task of giving the Opening Statement to the jury. It consisted of a PowerPoint slide show, which permitted her to explain the case while the facts were visually displayed on the screen behind her. She knew it was imperative to convince the jurors that Jana was actually dead even though her body had never been found. In order to prove this, she decided to show that Jana wouldn't have missed all of her appointments that weekend or not returned all the phone calls that had been made to the couple. First, the prosecutor had to prove to the jurors how reliable Jana was. Her first slide was a photo of Jana with a title on the top saying "Who was Jana Carpenter-Koklich? Then Eleanor

flashed on the screen behind her the words "Reliable," "Responsible," and "Dependable."

Then she wanted the jurors to understand all the things that Jana didn't do-things which would have been totally out of character for her. On her next slide, she showed all the appointments Jana had that she missed with various people like her physical trainer as well as her best friend. This slide showed how she didn't call to cancel and as a matter of fact didn't respond back to their voice mails. The inference was that the only way that could happen was if she were dead. *Both slides are shown on the following graphic page.*

Graphics Page

This slide illustrates that Jana was a predictable person.

This slide showed how the victim was contacted and didn't respond.

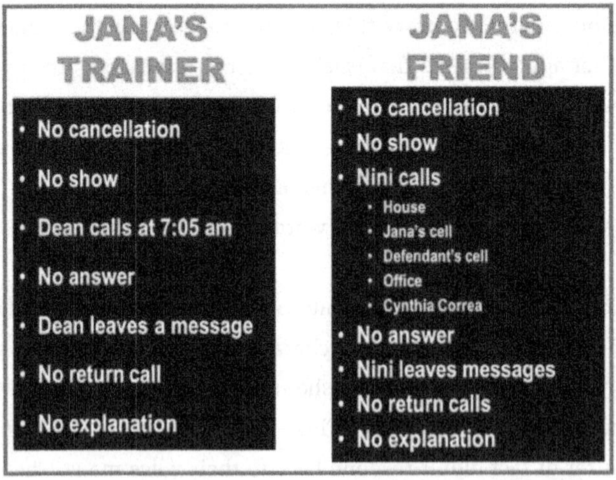

The next fact that the prosecutor was trying to convey to the jurors was how busy Jana was. On the next slide, she showed Jana's handwritten Calendar with all her appointments. That was followed by a slide comparing the activities of both Jana and her husband for that weekend. This illustrated how busy Jana was compared to Bruce who had nothing planned. *Both slides are shown on the following page.*

Graphics Page

This slide illustrated the plans the victim had in which she never kept.

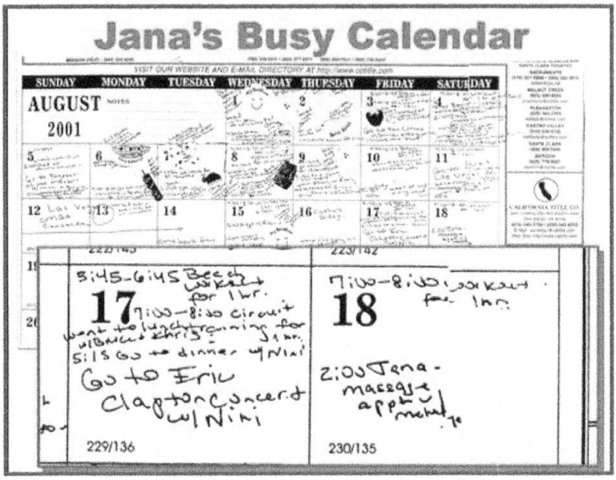

This slide compared the victim's and her husband's plans for the weekend.

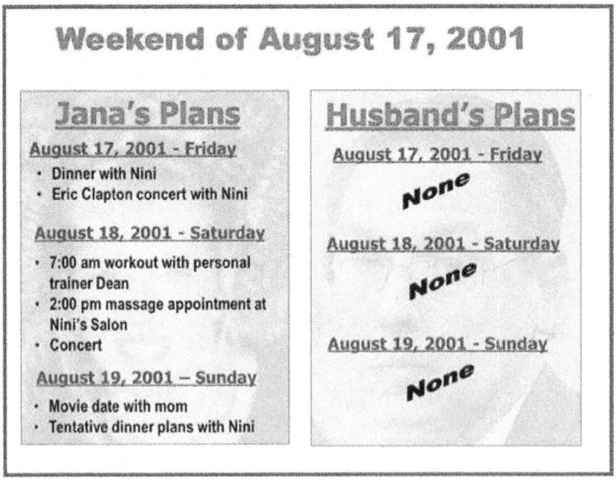

The next part of the prosecutor's Opening dealt with the fact that Bruce was trying to perpetuate the myth that Jana was alive all that weekend and spent it with Bruce at their house. So the next slide showed that no one saw Jana after she was dropped off at the house on Friday night by her friend Nini. No one saw her all weekend long except for her husband, who claimed he was with her. That was followed by the slide listing all the people he contacted to try to get them to claim that Jana wasn't a reliable person and that she often missed appointments. This slide showed how he was trying to deflect the focus of the police. *Both slides are shown on the following page.*

Graphics Page

This slide showed that it was only the defendant who claimed to see the victim.

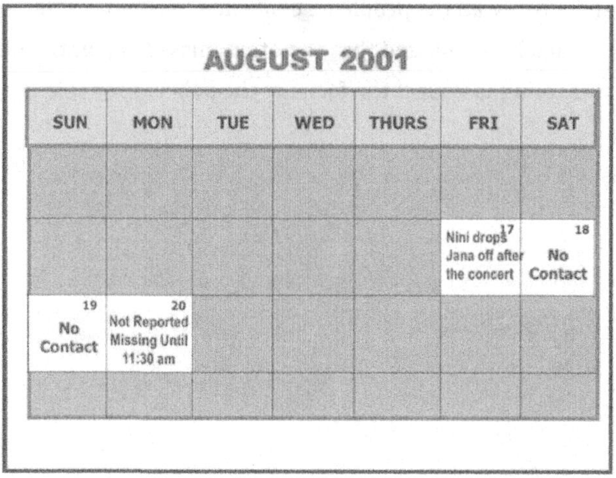

This slide summarized how the husband tried to make the wife look irresponsible.

Eleanor wanted the jurors to be firmly convinced that if Jana were alive she would have responded to the phone calls that had been made to her. She realized that merely telling the jurors that there had been 19 phone calls made to Jana didn't have the impact she wanted. That was when she devised a visual that illustrated the number of calls made to Jana in which there was no response.

Since this was the second trial, Eleanor knew that the Defense would try to spin the facts to make it look possible that a burglar might have broken into the house and kidnapped Jana. That was why she created a slide titled 'Condition of the Koklich Home' that permitted her the opportunity to show all the reasons why there was no such burglary. *Both slides are shown on the following page.*

Graphics Page

With this one slide the jurors could see all the calls that had been made to victim.

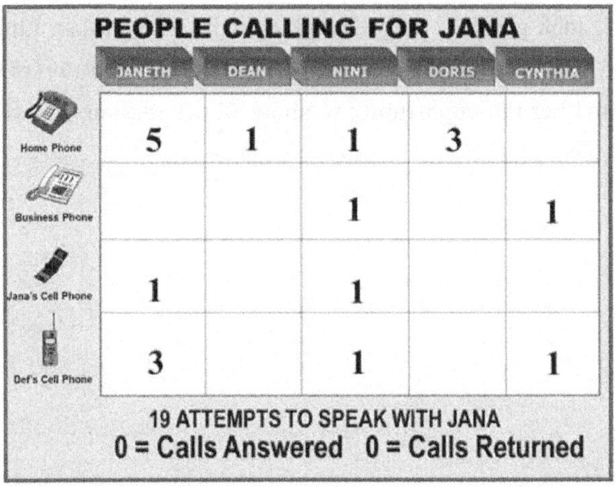

	JANETH	DEAN	NINI	DORIS	CYNTHIA
Home Phone	5	1	1	3	
Business Phone			1		1
Jana's Cell Phone	1		1		
Def's Cell Phone	3		1		1

This slide summarized the facts that didn't add up to a residential robbery.

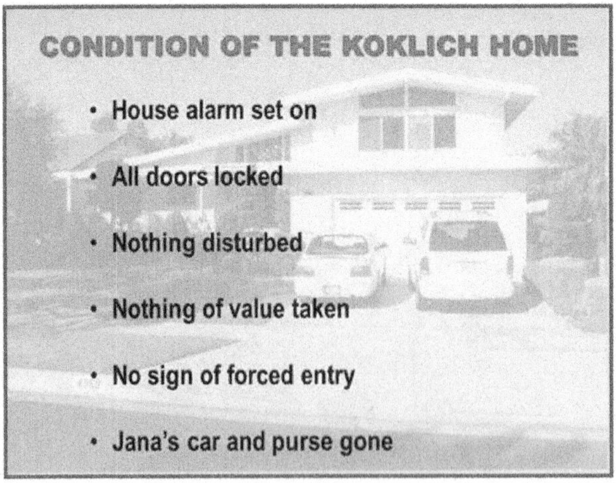

The next set of slides used by the prosecutor was about the housekeeper's findings involving the missing sheets. First, she used a slide that explained how the housekeeper determined that the sheets she had placed on the master bed the week before were missing. She found that someone had substituted a small size sheet for the original ones.

The following slide listed all the items that the housekeeper found missing, such as the Bed sheets for master bed; Pillow cases for master bed; Jana's Pillow from the master bed; and finally, a master Bath towel was missing as well. There were two possible inferences one could make: that Jana was killed on the master bed, or that the sheet was used to wrap the body in so it could easily be disposed of without being seen. *These slides are shown on the next page.*

Graphics Page

This slide showed how and when sheets were changed.

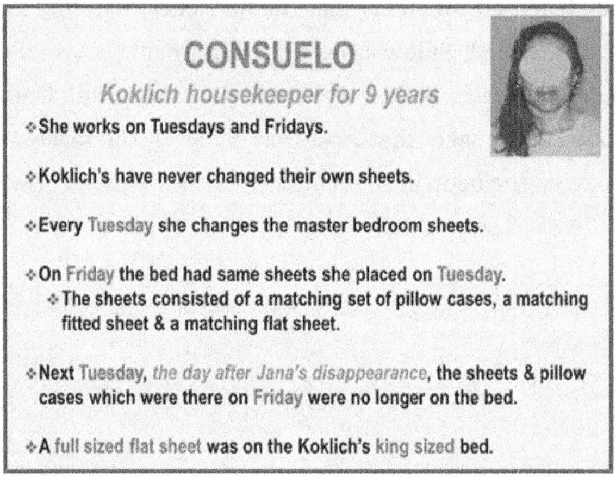

This slide was used to show all the items missing from the house.

The prosecution's case had to rely on the photos of the rear area of the car where the blood was found. Eleanor used a slide to show the rear portion of the car to illustrate to the jurors exactly where the blood was found. The other item found in the rear of the car was a 'down feather,' which might have come from a pillow. The logical inference was that someone had used Jana's car to dispose of her body.

Eleanor didn't want to take any chances that the jurors wouldn't be able to comprehend the various locations described by the witnesses. She prepared a slide that consisted of a map of the northern Long Beach area, including the city of Signal Hill. By using this graphic, the jurors could see how close the family house was in relation to their Real Estate office. Also, the map showed where Jana's car was originally spotted and later recovered. *Those slides are as follows:*

Graphics Page

This slide illustrate where her car was found with blood drops in the back area.

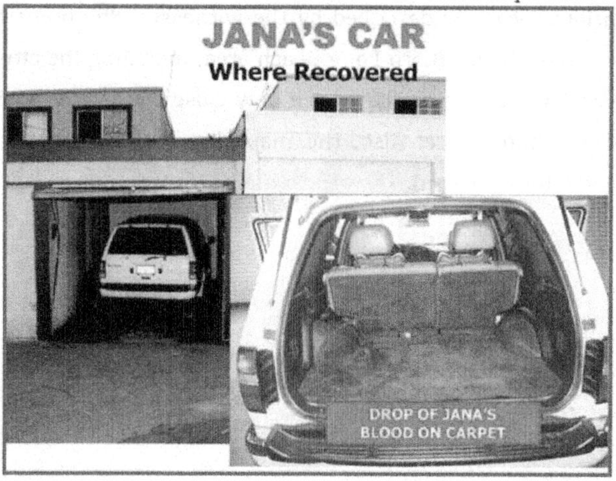

To orient the jurors, this slide was used to show how close everything was.

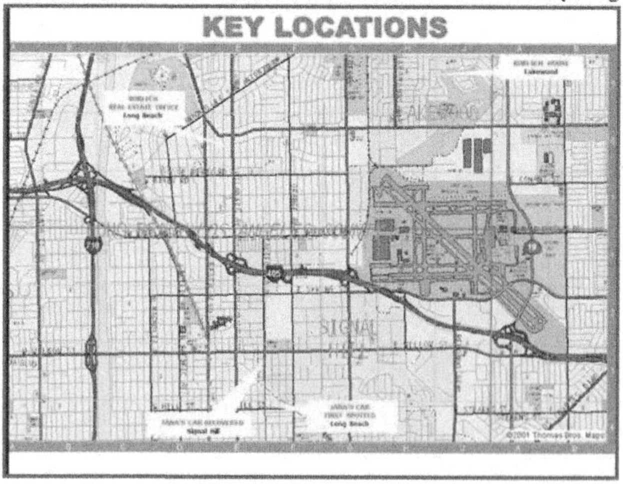

Throughout Eleanor's Opening Statement, the jurors were glued to her presentation. They seemed engaged and interested as she explained the facts. Their eyes were fixed on her, and when she went to another slide in her presentation there was a noticeable glance at the large screen behind her. Occasionally the jurors seemed to give a slight nod of their heads, as though to say 'I've got it.' Then they would redirect their eyes to the prosecutor.

Near the end of her slide show, Eleanor discussed how Bruce spent time trying to sexually hit on his young niece. The prosecutor didn't dwell on the more salacious part of the Koklich story but merely mentioned it to pique the jurors' interest. When Eleanor touched on Bruce's womanizing, several of the female jurors glanced at each other with a slight smirk on their face. Mentioning Bruce's sexual exploitation was like telling the jurors that there would be dessert served at the end of the trial. At least it was a little tidbit to keep the jurors' attention so they would be primed to hear those witnesses.

CHAPTER 18 KOKLICH-CONCLUSION OF CASE

The Defense was confident that the DA's Office was using the same witnesses and using the same approach they had utilized in the first trial. So the Defense's Opening Statement parroted their original Opening Statement, believing that the prosecution was going to rely on the theory that Bruce needed the life insurance money because he was in serious financial trouble caused by the new computer business they had started.

After both sides had finished their Opening Statements, the second trial began with Eleanor and Michael sharing the duties of questioning the witnesses. They started out with the workout trainer and Nini testifying to how reliable Jana was. This time the prosecution didn't introduce evidence that the killing was motivated by financial reasons. The prosecution relied on the theory that Bruce killed Jana because he was more interested in younger female companionship. The prosecution also put on all the witnesses involved in finding Jana's purse and her car.

The forensic testimony went well regarding the spot of blood on the rear carpet of Jana's SUV, as well as a spot that was found in the master bedroom. The DNA came back to Jana, supporting the idea that this was a homicide and not a mere Missing Persons case. This second trial seemed to go smoother. That may have been because the witnesses were well primed regarding what the questions would be so that they could give more concise answers. That was especially true with the housekeeper regarding the missing sheets. Since the jurors were alerted to the missing sheets in the Opening Statement, they seemed anxious to hear the testimony of the housekeeper. As Consuelo explained her suspicion of the bed sheets, she sounded like a character in one of Agatha Christie's detective novels.

Throughout the trial, the prosecutors continued to play various videos of Bruce being interviewed by TV reporters. In each of these interviews, Bruce professed how much he missed his wife and pleaded for her safe return. The videos showed Bruce appearing to be crying. However, witness after witnesses testified that they never saw any tears in Bruce's eyes. These witnesses thought it was odd that there was never any sign of visible tears.

Eleanor had promised the jurors that there would be some salacious testimony about Bruce hitting on women, such as at the bank and financial office. Then Eleanor called the niece, who delineated in detail all the attempts that Bruce had made in trying to convince her to have sex with him. What made this testimony so captivating was that the niece had been so outraged by Bruce's behavior that she had written a makeshift diary on butcher paper, which she read to the jurors.

After the prosecutors had finished calling their witnesses, it was the Defense's turn to call their witnesses, but it wasn't clear why some of the witnesses were called. The Defense seemed dead set on putting on the exact Defense they used in the first trial, not acknowledging that the prosecution had changed tactics and no longer was relying on the financial Motive for the killing. The Defense tried to suggest that Mr. Brooks, the computer business partner, was somehow the killer. The Defense tried to infer that Mr. Brooks felt cheated by the Koklichs, in that they had promised him a million shares of stock in the Software Company. When things were finalized, he only received 100,000 shares of stock.

The Defense tried to spin this so he would appear as a resentful co-employee who had a grudge against Jana and Bruce. There were two issues that the Defense tried to blow out of proportion. One was that Mr. Brooks had asked for a pillow back. When Jana's car was found, there was a small down feather next to the blood spot in the back of the SUV. The other issue was that Mr. Brooks had claimed that he **hadn't** spent the night at his girlfriend's place on the weekend in question. At trial, the Defense called his girlfriend to testify that he **had** spent the night at her place. This was to make Mr. Brooks look like a liar, someone the jurors could not trust. This was all much to do about nothing, since the prosecution had changed the strategy of the case.

The Defense called an expert witness who had training in psychology. He testified that it was not unusual for men who have lost a wife to immediately want to develop partnerships or liaisons with other women for comfort and support. He asserted that Bruce's conduct with other women and especially with his 18-year-old niece wasn't an uncommon reaction to a tragic loss. The expert may have believed what he was saying, but the jurors were more disgusted with Bruce's conduct and not buying the expert's reasoning, which they found devoid of common sense.

The witness expert went on to testify in front of the jury that he was a knowledgeable in the way that men and women cry. His contention was that men cry differently from women. He went on to say that men may not actually show tears when they are distraught. He tried to say that men's tear ducts may not stimulate tears in the same way that women become teary eyed.

One of the reasons that the Koklich murder trial was different than most was the fact that the defendant was out of custody. The judge had set bail at one million dollars. Since Bruce had property all over Southern California, it wasn't difficult for him to come up with the full amount of the bail. The fact of having a defendant out on bail in a murder case is devastating for the prosecution. The defendant is able to come and go like the jurors and even at times rub elbows while using the courthouse elevators or just the coming and going to the courtroom. Psychologically, the jurors get the feeling that the defendant must not be considered much of a threat if the court is permitting him to wander around like everybody else during the trial. In the eyes of the jurors, it is much more difficult to convict someone who you stood with in a cafeteria line or parked in the same parking lot.

The Defense tactic seemed more like a 'Shotgun' approach by showing that the prosecution hadn't answered where, when, or why the victim was killed. Everyone was waiting to hear from the defendant. In the first trial, he testified and was very combative with the prosecutor. But in this second trial, the defendant decided not to take the witness stand. Eleanor was looking forward to cross-examining Bruce. This time she had some incriminating evidence that she was going to ask him about. The Defense attorney was well aware that Eleanor was ready and well prepared for his client. He most likely thought it would be better not to have the jury see the arrogant and cocky side of Bruce, so the Defense attorney stood up in court and said, "The Defense has no more witnesses and the Defense Rests its case."

After both sides had finished presenting evidence, it was time for Argument. Although Michael was involved in part of the Argument, it was Eleanor who gave the bulk of the presentation. It was completely different from how she tried the case in the initial trial. In the first trial, she didn't use any slide show and used only a few visual exhibits. This second trial was what is called a 'Visual Trial.' Eleanor's presentation took every little piece of evidence and graphically showed the jury what it was and what it proved. By the use of visuals, the jurors were able to follow every step of her Argument.

The DA's Argument started out discussing the law that applied to this case. Eleanor always liked to explain to the jury the legal concepts, such as Circumstantial Evidence and Reasonable Doubt. Then she basically reviewed with the jurors the various slides from her Opening Statement and explained how she had proved each one of those points. This was highly effective, since the jurors could see visually that the prosecutor had proven everything she had said that she would prove.

However, there were several new slides that summarized certain witnesses' testimony. As to Eleanor's discussion of the niece's testimony, she used two slides. One was titled BRUCE'S CONDUCT WHILE JANA IS MISSING, and it listed all his questionable behavior with the niece. The second slide was titled BRUCE'S STATEMENT WHILE JANA IS MISSING, and it highlighted the statements that the defendant made, showing his cockiness and belief that he was going to get away with it. *See those two slides on the next graphic page.*

Graphics Page

This slide was used to illustrate the defendant's behavior after his wife went missing.

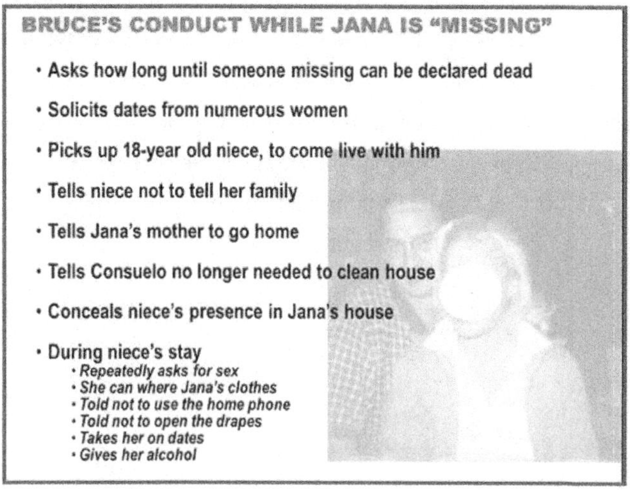

This slide listed some of the strange statements that the defendant made.

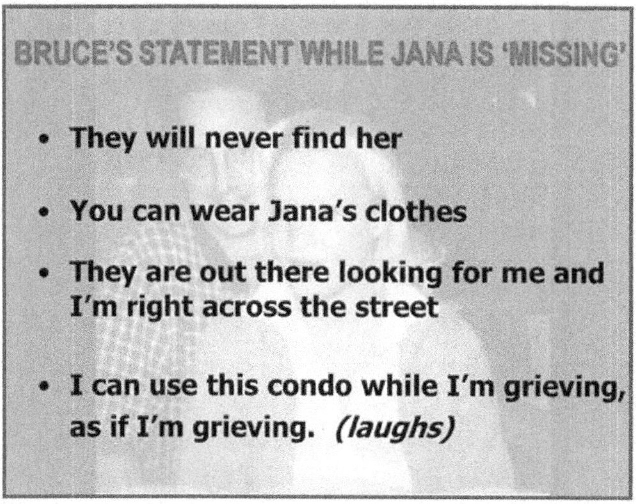

Other slides that were emphasized in the prosecutor's Argument were several of the videos of Bruce's interviews by TV reporters. Eleanor played those videos as part of her Argument and told the jurors to be the judge as to whether there were any tears in Bruce's eyes when he appeared to be crying during the interview.

Eleanor added a slide in her Argument that was titled DEFENSE TACTICS, in which she spelled out three words that she thought summarized the Defense actions, and they were **Delay; Distort; and Distract**. In some states an attorney is not permitted to criticize an opposing attorney. However, in California attorneys are given more latitude. Eleanor had been so outraged by the Defense tactics and felt it necessary to make some type of comment in front of the jury. Eleanor used those three words to describe the Defense's approach to the case. The jurors seemed acknowledge that was a good way to summarize the Defense. *Those slides are on the following graphic page.*

Graphics Page

There were several slides showing the defendant to be crying without tears.

During the Argument Eleanor wanted to discuss the Defense's approach.

Finally, Eleanor wanted to end her Argument by telling the jurors what she wanted them to do, and that was to find Bruce Koklich guilty of murder. She first used a slide spelling out the elements for MURDER. She knew that she would have a difficult time proving that the murder was of the first degree. So her slide was titled WHAT THIS CRIME IS—MURDER. In order to prove first degree Murder, Eleanor would have to prove Premeditation and Deliberation. It might have been a first degree murder, but there was no way of proving it. So she left it up to the jurors to decide whether it was first or second degree Murder.

Eleanor's last slide was meant to be dramatic. It stated 'Who is Bruce Koklich?' It showed a photo of Bruce, and under it were the bold letters **MURDERER**. *These slides appear on the following graphic page.*

Graphics Page

During the Argument this slide was used to show the jurors the elements for murder.

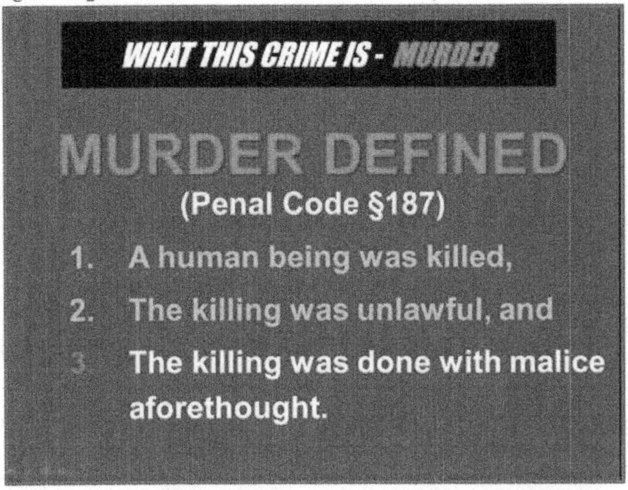

This was the prosecutor's final slide to her Argument presentation.

The Defense vigorously argued their case. The Defense attorney didn't use any slide show for his presentation. The Defense attorney was a strong advocate and continued to rely on his verbal skills to undercut the prosecution's evidence and presentation. He tried to sketch out some charts to counter Eleanor's Argument; however, it appeared too little too late.

The jury commenced their deliberations in the morning. By 2:00 p.m., they had come back with a verdict of MURDER IN THE SECOND DEGREE. After the verdict, the judge remanded Koklich into custody. Several weeks later, the judge sentenced Bruce to 15 years to life for the murder of his wife, Jana. Initially, it seemed like Bruce Koklich had pulled off the Perfect Crime, and few would have thought he would ever be convicted in a No Body case. Such cases are extremely challenging and seldom result in a conviction.

The DA's Office took a chance in filing this case. Without Eleanor's tenacious effort, the case didn't have a chance. Her extraordinary job in preparing and retrying this case made the difference. After the first trial, she was flexible enough to recognize that she needed to try another strategy in prosecuting the case. She made the adjustments, and most of all she recognized the effectiveness of putting together a visual presentation to persuade the jurors of the defendant's guilt.

Eleanor and her co-prosecutor Michael Latin made an effective team. They worked well with the witnesses and detectives to put all the incriminating evidence before the jury. It will never be known for certain whether it was Eleanor's visual slide show that made the difference between the first and second trial. When a prosecutor receives a hung jury split seven for conviction and five for not guilty, it takes an extraordinary attorney who can stand up tall with the self-confidence to say, "I can do it!" Eleanor was typical of all the **MAJOR CRIMES** prosecutors in that she rose to the occasion and did what seemed impossible, just like the Army's famed DELTA FORCE so often does.

PEOPLE VS. SANTE KIMES

Mother and Son Crime Wave

CHAPTER 19-KIMES-WHO ARE THEY?

Little did the Los Angeles District Attorney's Office realized that back in 1998 a body found in a dumpster near Los Angeles Airport would spiral into an infamous case with national implications. Because of the notoriety of the case, it was assigned to Major Crimes Division, requiring a top gun prosecutors, like Eleanor Hunter to handle the matter in court. The victim wasn't anyone special, and the cause of death was one bullet to the head by a small-caliber handgun. How could such a nondescript case draw so much attention?

Well, it is a long story, but it can best be described as one of a number of murders committed by the nefarious mother-and-son duo who wreaked havoc all across the country. They have earned a place on America's Most Wanted list, which includes Bonnie and Clyde; Leopold and Loeb; Jesse and Frank James; and Butch Cassidy and the Sundance Kid. Certainly the names of the wicked Sante Kimes (65) and her derelict son Kenny Kimes Jr. (25) should be added to this list.

Sante never won the mother-of-the-year award since she was a ruthless mother who terrorized her children and everyone around her. She gained the reputation of being one of the most devious and diabolical

Graphics Page

Sante Kimes **Kenny Kimes**

(Loving Mother **(Devoted Son)**

con artists in recent memory. She had a compulsive personality to manipulate and to control any and everyone who crossed her path.

Sante was a self-proclaimed criminal who thrived on committing crime despite the lack of motive or need for the theft. She had a habit of stealing to satisfy an inexplicable need that never seemed to be fulfilled. She was proud of her proficiency in lying to others about the crimes. She was like an addict who couldn't get enough of a thrill in trying to outsmart, outwit, and outfox anyone else. It seemed a logical conclusion that her scams and thievery would progress to murder. It is uncanny how a ruthless mother and an obedient son became known as the 'Gruesome Twosome' as they crisscrossed the country leaving peaceful towns in shambles from their fraudulent scams and rampages. *On the following graphic page is a summary of this case which may be helpful to better understand the facts of this bizarre case.*

Graphics Page

This graphics may help you better understand the two separate cases.

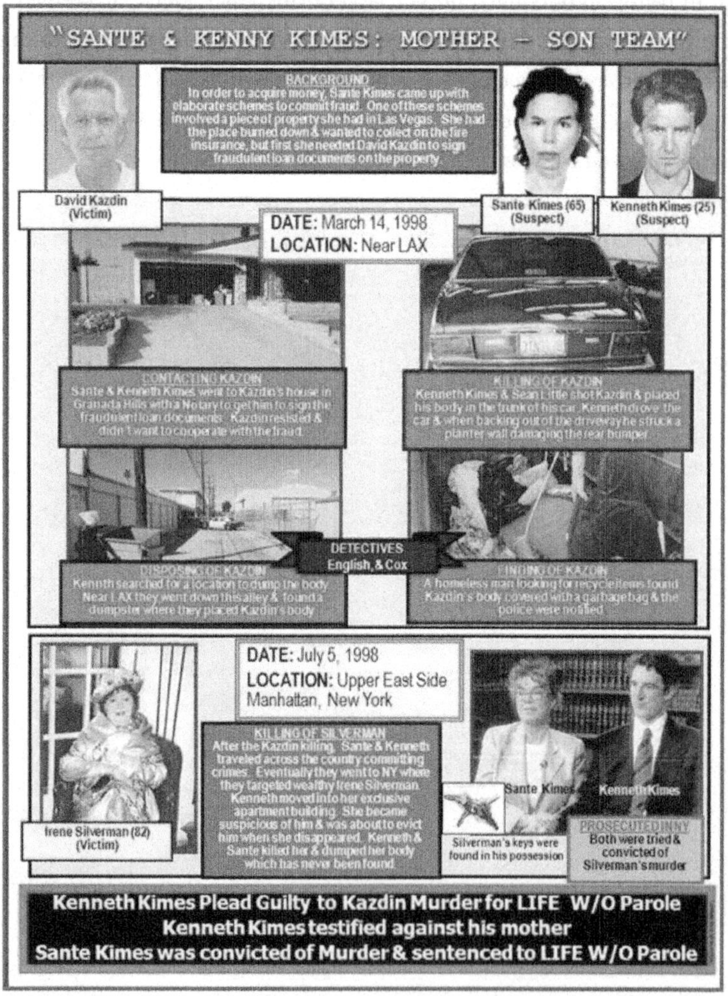

She was born in July 1934 and was named Sante Louise Singhrs. Her roots were planted in Oklahoma City in the heart of the Dust Bowl with a family consisting of an East Indian father and a Dutch mother. Along with her siblings, she and her family migrated to Los Angeles where their father deserted them. In order to survive, her mother brought in money for the family by working as a prostitute. Eventually, the family dissolved as a unit and the children rotated from orphanages to foster homes. Sante's family life was truly dysfunctional; however, by the time she was 12 years old she had the good fortune of being adopted by a stable family that settled in Carson City, Nevada. During her latter teenage years, she did well in school and was involved in all the normal school activities. Life seemed to be good for Sante, and during those years she was known as Sandy Chambers.

The high school and wild life style she was living were the turning point in her life. She was attractive, the boys were crazy about her, and she enjoyed all the attention. However, prior to graduation Sante was caught shoplifting at a local 'five and dime' store. (For those who don't remember such businesses, they were a form of a variety store selling a wide range of inexpensive household goods. These stores went by the names of Woolworths, Kress, Newberry's, Ben Franklin.) Because of her well-respected adopted family, Sante received a break, in that she was not prosecuted for her transgression. However, what she took away from this experience was not to stop shoplifting but how easy it was to talk her way out of it. She felt there were no consequences, so she continued to steal by using her adopted father's credit card.

Her high school graduation was a pivotal point in that she had the prospect to go to college to study journalism. However, she took a different road that included marrying a school sweetheart. As romantic as such a match should seem, the marriage lasted all of three months. She didn't seem to learn anything from that bad experience in that as soon as the divorce was final, she immediately married another high school admirer. That marriage lasted a little longer but produced a child by the name of Kent. Her husband stuck it out for several years, but he gave up on Sante as she continued to steal from others and became an adept shoplifter. The most accurate English word that described Sante's behavior is **kleptomaniac**.

After the divorce, she recognized that she had made some bad choices and returned to Los Angeles, where her main occupation was prostitution and stealing. Her proficiency as a larcenist was remarkable. Some might say that Sante was a **female thief with BALLS.**

To give you an example, one day Sante went into a Cadillac car dealership and asked the salesman if she could take a **'test drive'** in one of their new Cadillacs. She talked the salesman into letting her take the car on her own. She projected the appearance of a businesswoman who wanted to really test the car without being bothered with a lot of sales talk. The salesman didn't see any harm in giving this young damsel the keys for a drive around the block. Needless to say, Sante continued to drive the car for months before she was caught. When she was arrested, the police officer asked her what she was doing with the Cadillac, to which she nonchalantly said, "I was merely **'test driving'** the car as I told the salesman I wanted to do."

She didn't want to give up the incredible high she felt every time she pulled off a successful theft. To her it was an adrenaline rush that she was addicted to. As time went by, Sante was looking for a more stable life. One day out of nowhere came a 'knight on the white horse' and his name was **Kenneth Kimes Sr**. He was the perfect person for Sante in a peculiar way. He was from Oklahoma and migrated to California, where he worked the fields as a melon picker in the Central valleys. His life was like Horatio Alger's: a person who worked hard, saved his money, and became enormously prosperous.

He went into the construction business and carved a niche for himself by building motels in the 1950s. He had calculated that people were starting to travel by using their cars and they no longer wanted to stay in hotels but enjoyed the comforts offered by motels. He built over 30 motels and even built the Mecca Motel across from the entrance to Disneyland in Anaheim. The bottom line was that he had made millions of dollars. He was married with a wife and two children—a son and daughter—but he relished womanizing.

Eventually his wife had enough and the marriage ended in a divorce. He was a person who always wanted to be in control. Sante came along and knew exactly how to deal with Mr. Kimes. She would make sure his beverage glass was always full. When he became drunk, Sante took over and was in complete control of him. Even though he was 18 years older than Sante, she wasn't intimidated in the least. The two of them were ideal for each other. He came to the table with millions in cash and real estate. She brought to the relationship cunningness that allowed them to go from one scam to another, always making money.

In 1975, when Sante was 40 years old, she and Kenneth Senior had a son whom they named Kenneth Junior (Kenny). They as a couple didn't get married until Kenny was six years old. They maintained homes in Honolulu, La Jolla, Palm Springs, Santa Barbara, and a special house in Las Vegas. Kenneth Sr. and Sante lived well together and didn't need to steal. The couple loved the thrill of committing frauds, thefts, filing lawsuits, and suing people. Fires 'mysteriously' occurred at their homes, followed by efforts to collect on the fire insurance policies. An illustration of the boldness of the two was when they fraudulently gained access into the White House during a reception given by President Gerald Ford. Outsmarting the Secret Service was an extraordinary achievement for them. They cherished the photo of them shaking hands with the President and the First Lady in a receiving line in the East Room. Both thought this was one of their finest accomplishments.

Sante had a love affair with Cadillacs, diamonds, and fur coats. She liked to impersonate Elizabeth Taylor and enjoyed being mistaken for Miss Taylor. In February 1980, Sante and Kenneth were staying at the Mayflower Hotel in Washington D.C. One evening they went down to the Mayflower Town and Country lounge. A couple named Kenworth were seated near them, and the woman had left her dark ranch mink coat placed over a chair next to her. Kenneth Sr. went over to distract Mrs. Kenworth as Sante slunk behind to put on the fur coat. Sante returned to where she had been sitting and put on her own fur coat over Mrs. Kenworth's $6,500 fur coat.

People at another table saw what happened and were stunned at what they were observing in front of them. When Mrs. Kenworth discovered her coat was missing the police were called. The witnesses to the incident gave a description of the suspect as the lady who looked like Elizabeth Taylor. The hotel staff was only too familiar with that lady and told the police the woman was staying in a room up on the 7th floor. The police went to the Kime's hotel room, and when they entered they saw Mrs. Kenworth's mink coat lying on the bed with her name tag cut out by a razor blade. The police, while looking around the room, found several additional mink coats as well as a man's tall overcoat.

Sante was arrested and prosecuted for the theft of the fur coat. She used excuse after excuse to have the case continued time after time. It took five years before the case actually went to trial for her stealing the fur coat. When the jury reached a verdict Sante was nowhere to be found, so the judge took the verdict—guilty as charged—without Sante being present. Later, Sante appeared and claimed she had been in an accident and had gone home for medical attention. She appealed her conviction on the basis that she had been convicted in abstentia and that was illegal. The appellate court agreed with Sante, and later the conviction was thrown out.

She was like the 'Teflon Woman' on which nothing stuck. However, her next caper changed her life forever. Sante and Kenneth were constantly traveling to Mexico, and they would bring back numerous young girls as maids. They would use them around the house as servants and kept them locked up so they couldn't leave. While Sante was consumed with her lengthy trial over the fur coat, several of the girls escaped the house and went to authorities. As a result, Kenneth and Sante were prosecuted on human slavery charges. Prior to trial, Kenneth Sr. accepted a deal and pleaded guilty and was sentenced to attend an alcohol treatment program.

Sante went to trial in Las Vegas, and seven of the Mexican girls testified to the atrocities that Sante committed on the girls. The maids stated they were never paid, never permitted to take days off, nor were they allowed to contact relatives. They told the court they received physical and other types of abuse, mainly from Sante Kimes. After a long jury trial, Sante was found guilty and sentenced to five years in federal prison. That sentence impacted Sante's life forever.

While Sante was in prison, her 15-year-old son, Kenny, blossomed. He and his father began spending time together establishing a bond that was never there when Sante was on the scene. For Kenny's birthday, his father built a large swimming pool in the backyard of their house in Las Vegas. For the first time, Kenny was able to associate with the neighboring young people. He was permitted to go to public schools. For years the family traveled so much that Kenny had to be homeschooled with various tutors. This period of time, while his mother was in prison, gave Kenny a chance to be a normal kid and have friends. While Sante was away, Kenny had no contact with his mother and expressed hatred for her and felt ashamed for what she had done.

In 1989, after serving three years in prison, she was released. The prison authority hoped the prison experience was harsh enough to deter her from committing crimes in the future. However, for Sante it was a definite learning experience for an entirely different reason. She hated being in prison and vowed never to go back to prison. From that point on, Sante would do anything to avoid prison. To Sante, this didn't mean walking the straight and narrow but that there would be no witnesses to testify against her. In other words, anyone who was a witness to a crime committed by Sante would have to be eliminated, even if it meant murder.

As soon as Sante was out of prison in 1989, she and Kenneth Sr. were up to their old scams of burning down their property to collect on the fire insurance. They torched their Honolulu house, but the fire insurance company resisted paying the accidental fire claim. Sante demonstrated her new philosophy when the feds were getting close to making an arson case against her and Kenneth. The feds had persuaded the Kimeses' attorney to become an informant for the feds. When Sante started feeling the heat of possible arson charges against her, she and Kenneth Sr. invited their attorney friend (the new informant for the feds) to join them on a delightful vacation trip to Costa Rica. He joined them on the flight down; however, strangely he never returned, and as a matter of fact was never seen alive again. Now since the arson investigation lacked the key witness, the investigation against Sante and Kenneth Sr. had to be terminated and they walked away free as two love birds.

Unfortunately, Sante's release from prison was devastating for Kenny Jr. He had grown and matured during the three years his mother was away in prison. He had enjoyed his father's less controlling ways and living in a stable household. Kenny wanted to get away from his mother, so he worked hard to receive top grades so he could be admitted to the University of California at Santa Barbara, where he could be independent of his mother. It didn't last long, since Mommy decided to move to Santa Barbara with her husband. Sante wanted to be involved in every phase of Kenny's life. The residential area for the University was called Isla Vista, and on weekends it turned into a 'Party Town.' When Kenny had a party at his apartment, Sante would supply the beer kegs. She would attend his parties and often ended up as the life of the party. During this period, Kenny's hatred for his mother softened and evolved into an incestuous relationship.

By this time, Sante seemed to be showing more interest in her son's exciting life than her boring life with her 77-year-old husband. Then in 1994, Sante drove to the bank in downtown Santa Barbara with her husband, Kenneth Sr. She went into the bank to make a deposit, and when she came out her husband had passed away in the parked car. It was claimed to be a heart attack, and whether it was or not no one knew for sure. At the time of Kenneth Sr.'s death, Kenny Jr. was on spring break in Hawaii. Sante flew to Hawaii to join her son and together they spread her husband's ashes on the gentle teal blue waves of the Pacific Ocean.

Kenny Jr. was the only member of the family who knew that Kenneth Sr. had died. The reason for the secrecy was that Sante was never able to convince Kenneth Sr. to write a new Will, one which would include her as the beneficiary. His existing Will left everything to his original children. Whenever his older children asked about Kenneth Sr., Sante would say he was on a business trip in Japan. In the meantime, Sante went on a campaign to transfer over much of the property into her name or into names she had control over.

Sante moved back to Las Vegas to permanently live in the house on Geronimo Way. The Vegas place was a comfortable two-story house at the end of a development that overlooked a golf course. From the master bedroom they had a gorgeous view of manicured lawns covering the rolling hills, with various pine trees that provided shade on the fairways. The backyard had a curved swimming pool with a delightful spa. Sante loved to soak in the spa in the backyard while watching the country club crowd sauntering down the fairways. She had a gorgeous view of the sun setting behind the distant purple-gray mountains. By then the evening desert thermal air gave off a primrose scent.

Las Vegas was the perfect city for Sante to call home. Her house was a short drive from the Vegas strip, where the saying goes that 'what happens in Vegas stays in Vegas.' She fit in with the scammers and hustlers, which Vegas was full of. Sante understood human nature just like the casinos on the strip. Everyone understands that all the games are rigged so the house ultimately wins. The marketing concept is that certain lucky people can beat the house. The idea is to sell the people that they are those few special people who are WINNERS.

Sante was at ease with the Vegas crowd and life was good for her. In order to stay ahead of her creditors and various lawsuits she had transferred most of her funds to offshore bank accounts. This was to make sure that others weren't going profit from all the ill-gotten gains that she had made. Unfortunately, her 'money tree' somehow withered away as she discovered the bank accounts in the Bahamas had totally dried up.

Sante didn't want to be a 'Have Not' person. Kenneth Sr. was no longer available to provide the pecuniary support and personal attention that Sante craved. She had no other person to turn to other than her son Kenny Jr. In order to help his mother, Kenny obediently left college and moved to Vegas to be with her. From that point on, Kenny was mama's accomplice. An example of how Sante used Kenny was when she had him file malpractice lawsuits against a plastic surgeon in San Diego. Kenny filed a complaint stating that the doctor had botched his nose job. He also filed a claim against the doctor on behalf of his mother, who claimed that she fell from the operating table during one of her facelifts and that she suffered a traumatic head injury.

Those malpractice lawsuits didn't generate the kind of money Sante needed to live the lifestyle she had grown accustomed to. She and Kenny met with her attorney to find other possible money sources. The attorney suggested one way they could acquire money was by selling some real estate. Years before, the attorney had set up a corporation named 'AGAHAN' to hold title to property in Santa Maria, California, owned by Sante and Kenneth Sr. She was trying to develop the property for a sub-division. A dispute arose, and Sante's reaction was to refuse to pay for the plans for the project. A lien was placed on the property, which prevented her from selling the property or receiving any cash from it.

Since there was no easy way to sell the Santa Maria property, Sante realized her only option was to take out a loan on her residential property on Geronimo Way in Vegas. They had no mortgage on the Vegas property; therefore, it would be easy to obtain a loan. Over the years, to prevent creditors from placing liens on their property, they had years earlier transferred title of their residence to a **Mr. David Kazdin**. He had been a business associate of her husband. Kazdin had been involved in numerous business ventures with the Kimeses. Kazdin had moved from Las Vegas back to Los Angeles, where his daughter lived. Because of all the financial pressure, Sante decided to follow her attorney's advice and take out a home loan on the Geronimo Way, Vegas house.

Dsavid Kazdin

Nanette Wojdak (Pseudonym) lived in Las Vegas and worked part time as a bookkeeper for the Kimeses to assist them with all of their investments. Later, she became a Certified Notary in order to facilitate Sante's business transactions. Since the Las Vegas property was truly owned by Sante, she figured that it would be OK for her to have her bookkeeper sign Kazdin's name on the loan application. After affixing Kazdin's signature on all the documentations, she sent the material to the financial company, OCWEN Bank. The bank thereupon distributed the funds from the loan to the bookkeeper's personal bank account. Wojdak then transferred the funds from her account to Sante's offshore bank accounts. In this way, no creditor of Sante could intercept any of that money.

Sante was pleased how easy it was to obtain the loan and thought, why not double dip by taking out fire insurance? First she had to figure out how to obtain the maximum amount of fire insurance on the Las Vegas house. Sante and her late husband, Kenneth Kimes, were professionals at the old scam of burning down their property and collecting on the fire insurance. However, the insurance companies were familiar with the Kimes name. Sante knew they would need to use someone else's name to obtain the fire insurance. The question was, who could she find who would let her use their name? She went to a homeless shelter and found a transient by the name of Robert McDaniel (Pseudonym) and persuaded him to come work for her doing maintenance work on the house and on her other properties. She agreed to provide food and lodging for him. Part of the agreement was that Sante could use his name in various business transactions. She filled out a Quitclaim Deed showing that David Kazdin had transferred his interest in the residential property to Robert

McDaniel. Then she used McDaniel's name to apply for the fire insurance policy on the house in the maximum amount of $500,000.

The Kimeses' brains worked in devious ways. Sante thought what a waste to burn up all their luxurious furniture. Even though they were going to claim the furniture as a loss for insurance purposes, they thought, why not move the good furniture before the fire? Kenny's task was to find a storage unit and have the furniture relocated there. Kenny couldn't do all the heavy lifting by himself, so he hired a gentleman by the name of Stanley Pasternack (Pseudonym) to help him. Days before the fire, they went to the Vegas house and cherry-picked the best pieces of furniture and took them to a rental storage unit.

In order to establish an alibi, Kenny and Sante took their maintenance man, Robert McDaniel, to Los Angeles, where they stayed in a motel. On one of the evenings, Kenny quietly slipped away to return to Vegas to torch the house. After the fire was set, Kenny hastily returned to LA before McDaniel knew he was even gone. The next day, the Kimeses were notified that their Vegas house had burned under suspicious circumstances. Shortly thereafter, the Kimeses had their maintenance man Robert McDaniel file a claim for the fire damage of $500,000, which included the fire damage to the structure and the contents.

Taking out the loan had paid off for Sante, and it was just a matter of time before they would have the fire insurance money. Sante had done everything right and was proud of her meticulous planning of all the contingencies. She had been very careful in her dealings with the OCWEN Bank. She made sure that all correspondence about the loan would be sent to her residence at Geronimo Way, Las Vegas.

CHAPTER 20 KIMES-KILLING OF KAZDIN

However, Murphy's Law seemed to haunt Sante. Somehow, one of the employees at OCWEN Bank went through all the loan paperwork and missed the small piece of paper instructing the bank to send **all the correspondence to the Las Vegas address instead of Kazdin's house** in Granada Hills, CA. The employee mistakenly sent the mortgage monthly payment book to David Kazdin's house.

The result was that when David Kazdin received the loan payment book he immediately phoned the bank, asking them what loan they were talking about. He followed that up by sending the bank a letter explaining that he hadn't taken out any such loan and he didn't sign off on any property in Las Vegas. Needless to say, this made the bank quite nervous and it froze the distribution of the funds for the loan. Instantaneously, the bank started an investigation into the matter. Sante became aware of the mistake when the bookkeeper, Wojdak, indicated that the mortgage bank had frozen her personal bank account where she had transferred some of the money from the loan. Sante grasped the situation that she had 'opened a can of worms' and the fastest and best way to rectify it was to have Kazdin sign a Quitclaim Deed. She filled out a Quitclaim Deed showing that David Kazdin had transferred his interest in the residential property to Robert McDaniel. so that bank would leave him alone.

To carry out this new strategy, Sante and Kenny left Vegas with Nanette Wojdak, the notary public, and they travelled to Kazdin's house in Granada Hills, CA. They parked out of sight of Kazdin's house and had Wojdak approach the front door alone. She rang the doorbell and Kazdin's daughter answered the door and let her in. Wojdak started talking with David Kazdin about signing a Quitclaim deed on the

Vegas property. He denied any knowledge of a loan. She indicated her bank account had been frozen because of the problem of title to the Las Vegas property.

The conversation didn't go well, and in short order Nanette Wojdak left Kazdin's house without obtaining his signature. When she returned to Sante and Kenny, who were seated in their Town Car, she told them about his refusal. Sante became furious. Then it was now time to go to Plan B, which was to find a way to eliminate Kazdin. In order to carry that out, they decided to return to Las Vegas. There Kenny contacted Stanley Pasternack about the possibility of obtaining a handgun. Stanley had numerous guns, and he showed them to Kenny and explained the benefits of each one. After a lengthy discussion, Kenny selected a .22 caliber handgun and paid Stanley for it.

While in Las Vegas, Kenny went to the homeless shelter to find someone who he could use to help in the killing. There were several transients at the shelter. Kenny wanted someone who would be reliable and able to assist in killing someone. Some of the homeless seemed too old and feeble. Others seemed to be wasted on alcohol. Kenny needed someone he could trust but at the same time someone who would be willing to commit a murder. The task of finding the right person wasn't easy. Then he spotted Shawn Lipman (Pseudonym), who was younger and had a shady look. Kenny struck up a conversation with him; there seemed to be some type of chemistry between them. Kenny didn't tell Shawn what he would be expected to do, but Kenny was comfortable with his selection.

On Friday, March 13, 1998, Sante knew that Kazdin was having an Open House in the afternoon trying to sell his Granada Hills house. Kazdin was hoping that Friday the 13th would be his lucky day for selling his place so he could move to Florida. Or could Friday the 13th be a bad day for him, one on which he ended up dead?

Kenny and Shawn Lipman (the new homeless man) drove to Kazdin's place. Lipman was sent to the door and Kazdin opened it. As Shawn stepped in, Kenny came in from behind. Immediately, Kenny started talking about the loan situation. Kazdin didn't want to have anything to do with the loan or the Las Vegas property.

Kazdin, for whatever reason, walked back into the kitchen, and Kenny followed directly behind him. Kenny covertly stuck his hand into his pocket and slowly pulled out a handgun. Kazdin's was looking toward the kitchen. Kenny placed the gun to the rear of Kazdin's head and pulled the trigger. That was all that was needed to kill Kazdin. A small-caliber bullet from a .22 can be even more deadly than a larger-caliber bullet. What happens with the .22 bullet is it penetrates the outside of the skull and continues into the brain and begins to bounce off the walls of the interior of the skull and crisscrosses the cerebral cortex to cause extensive injury to the brain. Since the .22 caliber bullet doesn't have enough velocity to exit the skull, there isn't any collateral damage of a bullet flying around.

Shawn Lipman was shocked at the shooting, since Kenny hadn't explained all the details about the job. In order to dispose of the body, Kenny instructed Shawn to drive Kazdin's Jaguar into the garage so they could place Kazdin's body in the trunk of his car. Shawn wasn't familiar with driving a Jaguar, so he ran into a planter next to the driveway, causing damage to the rear bumper of the car. Eventually, Shawn pulled the Jaguar into the garage and Kenny closed the garage door. The garage was connected to the house by a hallway, and the two carried the body of Kazdin from the kitchen into the garage.

The shooting of Kazdin had been easy like a 'piece of cake' until they got into the garage. The challenge was how to get the body into the trunk. The Jaguar extended the full length of the garage. With the garage door down the only way to get on the other side of the car was to climb over the hood of the car. Kenny looked hurriedly at his watch and could see that the Open House 'lookie loos' would soon be arriving. Kenny instantaneously jumped on top of the hood of the car and told Shawn to lift Kazdin's body up to him. Kenny, standing on top of the hood, dragged the body across the hood and dropped it on the other side. Then he climbed down and yelled at Shawn to follow him.

What was strange about it all was that this Jaguar had been Kazdin's pride and joy. When he drove it, he would never park it near other cars in a shopping center parking lot. He was always willing to walk additional distance just to make sure no one scratched his classic Jaguar. Now the car had two big dents from Kenny's shoe prints on the hood. In addition, it had a dent to the rear fender that had occurred when they tried to pull the car into the garage.

Kenny quickly reached inside the car to push the button to pop the trunk open. Then they hastily dropped Kazdin's body into the trunk. They returned to the house to clean up any blood on the floor. Because of using a small-caliber gun, there was very little blood, and Kenny tried to wipe up any blood he could see on the floor. Since the handgun was an automatic, Kenny had to lean down on his hands and knees to find the single shell casing. It had rolled under the kitchen cabinets, where he picked it up and placed it into his pocket.

Kenny was convinced that they had sufficiently sanitized the crime scene, so both of them went to their respective cars. Shawn very carefully backed the Jaguar out of the garage into the street. He shifted the car into drive and started to follow Kenny in his Lincoln Town Car. Shawn, a homeless man who had been living in a shelter until several days before, was slightly traumatized driving an expensive vehicle. He was especially nervous because he had a dead body in the trunk. He was terrified that he might be stopped by the police. When he came to a stop sign, he obediently stopped all the way back at the 'Limit Line' before he ever entered the intersection. Shawn may have been homeless but he was no dummy.

They proceeded to the 405 Freeway and then headed southbound toward Los Angeles Airport (LAX). It was still mid-morning, and rush hour traffic had thinned out except for the interchange with the Interstate 10 near Westwood. They drove to the airport and exited to the Westchester shopping center. There they pulled into the parking lot and parked near the rear of the businesses. Kenny went over to Shawn and told him to park and lock up the Jaguar, since they had to wait until dark before they could attempt to get rid of the body.

Kenny knew it would take another eight hours before it would be dark. What should two killers do to kill time? They both got into the Lincoln and drove to the Beverly Center Shopping Mall, about 10 miles away. There they spent a leisurely day having a pleasant lunch. Afterwards they wandered through the shopping center, mainly window shopping. Since they still had to wait, they took in several of the recent movies at the multi-theater complex. One of the hit movies playing was *Saving Private Ryan*, which Kenny didn't care to see; and he didn't want to see *There's Something about Mary* since he heard it was a 'Girl Flick.' The only movie that appealed to Kenny was the *The Man With The Iron Mask*, so they purchased two tickets and a large bag of popcorn. From there they walked to the appropriate theater and found seats near the back. For the next two hours they escaped into a make-believe world while waiting to dispose of a body.

As the City of the Angels darkened for evening, they headed back to the airport area. Kenny drove the Lincoln Town Car to Westchester and at the parking lot pulled up next to the Jaguar, which had visible footprint dents on the hood. Kenny instructed Shawn to get out and told him to follow him to a seedy apartment complex that he was familiar with. Kenny headed east then slightly south which placed him directly under the flight path of the LAX North Runway. Kenny slowly drove down the rear alley, which had numerous trash dumpsters placed out in the alley for trash pick-up for the next day. Kenny was driving slowly as he looked around to see if anyone from the apartments could see them in the alley. The headlights of the Lincoln Town Car had spotted a dumpster that was well shielded by a set of detached apartments. Kenny motioned to Shawn to pull up to the dumpster so the trunk of the Jaguar would be next to it.

Kenny parked the Lincoln on the other side of the alley next to a closed business. Kenny continued to wave to Shawn to back the Jaguar even closer to the dumpster. Shawn cautiously got out of the Jaguar and waited for Kenny to gesture to him to pop the trunk open. Kenny had to lift up the lids of the dumpster. His nostrils received a whiff of the noxious stench of baby diapers mixed with dog droppings. Kenny abruptly turned his head away from the dumpster. Then he nodded to Shawn and leaned into the car and pushed the trunk button. Suddenly the trunk lid popped open, revealing a body partially covered in garbage bags. As Kenny quickly leaned in the trunk, his nose was hit by reeking smell like a decaying animal. As much as he wanted to walk away, he reached into the trunk and pulled the two trash bags together so the body couldn't be seen.

Kenny tried lifting the body and realized this was a two-man job. He told Shawn to come over to help. Shawn hesitated for a moment. He hadn't signed up for killing or dumping bodies. Kenny firmly stated to Shawn, "Come on, let's get this over with." Shawn knew that Kenny still had the gun, and he didn't want to end up like this corpus in the trunk. He leaned into the trunk and helped to pick up the body. They had to raise it high enough to reach over the side of dumpster. While they attempted to do this, the garbage bags continue to slide off the body. This was disheartening for Kenny. While resting the body on the top of the dumpster, Kenny tried to pull one of the garbage bags upward to cover up the victim's head. He did his best and told Shawn on the count of three to toss the body all the way into the trash-filled dumpster.

As they let go they heard Kazdin's body crash into the dumpster, crushing some cardboard boxes. Kenny had earlier taken out all of Kazdin's identification from his wallet and told Shawn that he would dispose of them elsewhere. Kenny wasn't thrilled with his immediate task, which included reaching into the dumpster and picking up trash to be placed on top of the body. While doing this, Kenny got another breath of the foul odors that had accumulated in the dumpster. Kenny walked away from the dumpster and wiped his hands together as though he was cleaning them.

He directed Shawn to follow him. He got back into the Town Car and drove slowly down to the end of the alley where he saw another dumpster. The Lincoln came to a halt and Kenny opened the car door and went over and lifted up the lid of the dumpster with his right hand. With his left hand, he tossed Kazdin's wallet and all his identification into the dumpster. He glanced in to make sure that it had fallen in. He could see that it had landed on top of a bag of used baby diapers in a Pampers box. In comparing the two dumpsters, this one clearly had a more pleasant scent, more like a compost pit on a warm evening.

Kenny quickly dropped the lid, and as it clanged shut Kenny thought to himself, "Why did I have to make so much noise?" As Kenny slowly walked back to the Lincoln, he could see the headlights of the Jaguar shining directly on him. At that moment a huge 747 jet came roaring overhead so loud he seemed to freeze in his tracks from the intense sound. Kenny stepped into the Town Car and sat down and closed the door. He looked up in the rearview mirror and could see the dumpster with the hidden dead body in it. He smiled to himself and thought, that must have been the way the mob did it during the 'Godfather' days.

Then Kenny motioned to Shawn to follow him back to the airport shopping center parking lot. There they pulled into a remote section and parked the Jag. Shawn carefully locked up Kazdin's Jaguar and climbed into the Lincoln. Kenny gave one last look at the Jag and gunned the Town Car engine as though he was glad to get out of there. He drove back to the 405 Freeway heading to the Sherman Oaks/Encino area. After travelling for twenty minutes, they turned off on Ventura Blvd. and then headed westbound. At the corner of Ventura Blvd. and Haskell Ave.

Kenny pulled over and stopped at the rear parking lot of a florist shop. Kenny exited the car and said to Shawn, "I'll be back in a few minutes."

Meekly, Kenny entered the back door of a small flower shop. The lady came to the counter and asked, "How can I help you?" Kenny looked around to see if he could point out a special flower arrangement. Nothing caught his attention, so he tried to explain what he was looking for. He told her, "I would like some flowers to celebrate a big event." She said, "Is it something for a Birthday or Anniversary? He said, "No, something like a graduation or doing something well." She said, "You mean a Celebration Bouquet." He didn't want to tell her the truth that it was to commemorate a successful killing of an old associate of the family. He just told her a 'Celebration Bouquet' would do.

Within 15 minutes, she amazingly created an arrangement that met all of Kenny's expectations. Kenny gave a broad smile of approval and paid $100 cash to the clerk. Shawn waited impatiently in the car and wondered what was taking so long. Kenny came back with this colorful bouquet. Shawn took a long look at it and, being a 'smart homeless man,' he knew it was best not to say anything. Then off they went, taking Sepulveda Boulevard up to Mulholland Drive, then over to the Bel Air house where they were renting rooms. As Kenny walked in, Sante had the TV on and slowly stood up and asked, "How did it go?"

Kenny strolled over to his dear mother and handed her the Celebration Bouquet. He said, "Everything is Okay." A huge smile lit up Sante's face as she said, "What a wonderful son!" Mother-Son love never shined so bright as it did at that moment between Sante and Kenny. For the rest of the evening everyone decompressed from all the excitement of a day in which a murder had been successfully committed.

Kenny was well aware of the family slogan of 'No Body No Crime.' Kenny knew that trash dumpsters are never checked by the trash-truck operators. So when you dump a body in a dumpster it is picked up by a trash truck, which takes it to a landfill where it is dumped. At the end of the day, three feet of top soil is covered on top of the trash. In other words, the body is well buried so it will never ever be found.

However, apparently Kenny wasn't aware of the new sport of **'Dumpster Diving.'** It might not be a legitimate sport recognized by the Olympic committee, but many people do it with the belief that 'One man's trash can be another man's treasure.'

The morning after disposing of the body, a homeless man was looking in the dumpsters before the big trash trucks arrived to empty them. He jumped into the dumpster and saw these trash bags covering something. To the homeless man it appeared that there must be something valuable inside. He pulled off the top garbage bag and discovered the head of a dead man. He was hoping for some beer or soda cans, not a dead body. He jumped out of the dumpster with lightning speed and scurried to a nearby apartment complex to find someone who would permit him to use their phone to call the police.

The police arrived and checked out the dumpster and sure enough, the homeless man was right: there was a dead body in the dumpster. A cursory search of the pockets didn't reveal any identification. The detectives were brought in to figure out who this victim could be and why he was killed. Because of the age of the victim, it didn't seem to be a gang-related killing. It could be a robbery, but robbers don't dispose of bodies in dumpsters. The one shot in the back of the head by a small-caliber gun didn't add up. There weren't any security cameras in the area to help piece together the identity of the suspect. The way the body was covered with garbage bags, it was obvious that the killer didn't intend for the victim to be found. The Dumpster Diver's unexpected discovery had given LAPD another 'John Doe' homicide. It seemed this murder was going to join all the other Cold Cases that accumulate over a year.

What are the chances that another Dumpster Diver would be working in the same area on the same day? Maybe it was the poor economy or the notion that apartment people tend to throw away more recyclables. The next day, the police received a call from another 'Dumpster Diver,' who indicated that he had found a wallet full of credit cards and a driver's license for a Mr. David Kazdin. The police were less than excited about checking out a smelly wallet that had been fished out of the bottom of a dumpster filled with dirty diapers, sanitary napkins, and maggot-filled, week-old rotten food.

The responding police officers had to wonder why they were responding to this call about a found wallet. Many people wouldn't have called the police but would merely have taken anything of value and thrown the rest back in the dumpster. For some reason this 'Dumpster Diver' was trying to be a Good Samaritan. Maybe this diver should have been rewarded with something similar to a Boy Scout merit badge for his honesty.

The officer, with his latex gloves on, thumbed through the wallet and looked at the driver's license and saw a photo of an older man with a full head of white hair. The officer remembered the detectives had mentioned finding the body of an older man just down the alley a block away. The officers contacted the detectives and told them that they had recovered a wallet that had the identification of a Mr. David Kazdin. The detectives were shown the driver's license and bingo, they then knew who their 'John Doe' was. The detectives then proceeded to converge on David Kazdin's house in Granada Hills.

They looked for blood and didn't find any, at least on their first cursory glance. (A later search revealed a small drop of blood on the kitchen floor next to the wallboard. This was found to be a DNA match to David Kazdin.) Kazdin's daughter mentioned that a stranger had come by to talk to her dad several days before. She didn't know what it was all about, but he had mentioned that he had received a mortgage book for a property in Las Vegas. Now the detectives had some clues to work on. What were the chances that two separate 'Dumpster Divers' would make unusual finds that pointed the detectives to a Las Vegas property that had just recently burned down? Without those 'Dumpster Divers,' the victim's body and his wallet would have ended up in a landfill, buried forever under tons of waste, and years later the dump would be transformed into new parkland with unaware children playing on top of buried bodies.

Kenny and Sante, with their homeless associates, were still staying in the rented rooms in Bel Air. Kenny's attention was focused on their so-called maintenance worker, Robert McDaniel. Kenny was concerned that he might be talking to the other tenants of the house. They had kept him locked up in one of the bedrooms so he couldn't leave or come in contact with others. They had threatened and even beaten him up on occasions to instill fear in him.

Then one evening Kenny, Sante, and Shawn Lipman took McDaniel out for dinner at a restaurant. While everyone was talking at the table, McDaniel excused himself to go to the bathroom. The restrooms were situated near the rear door. McDaniel saw his opportunity to escape and disappeared into the dark of the night. When Kenny realized what had happened, he became paranoid that McDaniel would go to the police. The next morning when the Bel Air landlord appeared unannounced at the house, Kenny freaked out and immediately decided to leave the rented room in that house.

Originally, Kenny was patting himself on the back for a job well done until the police started coming around asking questions. As proud as Sante was of her son's accomplishments, she knew it was time for them to move on. Thus began a Mother-Son odyssey resulting in a journey that crossed the entire continent of the USA. From that day forward, they would be known as the 'Grifters.'

CHAPTER 21 KIMES-GRIFTERS ON THE MOVE

Earlier in April of 1998, the Kimeses had bought a green 1997 Lincoln Town Car from a car dealership in Cedar City, Utah, and had it delivered to them in Los Angeles. They paid for the car with a check for $14,900. Unfortunately for the salesman, the check bounced as high as a kite. (Later, the dealership had the DA file criminal charges against both Sante and Kenny for fraud and auto theft.)

One of the reasons Kenny had selected the Lincoln Town Car was its amazingly soft, comfortable ride and incredible high-end sound system. As mom and son traveled across the heartland of America, Kenny wanted his mom to enjoy the Lincoln's surround-sound feature. Most important for Sante was giving the appearance of being affluent, and the Lincoln Town Car helped her to project that image.

The Kimeses' cross-country journey accumulated several thousand miles on that Town Car, stretching from Los Angeles to New York by way of Florida. While crossing one of the southern states, they committed another vehicle theft. It wasn't clear why they did this, but when they pulled into a small community they saw a For Sale sign on a huge, almost-new Recreational Vehicle (RV). Sante and Kenny had always had a RV in Las Vegas. However, their RV didn't weather well with all the heat and wind in Vegas. Their RV had passed the point of being reliable. Most people would have traded it in for a newer model. Nevertheless, for Kenny and Sante it was time for another 'con.' They could tell that this backward area hadn't seen a professional scam artist at work for a long time. This RV was listed for $83,000, and Kenny knew how to work the owner. Kenny didn't quibble over the price and agreed with the seller that the RV was worth the asking price. Then Kenny pulled out a checkbook and wrote a check for the full amount so they could take it immediately. The seller filled out the paperwork for the sale.

Kenny got in the RV and asked all sorts of stupid questions about how to use the RV. Undoubtedly, the seller had to be thinking what a sucker this buyer was. Within an hour, Kenny was driving out of the driveway with an $83,000 RV, and the seller waved good-bye to him. Kenny looked out his side mirror and saw that the seller had a slight smirk on his face. He wondered if the seller would be still smiling when he discovered that the check wasn't worth the paper it was written on. Sante followed in the Lincoln behind Kenny as he made his way to the interstate heading for Florida and disappearing into the countryside.

Several months prior, Sante had attended a seminar in Las Vegas where she met a man who told her about an elderly woman who operated a unique high-end bed-and-breakfast hotel in New York. This woman was a wealthy widow who was 82 years old and childless. Sante heard that she also maintained a large amount of cash in her apartment. Sante did a little investigation by using a title company and confirmed that **Irene Silverman** was the sole owner of the Manhattan property and she owned the property free and clear without any type of mortgage. The fact that she owned this property outright worth over $8 million and she had no heirs was a dream come true for a professional conniving con artist like Sante.

Irene Silverman (82)
(Victim)

Sante couldn't help herself from thinking up some type of scam to get access to that property. First, Sante knew that she needed some type of introduction to meet Irene Silverman. The person indicated that this woman was a good friend of Rudy Vaccari, who owned a specialty butcher shop in Manhattan. Sante called the hotel and used the excuse that she was the secretary for Manny Guerrin and he wanted to rent an apartment. She was able to contact one of the staff, who took down the information but said that no formal reservation could be made because Irene was unavailable.

On Saturday June 13, 1998, Sante and Kenny loaded up the Lincoln Town Car in Florida and started the long drive to New York. They took with them an assistant by the name of Jose Acosta (Pseudonym), who they employed to do the menial work Sante and Kenny didn't want to do. The three of them traveled up Interstate 95. In 1998, this was the main route used by drug dealers to quickly transport narcotics to the Big Apple. The question was whether the large Lincoln Town Car fit the description of possible drug dealers. Kenny and Jose would certainly fit the profile of drug dealers. However, Sante, with her grandmotherly appearance, rounded out the Town Car, and protected Kenny from being stopped by the narcotics officers.

To understand this new scam that Sante had plotted, one has to know a little about Irene Silverman. She owned and operated an unusual hotel in the Upper Eastside of New York at 20 East 65th Street near Madison Avenue. This old gray stone mansion had been converted into luxury apartments. The structure was built to give the appearance of a substantial city mansion with its carved-stone façade and sturdy wrought iron doors. The building projected opulence contained in a secure environment. Irene rented her rooms to a special clientele with an arty persuasion.

On Sunday June 14, 1998, a Mr. Manny Guerrin (the alias name Kenny Kimes was using) arrived at Irene Silverman's hotel asking for a room. Kenny was well dressed while turning on his charm and projected the image of a well-spoken member of high society. Irene was impressed, but she had certain standards that she never deviated from. She required her potential tenants to submit a resume with the names and numbers of references. If she didn't know the potential tenants personally, she conducted extensive background checks to verify that the person was of the caliber to fit in with her other avant-garde tenants.

When she requested Manny Guerrin to supply a resume with references, he agreed to provide her with one the next day since he hadn't brought any paperwork with him. Irene had learned to not make any exceptions. Manny (Kenny) knew that money talks extremely loud with business people. Irene continued to tell him that she had to have his resume before she could rent any room to him. Manny assured her that he understood and dropped the name of her butcher as someone he knew and who had recommended her place to him. As Manny started to leave, he pulled out $6,000 in cash and explained he would be willing to pay her in cash.

Irene Silverman's eyes were captivated by the 60 crisp one-hundred-dollar bills. Somehow, her mind snapped back to the days she was paid $36.00 per week in cash at the Radio City Music Hall. All of a sudden, she indicated that she could make an exception and told him she would get a receipt for him. Within minutes, Manny was escorted to the apartment 1B on the first floor. Kenny was pleased with his acting ability, and he had accomplished the first part of their plan, which was to get into the mansion and learn how the hotel operated.

As the week went on, Irene's impression of this new tenant changed. When Manny didn't hand over a resume the next day, Irene was slightly concerned. Then it was one excuse after another to the point that Irene was having second thoughts about renting room 1B. Irene noticed that this new tenant would cover his face when passing the security cameras. Then she noticed an older lady going into his room.

What actually caused Irene to become suspicious of this new tenant was the fact that he seemed to be sneaking around the building and often appeared to be listening to her conversations on the phone. Several of her servants complained to her that they thought he was 'trouble.' Irene was convinced that Manny had to be evicted. She explained to her accountant that she thought he was some type of drug dealer and she wanted him evicted even before the month was up.

During this first week of July, Kenny continually tried to find out Irene's Social Security number. They were able to set up an eavesdropping device on Irene's phone line. He used all sorts of excuses to ask her staff personal information about her. However, he didn't realize how loyal her staff was since she treated them like part of her family. Sante and Kenny were diligently gathering forms for property transfer, including a deed of sale, which would be needed for the fraudulent transfer of the hotel. However, to complete the fraudulent transaction they needed Irene's Social Security Number.

Sante and Kenny were professional scam artists, and they took pride in how well they could forge a person's name. They were able to obtain documents with Irene's signature and they practiced for hours to learn how to copy it to perfection. When they were pleased with their forgeries they were ready for the next step, which was to find a notary.

Kenny was able to line up a notary to come over to his room 1B. When the notary arrived, Kenny had her come in and then had his mother, Sante, play the part of Irene Silverman. Sante prided herself as being a great actress. Sante was wearing a nightcap and nightgown, posing as a bedridden Irene Silverman. She pretended to sign the grant deed, and then Kenny wanted the notary to affix her seal over the signature. For some reason, the notary became suspicious and reluctant to get involved with them. Was it Sante's performance that was over the top, or had the notary seen the switching of the documents? The notary refused to notarize the document and walked out.

On July 2nd, luckily Kenny rounded up another notary, who came over to his room. Again, Sante posed as an infirm Irene Silverman wearing a frilly nightgown and nightcap over a red wig. This second notary may have been in a hurry or overly impressed with the sizeable cash payment, in that she didn't seem too concerned to actually see Sante sign the document in front of her.

Sante and Kenny now had their sales agreements notarized, and the next step was to get someone to help them operate the hotel for a short time before they would sell it to someone for a price tag of eight to ten million dollars.

Kenny contacted Stanley Pasternack, their old friend from Las Vegas. Stanley lived in a tattered trailer park and eked out a living selling guns without asking too many questions. They promised to pay him well if he would fly from Las Vegas to New York and act as the manager of Irene Silverman's hotel. Stanley had held many questionable jobs, and he had confidence that he could wing his way through this one.

The one reason that Kenny contacted Stanley was that he could implicitly trust him. Stanley had come to the aid of the Kimeses on many occasions. He was the one who in fact had sold the .22 semi-automatic to Kenny that was used to kill Kazdin.

The police had been over to Stanley's place to ask about some of his transactions with the guns. Stanley didn't want to do prison time, especially for something he didn't get anything out of. The detectives also had spelled it out for Stanley that they wanted to know the whereabouts of Sante and Kenny Kimes. They made it clear that they weren't as interested in his transgressions with the sales of his guns. They could easily overlook the gun sales if he would alert the detectives where the Kimeses could be found.

Then one day Kenny called Stanley to ask him to come to New York to help them operate a hotel. When Stanley received that call, he must have felt he had been dealt a Monopoly 'Get Out Of Jail Free' pass. At the same time, Kenny thought he was so fortunate to have such a willing, trusting friend to help them out at a moment's notice. Unknown to Kenny was that his buddy was more interested in saving his own ass than helping an old friend.

CHAPTER 22 KIMES-DEATH OF IRENE SILVERMAN

Saturday, the fourth of July in New York in 1998, was a big deal. This is the city with the Statue of Liberty, and it takes pride having a gigantic fireworks show in New York harbor. To Irene, the Fourth was a big occasion for her. She was the perfect example of what an American could achieve, since she went from rags to riches with the help from her late husband. Irene knew the hotel would be quiet this weekend, since most of her guests would be off on trips or enjoying a holiday vacation. She had given most of the staff the weekend off.

Sunday morning July 5, 1998, was going to be a good day. During the morning around 11:00, Irene asked one of her remaining maids, Martha Rivera, to walk her dog on the roof garden. Her maid carried out her wish and took care of her dog. The hotel remained unusually quiet. Exactly what happened next is not known with certainty. However, the best inference from the facts is as follows: Sante and Kenny had everything in place to claim that they had purchased the Silverman's mansion and were going to take over the operation until they could find a buyer for this unique hotel. They had the notarized signature appearing to be that of Irene Silverman, indicating the selling of the mansion to them. They had the money to pay the property transfer tax. Furthermore, within several hours they would have a new manager for the hotel flying in from Las Vegas.

All that remained to complete their masterful fraud plan was to somehow dispose of Irene. What we don't know is whether Irene on her own went to room 1B to tell Manny (Kenny) that he was being evicted the following day, which was Monday, or if Kenny went to her office and asked her to come to his room so he could talk to her in private. What we do know was that Irene ended up in room 1B. Most likely there was an argument which led to a struggle. Irene was 83 years old, vs Kenny, who was six feet tall, a trim 180 pounds, and Sante, who may have been tipping the scales at 200 pounds.

Ultimately, there was a scuffle in which Irene didn't have a chance. Unfortunately, Irene thought of herself as being invincible and was surrounded 24 hours a day by loyal staff members who would do anything to protect her. She most likely thought nothing bad could happen to her in the house where she had created a loving, caring atmosphere for everyone who lived there. Sante zapped Irene with a stun gun, which most likely paralyzed Irene's frail body.

Kenny grabbed Irene by the neck and he painstakingly strangled her. The process took a long time and he had to continue to apply pressure to her neck. Because of her age, the shock of it all may have killed her, but Kenny didn't let off the pressure until he was certain there was no more life left in Irene's body. As Irene's body dropped to the floor, Sante reached for the shower curtain they had purchased. She took the liner from the shower curtain and laid it on the floor, and they rolled Irene's body up in it. In order for her body to stay wrapped tightly, Kenny took a roll of duct tape and started wrapping the tape around the ends of the shower liner. Two large trash bags were used to cover everything up.

Then Kenny rapidly walked down the hallway out the front door without anyone seeing him. He went to the garage down the street, where he had parked the Town Car. After waiting several minutes to retrieve the car, Kenny drove around the block and pulled up close to the front door of the hotel. Parking the car in a loading zone was the only place he could find. Kenny immediately entered the building and returned to his apartment, room 1B. They used a bedspread to cover the body, which had been rolled up in the shower liner and covered with trash bags. Kenny lifted Irene's body with the help of his mother, and they commenced their criminal exit down the hall out the front door. Kenny and Sante carried Irene's body that felt like dead weight, which it was! This was a strain on Sante and she didn't want to pull her back out of place. They approached the Town Car in broad daylight. No one seemed to notice this mother-son team struggling to carry something long in trash bags. Since the trunk wasn't open, the two of them gently placed the long wrapped item on the curb. Kenny got the key, pushed the button, and the trunk popped open. They both reached down and picked up the body and unceremoniously dropped it into the trunk.

As Kenny slammed the trunk lid closed, he gave his mother a half grin. Sante wanted to say job well done, but she knew there was much more to do to pull off the biggest fraud scam of her career, one that would be worth millions. So far, everything was going as planned. This Sunday morning was unusually peaceful compared to the usual hustle and bustle of New York.

Sante reminded Kenny that he needed to return to the room and remove all his personal belongings. They felt secure now, since the dead body was no longer in the room. They needed to collect all the paperwork and documents they had worked on, as well as scraps of paper they had used to practice writing Irene Silverman's signature.

They decided to take all their personal belongings first and place them in the backseat of the car. After several trips to the Lincoln Town Car, they had removed everything. Sante double-checked the room and was satisfied they had cleaned out all of their personal items. As they say in the old Western movies, "Now was the time to get out of Dodge."

Kenny got into the driver's seat as Sante entered from the passenger side, and they headed the Town Car in the direction of New Jersey. Over the years, Kenny had told his friends and associates that the family motto was 'No Body No Crime.' In order to stay true to the family slogan, Kenny drove to a construction site in a desolate swampy area off one of the New Jersey turnpikes. Kenny was a master of making bodies disappear so they would never be found. He learned that from his mother, who had experienced it the hard way, after serving several years in federal prison. With both Kenny and Sante executing the plan, it is no wonder that even to this day Irene Silverman's body has never been found and she most likely is resting in peace wherever they dumped her body.

After Kenny and Sante had successfully disposed of Irene's body, they headed back to Manhattan. Kenny dropped his mother off at the Plaza Hotel, and he looked for a nearby garage to park the car. Sante took a satchel and checked it in at the Plaza Hotel. The satchel contained many of the documents regarding the transfer of Irene Silverman's property.

Sante and Kenny had arranged to meet that afternoon with their old business friend, Stanley Pasternack from Las Vegas, who would actually run Irene's hotel until they could sell it. He was flying in to New York and would arrive in the afternoon. The plan was to meet him at the Hilton Hotel.

The police from the west coast wanted to arrest the Kimeses for the stealing of the Lincoln Town Car from a Utah dealer. LAPD detectives were also investigating the Kimeses for the murder of David Kazdin. When Stanley received the call from the Kimeses to come to New York to help them, he immediately contacted the law enforcement agencies. The detectives encouraged Stanley to fly to New York to meet the Kimeses. He was instructed to set up a meeting with them at the Hilton Hotel in New York. The police supplied him with a bulletproof vest and wired him for sound. Federal agents of the fugitive task force were helping out the Utah Police in this arrest. No one knew that the mother-son team had just committed a murder of one of New York's most prominent citizens.

At the assigned time, Stanley Pasternack was waiting nervously for this meeting to occur. Around 5:00 p.m., Sante spotted Stanley and went over to him. They found a location in the lobby where they could have a little privacy and sit down and discuss Stanley's new duties as manager of the hotel. It wasn't until 6:40 p.m. that Kenny arrived at the hotel after parking the Lincoln in a garage nearby. As Kenny went through the Hilton lobby, he continually looked around for his mother and Stanley.

The Hilton Hotel lobby was crowded with people who had come to New York for the Fourth of July celebration in the Big Apple. Sante and Kenny were on the verge of pulling off the biggest scam of their lives. Stanley Pasternack didn't want the Kimeses to realize that he was double-crossing them big time. The fugitive officers knew that they were in a difficult environment to make an arrest of these fugitives. The use of guns would definitely be highly problematic.

The officers noticed Kenny walking into the lobby, and he appeared to be pacing around looking for someone. The officers tried to approach Kenny without too much fanfare. But Kenny had spent most of his life running from the law. He had a sixth sense for recognizing cops. When the undercover officers came up on both sides of him, he definitely sensed something was wrong. Kenny took off running like a deer in hunting season. A foot race ensued. The NYPD undercover officers knew where the exits were and they were able to cut Kenny off before he got out the door.

After Kenny was apprehended, the other officers approached Sante, who was enjoying her conversation with their trusted friend Stanley. Sante looked up at the undercover officers, wondering what was happening. She seemed confused that the officers were arresting her while her good friend seemed to be standing idly by. When the police had handcuffed both Sante and Kenny, that action ended one of the most notorious mother-son criminal careers. When the cops were leading Kenny away, they noticed that he had soiled his pants. Apparently, the act of finally getting caught had scared the S--- out of him.

The lead detective informed the two of them they were being arrested for Auto Theft of a Lincoln Town Car from the Utah dealer. A smile came over Kenny's face when he realized that the cops weren't aware of the murder of Irene Silverman. However, his smile faded as the officers started searching him, finding the identification in the name of Manuel Guerrero and numerous documents in the name of Irene Silverman. He also had a knife and brass knuckles on his person. Also on Kenny's person was Irene Silverman's personal set of unique hotel keys. Kenny also possessed a black vinyl bag that contained more than $10,000 in cash and several documents bearing the name of Irene Silverman. They also found a parking stub for a nearby garage, where they found the stolen Lincoln Town Car. It was towed over to the FBI headquarters, where it was searched pursuant to a search warrant.

When they searched the car they found documents in Irene's named, blank legal forms, notebooks, and other items including a can of mace, handcuffs, a jar of sedatives, rubber gloves, 10 wigs in various colors, black garbage bags, and an empty stun gun box and a semi-automatic handgun with ammunition. They found documents of power-of-attorney forms, real estate transfer forms, and pieces of paper on which someone had been practicing Irene Silverman's signature, as well as $30,000 in cash. In the trunk was an empty duffel bag that was large enough to hold the body. Other items found were two rolls of duct tape, a shower liner, heavy-duty garbage bags, and clothesline.

The FBI fugitive unit was pleased that they were able to take both Kimeses into custody. They were coming up with all these items and documents with the name of Irene Silverman. None of the officers were aware of the Missing Person Report about an 'Irene Silverman.' However, the gods were **NOT** looking down on Sante and Kenny. One of the fugitive detectives just happened to glance at a TV set that was on. He heard the TV reporter mention the mysterious disappearance of an elderly socialite by the name of **Irene Silverman,** and that the police wanted to speak to a tenant at her hotel by the name of **Manny Guerrin**. The detective thought that was strange, since that was the same name used by Kenny Kimes when he was arrested. That detective called the 19th Precinct and told the Inspector working the Missing Person case that they had the missing tenant in custody.

Then the FBI agent mentioned they had numerous documents in the name of Irene Silverman, such as a passport and Social Security card. The Missing Person Inspector went over to talk to Sante, who was waiting to be booked on the fugitive Auto Theft Warrant. He asked her if she knew an **Irene Silverman,** to which Sante denied knowing her, indicating that maybe she was out walking her dog. (This seemed to be an odd response if she really didn't know her.)

The satchel that Sante had taken to the Plaza Hotel contained considerable incriminating evidence. After Sante and Kenny were arrested, they hired an attorney to represent them. There hope was to have the attorney get both of them out on a low bail before the police realized that Irene had been murdered. Sante told the attorney to have someone go to the Plaza Hotel and retrieve the satchel she had checked in. None of the detectives knew anything about it. The Kimeses' attorney hired a private investigator to go to the Plaza Hotel to pick up the satchel. The private investigator didn't have any difficulty locating the satchel and notifying the attorney. At that point, the attorney notified the police, who had obtained a search warrant for the satchel. (Apparently, the attorney didn't want to be suspected of being an 'assessory after the fact' to murder.)

After the satchel was seized, it was taken to the DA's Office, and in the presence of the Kimeses' Defense attorney, the satchel was opened and all the items were itemized for use in court. When they inventoried it, they found a treasure trove of items including a loaded .22 caliber Beretta and numerous incriminating pieces of evidence, including a folder titled 'The Final Dynasty' which contained the notarized deed, notarized transfer tax forms, and the other documents with the forged signature of Irene Silverman selling the hotel to Atlantis Group Ltd., a corporation set up by Kimes.

The murder trial of both Sante and Kenny Kimes was heralded as the Trial of the Millennium. It was believed that the Kimes trial would likely be the most sensational and widely covered trial since that of the O.J. Simpson trial (1995). One newspaper heralded this case as one with no body and no direct evidence and that it was the type of case that would really tax the prosecutor's skills.

Just days before the big trial, both Sante and Kenny granted an interview to *60 Minutes*. During the broadcast of the interview, Sante, who had turned 65 years old, and Kenny, then 25 years old, appeared stoic and confident they would be acquitted. They both explained, "There's no truth to any of this." Sante had on a gray oversize suit with her hair up and looked like a professional business executive with her horn-rimmed glasses. Throughout the interview, Sante clutched her dear son's hand as Kenny smiled wearing a black double breasted suit with a somber blue tie. Kenny gave the appearance of a happy mortician who was being overly protected by his dear mother.

It was hard to fathom the purpose of doing the *60 Minutes* interview. It did make this mother-son scam team look like human beings. However, the audience was informed about all the people who had been ripped off by the Kimeses or disappeared after meeting them. However, most TV viewers might get the impression that this mother-son team was a little too slick and slippery. Their rehearsed, polished answers only reinforced how good they were. There was the comparison with Bonnie and Clyde, who traveled across the country wreaking havoc wherever they stopped. Some reporters were saying that they were the new 'Mommy and Clyde' team. As Sante held her head up high throughout the interview, she had to be thinking that she and her son had made it to the top. They were being recognized and admired for their accomplishments.

In New York, Prosecutor Connie Fernandez in her Opening Statement said to the jury, "They murdered Irene Silverman to get her out of the way. It's as simple as that." "They used a stun gun to knock out Mrs. Silverman and then strangled her." "They wrapped her body up, and loaded it into the trunk of their car."

The prosecution wanted to establish that the Kimeses had a **<u>Motive</u>** to get rid of Irene. The way they established a motive to the jury was to show that the Kimeses wanted Silverman's hotel and that Irene would never be willingly give up her hotel/house to them. Irene had planned to leave her place to a charitable foundation she had established in memory of her mother. The directors of the foundation would not personally benefit from Irene's death. However, the Kimeses would unquestionably benefit from her death. They had arranged for the transfer of her business and building to their 'shell corporation.' They could not assume full control of the property and reap the benefits of the house if Irene were still alive. The Kimeses knew that Irene would not allow them to take over the house so long as she was alive. Therefore they had a strong motive to kill Irene.

Besides Motive, the Kimeses had the **Opportunity** as well as the means to kill Irene. Cellphone records showed that the Kimeses were in the mansion at the time of Irene's disappearance. The records show two calls made from their cellphone to the Plaza hotel. Those calls were made from inside Irene's place or in the immediate vicinity of her hotel at 11:06 a.m. and 11:26 a.m. The only people in Irene's hotel at that time were the Kimeses, Irene, and her maid Ms. Rivera, who was busy doing her chores. The Kimeses had the exclusive Opportunity to be present when Irene disappeared.

The Kimeses were also well equipped with **Tools to Murder** Irene Silverman. Various instruments that would assist in the murder and disposal of Irene were found in the Lincoln and the satchel that had been checked in at the Plaza Hotel. These instruments included two loaded guns, an empty stun gun box, drugs, syringes, large duffel bags, duct tape, and masks. Also found in room 1B were an open roll of duct tape bearing Kenny Kimes' prints, four heavy-duty garbage bags missing from a box of ten, and a shower curtain missing a plastic liner.

In order to answer the claim that there was no evidence of a struggle at the hotel, the prosecution argued that the Kimeses overpowered Irene Silverman without a struggle. The victim was 83 years old, four feet eight inches tall, and weighing 115 pounds, compared to Kenny, who was six feet tall and weighed 180 pounds, and Sante, who was five feet five inches tall and weighed 200 pounds. They could easily overpower Irene Silverman with sheer bodily force.

The prosecution showed the jury the **14 notebooks** that Sante kept containing minute details of the scheme, as well as tape recordings they made of wiretaps they placed on Irene's phone. These notebooks explained in Sante's words how they planned and carried out their various scams and murders. In Sante's handwriting were the words "Rich, elderly, easy marks." The notebooks listed the documents needed to transfer title of Irene's building and included a to-do list: get Silverman's Social Security number and examples of her signature, buy rope, stun gun, and gloves.

The New York prosecutors called as a witness a Ralph Pellman (Pseudonym), an insurance salesman, to testify to the origin of the scheme to take Irene Silverman's hotel. It all started in 1996 when he and Sante were attending an anti-aging seminar in Las Vegas. He had met Mrs. Silverman and told Sante how Silverman ran this unique hotel in New York in which she rented the rooms for up to $10,000 per month. Witness Pellman testified that Sante was extremely interested in the fact that this widow owned this property outright without any mortgage. She wanted more information, and he told her that she could use the name Rudy Vaccari as a reference.

Then the prosecutors called members of Silverman's staff, who testified that two months before the disappearance of Mrs. Silverman, a woman called about renting a room and used the reference name of Rudy Vaccari.

The Kimeses' Defense claimed that there was no forensic evidence connecting the Kimeses to the alleged murder. They explained it was a case based on speculation and misinformation. There wasn't a body; there were no eyewitness accounts, no fingerprints, no hair, no blood or fibers to link them to the victim. On top of all that, there was no confession or admissions by the Kimeses. The evidence was entirely circumstantial. The Defense claimed that "There are other individuals who would have benefited from Ms. Silverman's death, such as people who had an interest in the property who were beneficiaries in her Will. Further, there was dissension between her and some business associates. She'd made enemies and the prosecutor should be investigating those people because we, the Defense, certainly have."

During the trial, the judge ordered the mother and son to stop holding hands in front of the jury. Further, the judge ordered the Kimeses not to speak to the news media. But Sante couldn't restrain herself and was caught passing a note to a reporter. The judge threatened to have Sante handcuffed during further proceedings if she continued to contact the media. The judge restricted Sante's phone access to only her attorneys. The judge sustained a motion that Sante was attempting to influence the jury, since they might hear stories about the case through the news media.

The judge had ruled that Sante's prior slavery conviction could be used to impeach her if she decided to testify. Since the Defense attorneys didn't want the jury to hear about her prior conviction, Sante decided not to take the witness stand.

The prosecutor in her final Argument said, "Do not reward these defendants because they were clever enough to dispose of the victim's body."

After the 15-week trial involving the testimony of 130 witnesses and 430 exhibits, the jury comprising eight women and four men deliberated for four days. When the jury buzzed that they had reached a verdict, Sante and Kenny were brought into the courtroom and sat at counsel table. They were apathetic and listened to the guilty verdicts, which took 20 minutes for the forewoman to read. Partway through the reading, Kenny leaned over to his mother and whispered, "Mom, it'll be OK."

They were found guilty of multiple counts of murder in the second degree, robbery and burglary in the first degree, criminal possession of a weapon in the second and third degree, 16 counts of forgery in the second degree, criminal possession of a forged instrument in the second degree, 29 counts of eavesdropping, criminal possession of stolen property in the third degree, conspiracy in the fourth degree, and attempted grand larceny in the first degree.

Later, at the time of sentencing, the judge gave Sante an opportunity to make a statement. Sante seemed like a clock wound too tight. She sprang forth with a mouth full of words that few courtrooms have ever heard. Her statement pointed the blame to authorities, including her lawyers, all of those who had framed her. She continued on to compare their trial to the 'Salem Witch Trials' and indicated that the prosecutors were guilty of 'Murdering the Constitution.' The judge then had the opportunity to express her opinion about Sante. The judge said that Mrs. Kimes was "a sociopath and a degenerate" and her son was duped and "a remorseless predator." Then the judge imposed the sentence of 120 years in prison for Sante, while Kenny received slightly more with a sentence of 125 years in prison.

Sadly, Sante said in a dejected voice to her attorney, "What's next? Is this the end of everything for us?" But an hour later Sante was in better spirits as the TV cameras were focused on her, and in a strong defiant voice she said, "The verdict is an insult to justice and a temporary setback."

The interview was lengthy but gave Sante what she wanted more than anything else, a chance to commit the biggest fraud of all. Throughout her whole life she was trying to persuade people that whatever she was doing or selling was the truth. Could she con the world? She had just been sentenced to 120 years in prison, which might depress most people and even make them contrite, but not Sante. She wasn't about to demonstrate any remorse or change her evil ways. She was about to be transported to Los Angles, where she could face the Death Penalty for the murder of David Kazdin.

CHAPTER 23 KIMES-LET'S MAKE A DEAL

Shortly after the New York verdict and sentencing, Kenny's life took a bizarre turn. He was doing an interview in prison with a freelance Court TV reporter when he took her hostage by grabbing a ballpoint pen and placed it against her throat. He told authorities he would stab her if they didn't comply with his demands. After three hours of negotiation with Kenny, he finally dropped the pen. As a result of this hostage taking, Kenny was given eight years in solitary confinement.

It was extraordinary that Larry King was willing to do an interview with Kenny, but apparently they took all the ballpoint pens away from Kenny. Undoubtedly security was tight when the CNN TV interview occurred. Kenny was even smoother than his mother. He could take any question from Larry King and spin it into whatever he wanted to complain about. Larry asked Kenny why he and his mother were convicted. He laid the blame on the fact that the investigators didn't take any notes for the last two years. His other excuse was that there was a photo that showed a possible security camera viewing of the front of Irene's hotel and its film was never seized and examined by the police. Kenny took the lack of notes and non-seizure of the camera to illustrate how the police and DA were out to get Kenny and his mother.

The following is part of the interview between Larry King and Kenny Kimes:

KENNY KIMES: Which tells me, no notes over two years. And if they wanted us, and if they wanted to prove our guilt, they would have taken the film and they would have used that camera as an aspect of their leading evidence in the case....They could take the camera out, and they did it intentionally.

LARRY KING: And why do they want to get you, so you think? New York City police don't know you.

KENNY KIMES: I think we're the easy whipping boy.

LARRY KING: Why would you be whipping boy when someone is just missing?

KENNY KIMES: It's an election year. Publicity, negative publicity, the public loves it. We're selling papers, clearly....But why me? Because I'm easy. I'm a foreigner, I'm out of town. They can just point the finger at the out of towners. There's always been an easy ability for people to just pick on someone who's not the local.

Kenny was good at playing the 'Minority Card,' that he was treated unfairly since he was an outsider. But when Larry asked why he didn't testify he gave an incredible response.

KENNY KIMES: Why didn't I testify? Because I thought my mom was going to have a shot at testifying on her own.

LARRY KING: But when she didn't, why didn't you?

KENNY KIMES: Well, why didn't I? I figured at the beginning, we wanted to get Court TV to come in. I figured, if this judge isn't going to let Court TV come in, and is only going to allow a one-sided print media to get only what the DA feeds them, I might as well be careful and stand guard knowing what kind of unfairness is going to take place.

LARRY KING: Even though the jury would have the ability to see you.

KENNY KIMES: Never. It was too late. At that point, there was not a chance.

It is difficult to follow Kenny's reasoning that the fact that Court TV was excluded therefore he couldn't testify doesn't add up. But he did give an answer that some people might take under consideration. Next Larry asked directly if they were involved in Irene Silverman's disappearance. Kenny answered unequivocally that they had nothing to do with the crime.

KENNY KIMES: Well. Larry, I did not do this. I did not commit this crime. I was arrested at the Hilton. There are no eyewitnesses. There was no physical evidence. I have no motive to commit this.

LARRY KING: I'm trying to figure out your motive?

KENNY KIMES: They said that we wanted to rob the house. They said we wanted to steal the mansion. For the love of God, how do you steal a mansion? How do you steal a mansion?

LARRY KING: Do you believe she's dead?

KENNY KIMES: This woman? Honestly? I have no idea. And for me to speculate would make me as bad as the jury who speculated upon us.

Some people look at any defendant charged with a crime as the underdog and in some way they may want to believe the person is innocent. Undoubtedly some readers may feel sorry for Kenny, since he so adamantly claimed that he had nothing to do with Silverman's death. Maybe he is telling the truth. For those readers who believed him, the next paragraphs may be disconcerting.

Only a short time after the Larry King interview, Kenny was showing authorities where Irene's body was buried. He did this so the authorities would reduce the amount of time he had to spend in solitary confinement. Kenny's change of heart shocked his attorney, since now he admitted he had been involved in the victim's death. This would wipe out his claim on appeal that he was an innocent person who was unfairly convicted. Kenny was having a 'reality check,' since he now accepted the fact that he was going to spend the rest of his life in prison. As a professional schemer, why not make it as pleasant as possible for one's self? Solitary confinement was not the way he wanted to spend the next eight years of his life.

What Kenny told law enforcement was, "I packaged Mrs. Silverman's body ..., placed it in the trunk of the car and drove through the Holland Tunnel. I dumped her body at a New Jersey construction site 35 to 40 minutes from Manhattan."

In New York, Kenny had been sentenced to 125 years to life and Sante had been sentenced to 120 years to life. The question becomes, what is enough of a sentence? Some people would say that was enough, since Sante wouldn't come up for a parole hearing until 2119. Would California want to bring them back to be tried for the murder of David Kazdin? The Los Angeles County District Attorney's Office had to make the determination. One of the advantages that Los Angeles DA's Office had was that it had an incredibly knowledgeable Extradition Unit. (One of the duties of the author over the years was to supervise the DA's Extradition Unit). This Unit at any one time had hundreds of extradition cases it was pursuing in the other 50 states and dozens of foreign countries. One of the advantages of the LA DA's Office is that it has incredible patience. Some extraditions will take years and sometimes require special documents to be translated into various foreign languages.

In a classic statement when she was in court waiting for the extradition hearing, Sante said, "When is this all going to end?" Apparently, Sante was tired of court proceedings. What she didn't realize was that the Los Angeles DA's Office wanted defendants to be accountable. Many jurisdictions don't have the experience or resources of the LA District Attorney's Office, and the smaller DA's Offices will refuse to spend the time and resources to extradite many of their fugitives.

When the LA DA's Office heard about the arrest of Sante and Kenny in New York, they set in motion the extradition request for both of them. California has the Death Penalty on the books while New York does not have such a law. This fact created an interesting issue. Should California have the opportunity to try the Kimeses first, since they could impose the Death Penalty in California? The LA DA's Office felt they should have the first opportunity. Therefore, it started the extradition proceedings by sending a formal request to California's Governor Gray Davis. The Governor's Office then submitted the application to New York's Governor, George E. Pataki. This required considerable bureaucratic paperwork that has to contain the approved extradition documents with the governors' seals affixed to them.

Although the extradition documents are impressive with all their seals and ribbons, the process is quite unusual compared to other legal proceedings. In extradition hearings, the state and federal law requires that a court hearing be held as in this case in New York, at which time the defendants can waive their rights or oppose the extradition request. Extradition hearings are limited to determining whether or not the person named in the extradition request is the person in custody. Also, whether the offense of which they are accused is a crime and whether the defendant was in the requesting state at the time of the offense charged and fled it to avoid prosecution. How this hearing is different from other criminal proceedings is that the burden is on the defendant to disprove these issues. No evidence is permitted on the strength of the requesting state's case or the guilt or innocence of the defendant.

Governor Pataki approved the extradition and stated, "These murderers must be held accountable for each and every one of their vile acts." He agreed that both Kimeses could be extradited to Los Angeles **at the completion of all proceeding in New York**. In other words, California would get them but New York wanted to try them first.

In May of 2002, the Los Angeles Grand Jury indicted Sante and Kenny Kimes, charging them with the murder of David Kazdin. A special circumstance allegation for financial gain was added to the murder charge.

It became apparent this dynamic duo would require the attention of the DA's **Major Crimes Division**. By the time Los Angeles County was able to bring them back for prosecution, both mother and son were infamous. Their trial was guaranteed to be a big public spectacle. The DA's Office needed to put a high-octane prosecutor on the case so the trial didn't turn into a Sante Kimes 'Circus Side Show.' Eleanor Hunter had gained the reputation of being able to handle the pressure of the big cases and get good results.

The assignment of the case to Eleanor seemed like a good fit for the DA's Office. However, the unanswerable question is what is the prosecutor's availability to try such a case? The problem is that it is next to impossible to be able to predict when such a case will be required to go trial. Since the defendant has an absolute right to a speedy trial, the Defense can demand a speedy trial when the prosecutor is tied up in trial on another case. There are so many factors that come into play in deciding the trial date for a case, such as a defense attorney's readiness and availability to try the case; the court has to find a time slot when it is available to start the trial as well as the availability of the witnesses.

Eleanor Hunter tried to schedule her cases so she would have sufficient time to prepare. When she received the Kimes case, she knew that it would be more than a year before she would ever see them in court, since they were first being tried in New York. As a result, Eleanor took on the Koklich case, since she had more than enough time to try it. What she didn't factor in was the fact that the first Koklich trial would result in a hung jury, thereby requiring a second trial that started in October 2003.

As if Eleanor wasn't busy enough retrying the Koklich case, she became entangled in the Kenny Kimes case. Both Kimeses were back in California, and a major decision had to be made regarding the trials of these two cases. The DA's Office had approved the Death Penalty on Kenny Kimes, since he was the one who shot and killed David Kazdin. One of the tenets that the LA DA's Office holds up as non-negotiable is that they won't agree to drop the Death Penalty if the defendant is willing to plead guilty and agree to a sentence of Life without the Possibility of

Parole. The purpose of having such a policy is that it is considered to be unethical to charge the Death Penalty only to withdraw it if the defendant agrees to plead guilty to the murder charge. This is held to be unfair coercion to get a defendant to plead guilty.

When Kenny's attorney indicated that Kenny was anxious to work out some type of plea bargain, the DA's Office's initial reaction was that once the decision is made to pursue the Death Penalty, there is nothing that can be done unless there is a proof problem with the case. However, Kenny's attorney indicated that he had already been sentenced to 125 years in prison and all he wanted to do was bring all the court proceedings to a conclusion. His attorney indicated that he was willing to plead guilty to the charge of murder of David Kazdin. All he was asking for was that the Death Penalty be dropped and that the DA allow him to receive a sentence of Life Without Possiblity of Parole (LWOP).

As repugnant as such a plea bargain was, there was a pause by the DA's Office when they started reviewing the strength of their case against Sante. Factually, it was Kenny who actually did the killing while his mother remained miles away. The prosecution of the case against Sante was based on the strength of the testimony of Shawn Lipman. The DA's Office, as well as most of the public, considered Sante Kimes to be one of the worst of the worst human beings who ever walked the face of the earth. It seemed like Sante truly was a vile person who the DA's Office wanted to convict of the Murder.

All of sudden the DA's Office found themselves in a position of having a weak case against a person (Sante) who almost everyone would agree totally deserved to be convicted. At that point it became clear that if the prosecution could get Kenny to testify against his mother that would strengthen the chances of obtaining a conviction against Sante. When asked, Kenny's attorney clearly stated that he would be more than willing to testify against his mother.

The DA's Office had a dilemma. Should the DA's Office enter into a plea bargain with Kenny and violate their highest tenet of not plea bargaining the Death Penalty? Could any legal justification be found that the case against Kenny had been substantially weakened, thereby meriting some type of plea bargain in order to successfully prosecute him? The case against Kenny hadn't been lessened. The only gain for the DA's Office would be that by getting Kenny to testify against his mother the DA's Office would be better able to convince the jury to CONVICT Sante.

The DA's Office found itself in a very delicate situation. It was damned if you do and damned if you don't. It wasn't that one side was GOOD and the other side was EVIL. The DA's administrators had many discussions on this subject, and eventually a decision had to be made. Finally, it was decided that the DA's Office would drop the Death Penalty against Kenny and he would receive a sentence of LWOP, if he agreed to testify truthfully against his mother.

Then it fell on Eleanor Hunter to try to carry out this deal, which many felt was the same as making a pact with the Devil. Eleanor and Kenny's attorney arranged for the lengthy interview with the prosecutor and the detectives. They were shocked to learn all the details of how this mother-son team scammed their way across America.

On November 17, 2003, Kenny appeared in the Los Angeles courtroom of Judge Kathleen Kennedy-Powell. The DA's Office and Kenny's Defense attorney announced to the judge that a plea bargain had been agreed to and the defendant would be pleading guilty to the murder of David Kazdin. The prosecutor, Eleanor Hunter, stated in open court that the prosecution would **not** seek the Death Penalty against Kenny. Then the judge instructed the prosecutor to take the plea. Eleanor turned and looked at Kenny as he was standing next to his attorney and said, "In this case, Kenneth Kimes Jr., how do you plead to the murder of David Kazdin?" Kenny with a contrite soft voice uttered the word **"GUILTY."**

In order to get a factual basis for the plea, the prosecutor asked Kenny if he had been to Kazdin's home on March 19, 1998, and shot David Kazdin. Kenny very calmly and resolutely said, "Yes." He further admitted to disposing of the body in order to conceal a fraud committed against the victim. The prosecutor indicated that this plea was based on the fact that Kenny Kimes had agreed to testify against his 64-year-old mother.

After that court proceeding, the news media and the general public were buzzing with excitement as to what was going on in both Kenny's and Sante's cases. When the reporters heard the word that Kenny would be testifying against his mother, they were full of questions that they wanted to ask Eleanor. However, she was preoccupied with the retrial of the Koklich case in the Norwalk courthouse.

Later that day, Sante Kimes appeared in the same courtroom of Judge Kennedy-Powell with her attorney Charles Maple. Sante pled **Not Guilty** and the matter was set for trial. On that day, Sante played the 'sympathy card' by complaining about her poor health as she sat silently in a county-issued jail wheelchair. Throughout her many court appearances she would arrive in a wheelchair. During the proceedings she might claim to have a fainting spell, or claim to be having a heart attack, but there was always the constant weeping, claiming she was just a poor elderly lady who was being picked on by the court system.

It wasn't until June 14, 2004, that her jury trial began. By that time, Eleanor had successfully convicted Bruce Koklich and now was in the middle of the Govin Indian Motel case. She had gotten Victor Govin convicted; however, the other brother Peter Govin's case had resulted in a hung jury and would have to be retried. Since that case was being tried in Judge Kennedy-Powell's court, Eleanor was able to have the Sante Kimes case squeezed in between the two Govin brothers' trials.

No other attorney would take three of the most challenging cases and try them interchangeably over the same time period. It was a wonder that Eleanor was able to keep the facts straight from three totally separate cases. However, what the media and public have no way of knowing is what an extraordinary job certain people do. Eleanor stepped up to the plate and was able to juggle three significant cases all at the same time.

The point is that Major Crimes Division is made up of some of the most remarkable attorneys I have ever worked with. It is amazing what certain people are capable of doing under tremendous pressures. What has astonished me about the Major Crimes prosecutors is that they exhibit a 'Can Do' attitude. They aren't looking for excuses as to how tough things are. Many attorneys are willing to find fault with their cases and willing to find any way possible to dispose of them.

Eleanor was typical of the other prosecutors in the Major Crimes Division. When she realized that the Sante Kimes case had to be tried she answered, "Ready for the People." In her Opening Statement she said, "Kenny was Sante's enforcer, the one she would send to do all her dirty work." She went on to outline the case to the jury. Next, Sante's Defense attorney said, "Sante cannot accept that her son would commit such a violent crime. My client did not order any killing and there was no motive for her to want Kazdin dead. It had nothing to do with Mrs. Kimes."

The Kimes case was one of the most challenging for a prosecutor to try in front of a jury. Eleanor needed the jurors to believe the testimony of Kenny and Shawn Lipman. In order to use accomplices as prosecution witnesses, she had to corroborate everything they were saying. In this case, the key witness (Kenny) was one of the boldest scam artists of all times. The prosecutor was trying to prove to the jurors that this time Kenny was being totally truthful. Kenny Kimes most likely had told more lies than any other human who had ever stepped foot in that courtroom.

So how do you know when he is telling the truth? On June 17th he took the witness stand and the court clerk had him swear to tell the truth and nothing but the truth. He testified that his mother said to him, "We're going to have to kill him." He went on to say that his mother had planned the murder on March 13, 1998, after Kazdin had confronted the bank about the loan and told them he knew nothing about it and certainly hadn't approved it. Kenny testified that his mother said to him that he had to take care of Kazdin. Her words were, "She wished me luck and told me to do a good job."

Kenny related to the jury that he and his accomplice, Shawn Lipman, went to Kazdin's house that morning with trash bags, a .22-caliber gun, gloves, and duct tape. He indicated that he confronted Kazdin about the loan and Kazdin told him not to worry. Then Kenny followed him into the kitchen and took out the gun. He testified, "I shot him in the back of the head at point-blank range to minimize the risk of error." Then he and Shawn Lipman cleaned up the crime scene and threw Kazdin's body in the trunk of his Jaguar and drove to an area near LAX. Since they had some time to kill before it was dark, he explained to the jury that they went to the Beverly Center, where, he said, "We ate lunch and went to see the movie '*The*

Man in the Iron Mask' and shopped for clothes. In the evening when it was dark we returned to the airport area and disposed of the body in a trash dumpster." They also threw out the gun and Kazdin's wallet a short distance away in another dumpster.

"Afterwards we headed to the Valley, where I stopped to buy some flowers." When asked by the prosecutor what he did with the flowers he said, "I kissed my mother and handed her the flowers and told her everything was OK." When asked why he did that, he said, "In my mind-set, I thought I had completed a great duty for my mom. It was a significant completion, and I wanted to celebrate."

CHAPTER 24 KIMES-SANTE'S LA TRIAL

After Kenny was cross-examined about his testimony, Eleanor continued to put on evidence about the killing by having the jurors hear from **Shawn Lipman,** who was the other person who took part in the killing and disposal of the body. However, Shawn Lipman was unavailable to testify in court, but he had testified at the Grand Jury and the parties stipulated that the transcript of his testimony could be read to the jurors. The reading of the transcript permitted the jury to hear some corroboration of Kenny's testimony.

Nannette Wojdak testified next that she met Sante in 1993 and she was hired as a part-time bookkeeper and worked at the Geronimo Way residence in Las Vegas. Sante encouraged her to become a notary. Over a period of weeks, she saw McDaniel do maintenance work around the house. He was given a room to stay in and was strictly not permitted to leave the house.

Sante instructed her to sign and notarize Kazdin's name on the loan documents, including the Quitclaim deed and a deed of trust. The notary claimed that Sante said she had a power of attorney for Kazdin. Sante used Wojdak's bank account much like her own without the Kimes name on it. When the bank loan was funded, the money was placed in Wojdak's bank account and later she wired $120,000 to a bank account in Florida that the Kimeses used.

Later, Sante and Kenny had her join them on a so-called shopping trip to Los Angeles, where she was to meet with Kazdin. She went to his house while the Kimeses waited in their car down the street. She knocked on the door and Kazdin's daughter let her in. She talked to him about her problem with the bank, to which he claimed he didn't know anything about a loan with that bank. Without getting his cooperation and signature, she went back to the car and met with the Kimeses.

She further testified that Kenny wanted her notary book, which she gave to him. He immediately destroyed it. Months later, **after the Kimeses were arrested in New York,** Wojdak received a letter from Sante that urged her **not** to talk about the Kazdin transaction, explaining that Kazdin had authorized her to sign his name. Sante wrote in the letter, "If DK (David Kazdin) is really gone, we certainly can't be connected to that. David is the only one who could at this time say he didn't sign papers or tell you to notarize." Nannette Wojdak was able to explain how the property was transferred by using forgeries.

The next witness was the person that the property was supposedly transferred to. **Robert McDaniel** was called next to the witness stand to relate his role in the property scam. He stated that he met Sante on November 8, 1996, when he was a homeless person. He agreed to work as the Kimeses' maintenance person in return for room and board. They took his identification and ordered him not to leave the house. They cashed his Social Security checks and seldom gave him any of the money.

For whatever reason, they used his name on a Quitclaim deed purportedly signed by a David Kazdin conveying the Geronimo Way property to McDaniel for the full sum of $10. They also used his name on a fire insurance policy on the house without his knowledge.

McDaniel went on to testify that he helped Kenny move some furniture out of the house. He explained they moved into a duplex to live on the other side of Las Vegas. Later, he traveled with the Kimeses to Los Angeles and stayed at a motel. While there, they told him that the Geronimo Way house had burnt down because of an electrical fire. When they returned to Las Vegas to live in the duplex, he was told that the title to the Geronimo Way property was put in his name because of some legal problems they were having.

He related that they wanted him to meet with a fire insurance company investigator to answer certain questions about the $500,000 fire loss. He did his best at the meeting, claiming that he was the owner of the house that burned. After the meeting, he returned to a place in Bel Air, in the Los Angeles area where they were all staying. He was ordered not to tell anyone who they were or what they were up to. However, he told another tenant who the Kimeses really were and what they were planning to do. As a result, he described to the jury how Kenny and Sante beat him up for talking to the other tenant.

McDaniel further related that one day he overheard Sante tell Kenny, "He knows too much. We have got to do something about him." Kenny replied, "What about Kazdin's daughter?" Sante responded, "She won't be any problem." A few days later Kenny and Shawn Lipman left the Bel Air house early in the morning. They returned later that night, and Kenny gave his mother a bouquet of flowers and kissed her. On the next day, the landlord came by and that was when Kenny went ballistic and they all moved out. They all went to a restaurant to regroup, and that was when McDaniel ran away and escaped from the Kimeses' control.

Sante's Civil Attorney George Rogers (Pseudonym) testified that he worked at a company called Nevada Corporate Services. Rogers worked as a resident agent for Nevada corporations and Sante wanted his help to bring her Agahan corporation out of default. The main asset of the corporation was the Santa Maria property that was tied up in the civil lawsuit. Later in 1998 she wanted David Kazdin to be made an officer of the corporation. Rogers claimed that he was contacted by phone by a person claiming to be Kazdin and that he consented to be added as an officer.

Sante later asked him to take out a loan on the Geronimo Way residence; however, he needed Kazdin's consent since his name was on the land title. Sante assured him that the property was really hers so Kazdin would be no problem. Rogers never contacted him to obtain his consent, but when he received the loan documents they had Kazdin's signature on them. When the loan money was paid, part of it went to Sante's off shore bank accounts. It was not until February 1998 that he became aware that Kazdin denied signing the loan, at which point Rogers said he terminated his relationship with the Kimeses.

To continue with the loan testimony, **Brenda Ross** (Pseudonym) was called as the next witness. She testified she worked for OCWEN Financial Services and she was the one who received the loan documents for the property on Geronimo Way. She had Kazdin's signature on the Quitclaim deed, which transferred the property to McDaniel and had been notarized by Wojdak. The loan amount of $280,000 was funded, and part of the money was wired to Wojdak's account. There was a request by the loan applicant (Sante Kimes) that **all correspondence be sent the Geronimo**

Way address. Unfortunately, the bank made a mistake and **sent a billing statement and payment book to Kazdin's residence**.

That ended up as a deadly mistake, because this witness testified that she received a call from Kazdin. She related that Kazdin was upset that he had been sent the material in error. He claimed that he didn't sign any loan application and indicated that the loan was a fraud. Since she had distributed most of the funds to a Nannette Wojdak's bank account, she immediately placed a hold on any more distribution of funds.

Clifford Mitchell, an expert in arson detection, testified that he investigated the Geronimo Way property fire on January 31, 1998, and found it was intentionally set. He testified that he was able to locate several points on the floor where an accelerant had been poured. As he examined the remains of the house, he determined that there was no evidence of an electrical or gas fire.

Stanley Pasternack testified that he had helped the Kimeses do some moving. Then Kenny had asked him if he could obtain certain types of handguns. This witness said he could provide Kenny with any kind of handgun he needed for $1,000. Eventually he returned to Los Angeles and brought Kenny a .22 Jennings handgun, along with two other handguns. After the shooting, he drove the Kimeses' RV from Las Vegas to a restaurant in LA, where they all met.

The next witnesses testified to their contacts with the victim, David Kazdin. **Phillip Eaton** stated that he was a longtime friend and attorney of David Kazdin. Kazdin had told him that his name was used on the title of the Geronimo Way property to help out his old friend Kenneth Kimes Sr. Kazdin had asked that his name be removed from the title of the property but it was never removed. Kazdin told him that in 1998 there was an unauthorized loan on that property using his name. Kazdin told him that he had not signed a Quit Claim deed in favor of McDaniel.

To continue to show the victim's involvement, **Linda Kazdin** was called as a witness and testified that she was the daughter of the victim. She realized something was wrong when she went to her father's home and noticed that his bed was unmade and his shoes were beside it. Also, his car was gone, and the answering machine was blinking with more than 10 messages.

Daniella Scott (Pseudonym) testified that she lived on El Vido Drive in Bel Air and the Kimeses were renting rooms there. In their room was a map to Kazdin's house that they apparently had left behind.

Officer Dale Best of LAPD testified he was the officer who was sent to check out a dumpster with a body in it. He verified that the dumpster did contain a body covered by black plastic trash bags. The body didn't contain any wallet or identification. The victim's Jaguar was found about a mile away parked in a shopping center parking lot.

Finally, the prosecutor addressed the issue of the cause of death. **Dr. Irwin Golden** was called to the witness stand as the medical examiner, and he testified that he performed the autopsy on David Kazdin. He was able to determine that the victim had been killed by a single gunshot wound to the back of the neck at the base of the skull. The gun had been fired from very close range. A small-caliber bullet was recovered from the victim's jaw.

James Bell (Pseudonym), an attorney for the victim Kazdin, testified that Kazdin contacted him when he discovered the loan fraud. He did state that Kenny was a loose cannon. When he was cross-examined, he indicated that Sante had threatened Kazdin and left threats on his voice mail.

Allen Glass was not a lengthy witness, since he only testified that he was the one who was instrumental in obtaining the loan on the Geronimo Way property. With all of his contacts, he was able to find the best loan rates from a bank in Florida, which was OCWEN Bank.

The head LAPD investigator on the case was **Detective English.** It seemed strange when the Defense called him to testify for them. They asked him whether witness James Bell had said that Kenny was a loose cannon. The detective related that Bell had said something to that effect. Everyone in the courtroom was befuddled as to what that had to do with the killing of Kazdin.

Against her attorney's advice, Sante testified that she had absolutely nothing to do with Kazdin's murder. **Sante Kimes** emphasized how fond she was of David Kazdin and how she loved him more than anyone in the world except for her husband. On cross-examination, the prosecutor asked her if she had been convicted of a felony. She denied any conviction. When she was asked specifically about the five federal felony convictions for slavery in 1985, she said that she didn't consider herself to have been guilty of those offenses. The prosecutor asked if those convictions involved five young women she had brought to Las Vegas from Mexico who testified that she physically abused them. She adamantly denied there was any abuse.

Nevertheless, when asked about her convictions in the Irene Silverman case she indicated she was wrongfully convicted and she insisted that she was truly a good friend with Irene Silverman. When she denied the murder and offered an alibi, the prosecutor asked her whether she had any of Silverman's property in her possession at the time of her arrest. Sante thought for a moment about Irene's passports and Social Security card said to the prosecutor, "I don't remember."

She spent nearly three hours on the witness stand either crying or sniveling. She accused a detective of planting evidence, and called the prosecutor a monster and launched into several diatribes that prompted the judge to tell her to be quiet. Then Sante referred to Kazdin and said, "God bless him, wherever he is, I wish he were here to help me, I need help." She went on to say that she had been to his Granada Hills home more than 200 times and that neither she nor her son had anything to do with his death. She blamed his death on a former attorney who she said had helped her set up an offshore bank account.

As to explaining Sante's son's testimony, she told the jurors that it was the prosecutor who had forced her son to testify against her by threatening him with the

Death Penalty. She went on to praise her son and stated that he was a wonderful boy and a hero, and she begged the prosecutor to leave him alone. She accused the prosecutor of paying witnesses to lie. Then Sante said to the prosecutor, "You're the real murderer here. You don't know what justice is." The prosecutor could have fired back about all the murders Sante had been involved in. However, Eleanor exercised restrained and didn't call Sante the 'real murderer,' since that was the job for the jury to do.

At the time of the Rebuttal, the prosecutor recalled Kenny to explain in more detail Sante's role in the killing of Irene Silverman. This recall was to answer the Defense's claim that Sante wasn't at all involved and knew little or nothing about it. This seemed to end the evidence stage of the trial. However, Sante insisted over her attorney's advice to testify again in surrebuttal.

Sante testified to her affluence at the time of her husband's death. She wanted the jury to know that she was wealthy and had no need to commit crimes for financial gain. It may have seemed like brag contest in that she had more money than the jurors. Then, after being cross-examined, Sante sat down at counsel table and everyone thought it was over.

The old saying seemed true, "It's over when the Fat Lady (to be PC when the Heavyset Lady) sings." Both sides had rested their case and it was time to start the Argument. Sante all of a sudden requested one more time to testify. Everyone wondered what was going on. The judge, not wanting to create an issue on appeal, agreed that she could testify for a third time. Sante walked up to the witness stand and the judge instructed her that she was still under oath to tell the truth.

She seemed to ramble on about the Silverman murder. She testified that she never intended to steal from or kill her, since she loved the woman. She explained to the jury that she had no motive to steal from her since she had lots of money. Sante's attorney, who seemed to be shaking his head, asked the judge to erase all of Sante's testimony. This objection surprised the judge, since there was no such legal objection. The judge denied the objection and must have pondered how this case could get any stranger.

Finally, it was time for Argument. Prosecutor Eleanor Hunter was in a league all by herself. She had taken on some of the toughest cases ever handled by the LA DA's Office

Eleanor Hunter had a ‘No Fear’ attitude as to any defendant or defense attorney. She knew how to take whatever evidence the police were able to acquire and she knew how to present it to the jury. Her litigation skills were finely polished, with a strong emphasis on using graphics to tell the story. In this **Sante Kimes case,** she used numerous charts to assist the jurors in understanding the facts. She utilized a Timeline chart to show all the key dates that the jurors needed to remember. Her dilemma was that there were 24 crucial dates that the jurors needed to remember. She wanted them all to be on one poster so the jurors could see all the events at one time. However, with 24 lines it made the font so small on the chart that it was difficult for the jurors to read from a distance. The solution was to use one tall vertical chart to show all the critical dates. *On the following graphic page is the Timeline exhibit.*

Graphics Page

This Timeline poster was used in the Sante Kimes' case so jurors could keep track of what happened and when.it happened.

TIMELINE OF EVENTS

Date	Event
11/1997	Begin process for loan
12/19/1997	• D. Kazdin receives loan documents at home • Writes letter to Phil Eaton
01/06/1998	Ocwen funds the loan for $280,000
01/11/1998	Quit Claim Deed D. Kazdin → McDaniel
01/15-20/1998	Sante Kimes obtains insurance on home (Fireman's Fund)
01/23/1998	• D. Kazdin gets payment book at his home • D. Kazdin notifies Ocwen of fraud
~01/23/1998	Kenneth Kimes & others move furniture out of Geronimo home
01/26/1998	Move McDaniel out of Geronimo home
01/31/1998	Fire at Geronimo home
02/01/1998	• Sante Kimes, Kenneth Kimes & McDaniel leave LA & go to Las Vegas • Furniture at new home
02/12/1998	Sante Kime, Kenneth Kimes and Wojdak in LA Super 8 Motel
02/13/1998	• Sante Kimes, Kenneth Kimes & Wojdak go to D. Kazdin's home • Wojdak confronts D. Kazdin
~02/14/1998	Wojdak leaves message on D. Kazdin's phone
02/20/1998	McDaniel interviewed at Marriott regarding arson
02/22/1998	• Move to Elvido Dr. • Aliases
~02/24/1998	Stanley gives 22 Cal. gun to the Kimes'
03/09/1998	Sante Kimes & Kenneth Kimes brin Shawn back to Las Vegas
03/12/1998	D. Kazdin last contacted by his daughter
03/13/1998	• Shawn & Kenneth Kimes leave early • Kill D. Kazdin • Return late with flowers
03/14/1998	D. Kazdin found
03/19/1998	• Sante Kimes & Kenneth Kimes learn McDaniel talking • Take him to motel and beat him
03/20/1998	McDaniel beaten by all 3
03/21/1998	Pasternack arrives in LA with motor home Pasternack leaves
03/22/1998	• All leave Elvido & go to IHOP McDaniel escapes

Prosecutor Hunter used visuals that showed the Relationship of the Parties in the case. One of the visuals used was of the various locations that the jurors needed to be familiar with. The most confusing part of Sante's case was all the documents involving the loan transaction. So the prosecutor labeled them and displayed them on one large visual aid poster board. The prosecutor gave an insightful Argument explaining all the pieces of evidence and how they all fitted together. She realized that her main job was convincing the jurors that they could believe Kenny Kimes as a witness. She continually used visuals that corroborated every part of his testimony. She used two photo exhibits showing Kazdin's house, where he was shot, and another one of photos of the alley where Kazdin's body was found in a trash dumpster. *The following visual is on the next graphic page.*

Graphics Page

This visual was used so jurors could see the crime scene

This depicts where the dumpster was located that contained the body.

She knew that some jurors might look at Kenny as the biggest Judas, since he was selling out his mother in order to save his life. Neither Kenny nor Sante was a likeable character, and some would say they were high on the list of being the most despicable human beings on this earth. Eleanor knew that she could only use Kenny's testimony as the basic framework of the case, and that she needed all those other witnesses to provide the details.

After the prosecution Argument, the Defense attorney commenced his Argument. He did his best to hammer away at Kenny as being unbelievable. He stressed that Sante wasn't anywhere near the killing of David Kazdin in Granada Hills. He harped on the fact that the prosecution hadn't proved their case beyond a reasonable doubt. He reminded the jurors that other people might want the victim killed. Unfortunately for her attorney, Sante didn't make a good witness for the Defense. Her continual broad-brush denials made her far from a sympathetic witness. All he could hope for was that some juror might hang up the jury.

After five days of deliberation, the jury had reached a verdict. Sante was brought into the courtroom and sat down. She leaned her elbows on the table as though she was praying and bowed her head as the guilty Murder verdict was read with the special allegation of Financial Gain found to be true.

On March 21, 2005, it was time for sentencing. Sante was fighting to the very end as she told the judge, "We are INNOCENT! I pray for justice. I ask for all Americans to help us. We have only just begun to fight." The judge was unmoved by Sante's plea. The judge said, "You are one of the most **EVIL** individuals that I have ever encountered in 16 years on the bench." Thereupon the judge sentenced Sante Kimes to Life With Out the Possibility of Parole (LWOP). Shortly thereafter, Kenny received the same sentence, even though the judge said, "At least he finally stepped up to the plate. I do think it was a real turning point in his life to cut that umbilical cord or whatever, the stranglehold she had on him. I know that his testimony was crucial to her conviction."

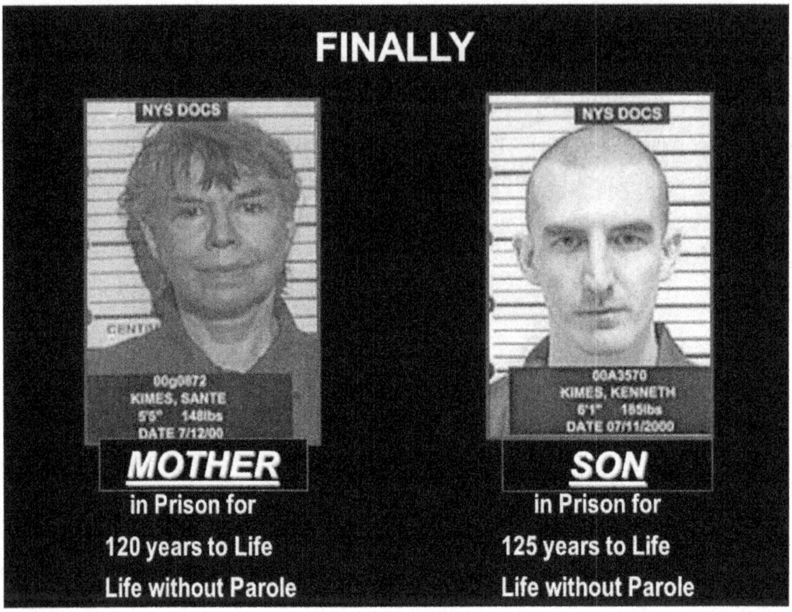
FINALLY
NYS DOCS
00g0872
KIMES, SANTE
5'5" 148lbs
DATE 7/12/00
MOTHER
in Prison for
120 years to Life
Life without Parole
NYS DOCS
00A3570
KIMES, KENNETH
6'1" 165lbs
DATE 07/11/2000
SON
in Prison for
125 years to Life
Life without Parole

PEOPLE VS. VICTOR & PETER GOVIN

Motel Alley Massacre

CHAPTER 25 GOVIN- DISPUTE BETWEEN MOTEL OWNERS

It was a balmy evening in Los Angeles as Victor Govin drove his way up the windy road in the East Hollywood Hills to visit an Indian family's home. He was anxious to meet with Gita Kumar in hopes of resolving a crucial issue regarding the expansion of his motel. What it was all about was the use of an alleyway that ran through the rear area of his family's Studio Place Motel as well as the Gita Kumar's Universal City Inn.

The Govin family had owned the property for years, making a good living from operating the aging motel, which was located directly across the street from the main entrance of Universal Studios. Millions of tourists who have visited Hollywood have gone by his family's humble motel. Because of its prime location, it was like a gold mine with unlimited potential if only they could close off a city alley in the rear of the property in order to expand their motel. With additional motel units, they could attract a national motel chain to become interested in their location.

It didn't seem like a big deal, since the alley had been closed for years and basically had been walled off from use. The other property that used the alley was the adjacent motel, the Universal City Inn, which was to the east of the Govin's motel. This neighboring motel was larger and was operated by Gita Kumar and her husband Michael Patel (In order to simplify this story, he will be referred to as Mr. Kumar). This motel didn't use the short public alley that ran the length of rear of the property. As a matter of fact, Gita and Michael liked the fact that the alley had been temporarily closed off by the Govin brothers. With the alley closed off, the Universal City Inn could better control activity in their rear parking lot, since everyone had to drive by the motel office to enter or exit the rear parking lot. Having the alley blocked off was certainly a security benefit for all their motel guests.

In other words, both motels were pleased that the public alley was blocked off. Since it had been that way for years, everyone liked the status quo. Five years earlier, the Govins had submitted a building plan to the City of Los Angeles in which they showed that the alley would be closed. Back then, the City Planning Department approved the Govin's building plan. Everyone was happy, and if they had started the construction the old alley would have been totally closed and would have been forever forgotten. Unfortunately, at that time, the economy suffered a recession and as a result the Govins abandoned their remodeling project.

Since the recession cut down the number of tourists coming to Universal Studios, the Govins just wanted to survive the bad times. The City building plans were still good and valid for five years. Time went by and six years later the Govins dusted off the building plans and decided to try again on their remodeling project. Since the plans had lapsed, the City required that they re-submit an updated set of plans. Again they needed to obtain the consent of the owners of the neighboring motel to have them sign off on the abandonment of the small city alley.

However, this time Gita Kumar from the neighboring motel indicated that they were exploring the possibility of expanding their motel. When Gita and her husband submitted their plans to the City Building Department, they were surprised that the city planners insisted that they have a secondary source of ingress and egress. In other words, the city said that they had to reopen the alleyway in the rear of their property for delivery trucks to have access to their Universal City Inn.

The City was saying that the Govins had to permanently close off the alley to have their building plans approved. At the same time, the City was telling the Kumars, the next door neighbor, that if they wanted to expand their motel they had to have the alleyway reopened in order to get their building plans approved. Both Indian families found themselves at odds with each other. Gita Kumar told the Govins that she could NOT sign off on the closing of the alley because she now needed it to be open. These two families, who had spent many years peacefully operating their motels next to each other, now found themselves with a major disagreement. For both families there were significant financial consequences revolving around this small alleyway.

Both families knew that they had prime pieces of property that could make both families extremely wealthy, since Universal Studios had plans to expand to be an even larger tourist attraction for Los Angeles. How could this matter be amicably resolved for both families? The Govins contacted their business attorney, and he drafted an agreement that they thought might be acceptable to Gita. It fell on Victor Govin to take a copy of the drafted Agreement to Gita and explain it to her. That was the purpose for the meeting Victor had set up. Both sides had a lot at stake.

As Victor finally reached the top of the hill, he turned down a long driveway to the Kumar's home and parked in front of their house. He grabbed the folder lying on the passenger seat and looked inside to see that he had the copy of the attorney's drafted Agreement. Seeing that everything was in order, he opened the car door and stepped out. Within ten steps, he was standing at the front door ringing the bell. Victor waited anxiously. As he stood there, he felt the enormous pressure on his shoulders. His family's financial wellbeing was on the line.

To Victor, it seemed like he had been waiting a long time before the door was opened. He didn't know if the Kumar family was intentionally making him wait or what was taking them so long to open the door. Eventually, Gita opened the door a crack and, upon seeing Victor, swung the door wide open and warmly greeted him. Victor tried his hardest to appear agreeable to Gita, but as an Indian man he didn't want to appear to be condescending or begging an Indian woman, for a favor.

After the exchange of pleasantries, Victor placed his right hand into the folder and pulled out the Agreement. He explained to Gita that he would like her to look over the document, which had been drafted by his attorney. He explained that the document addressed all the issues regarding the closing of the alley behind both their motels. Gita took the document and sat down to read it. Her eyes glanced over the various paragraphs. She quietly looked over the papers, and several times she seemed to jerk back in the chair when she came to the various paragraphs discussing the alley.

After reviewing all the pages, she started asking questions about how this was going to impact their plans to expand Universal City Inn. She zeroed in on the point that the City was telling her that she had to have access to the alleyway for delivery trucks. The document didn't address their problems that they had with the City. She stated that the alley was really the property of the City and she didn't have authorization to give up the City's rights to the alley.

She pushed the document away and outright stated that she couldn't sign it. This was slightly different from her saying that she wouldn't sign it. Victor tried to think of anything he could say to persuade her to sign her name to the Agreement. Gita, with her piercing dark eyes, stared at Victor and outright stated "I won't sign this Agreement." At that very moment it was clear that a bright red line had been drawn in the sand. The negotiation phase was over; both sides had dug in their heels and no one was going to budge.

Victor meekly picked up the copy of the Agreement, not knowing what to say next. He slowly turned and headed for the door, which he opened on his own, and left the Kumar's house. He bristled with utter humiliation. How could an 'Indian Woman' treat him so badly? His male ego was bruised by the manner in which Gita had outright rejected his request for her to sign the Agreement. As he drove back to his small motel, he kept thinking how his brother Peter and the other members of his family would look upon him as a failure for not getting her to sign her name to the Agreement.

Then his thinking switched to how he could force Gita to sign the Agreement. How could he apply pressure on her to make her more agreeable? Victor was realistic to recognize that he was small in stature and certainly wouldn't project fear in the mind of another. But who could he get to frighten Gita? He thought maybe if he and his brother approached her together that they would look stronger. But he continued to come to the same conclusion: that he and his brother, as short Indian men, looked anything but menacing. All the Indian men he knew and associated with were docile looking and didn't project a feeling of fear.

When he returned to his motel office, he telephoned his brother, Peter, and gave him the bad news. Peter was livid that his brother had failed again in not getting the cooperation of an Indian woman like Gita. The two brothers weren't going to accept defeat. Their frustration turned to finding a way to exert pressure on Gita that would make or force her to sign the Agreement. After much discussion, the brothers decided to find someone who could accompany them when they next met with Gita. This person had to look menacing and scary to persuade Gita to sign the Agreement. This so-called 'Muscle Person' would act as an INTIMIDATOR.

CHAPTER 26 GOVIN-BACKGROUND OF PARTIES

To better understand how two families from India found themselves involved in such a high-stakes drama, one has to go back several decades to India. Conditions in India were less than desirable for many Indians who were living in deplorable conditions and wanted a better life for themselves and their families. After World War II, the government in India decided to make major changes in their economy. They wanted to break its ties with the old British Empire, but the government wanted to concentrate on having a business model that would guarantee uniform development for everyone.

The Indian government adopted a Soviet-style economy system called **License Raj**. It was a comprehensive plan as to how to build the infrastructure for a vibrant economy for the entire country. The idea was that the government would control the economy by selecting who could be given a license for a particular business. That meant that the government gave out the licenses for a certain products and it was the government that decided what was produced, how much to produce, and what the price would be as well, as what sources of capital could be used.

It seemed like a good idea for a developing nation; however, it had devastating consequences for the economy and the public. The licenses were given to select groups, and most of the population was excluded from being able to obtain a license. In practice, it took dozens of government agencies just to obtain the license. The process required a massive bureaucracy, which placed absurd restrictions on each business. The bottom line was the **License Raj** plan created few jobs and little wealth for the masses. It led to unreasonable constraints on businesses and caused widespread corruption.

From 1947 to 1990, the **License Raj** concept created massive poverty and a failed economic system. Many Indian families were shut out of the benefits of the Indian economy and began to look for other countries where they had a better chance to succeed.

Some of them left India to take refuge in England, where they stayed for a short time. But when they had an opportunity to migrate to the USA, they took advantage of it. This criminal case revolves around three families which included the Govin family, the Patel family, and the Kumar family. They all came to America with great hopes. They believed in working hard and soon learned to be shrewd business people. For years there was a stereotype regarding Indian immigrants that involved them buying and operating small convenience stores. In many communities, Indian clerks were seen as a fixture making Slurpees at the local 7-Eleven Markets.

However, these families in our story took another route to climb out of poverty, and their ladder of success came by buying and operating older motels. These Indian families would scrape together the small amount of resources they had saved up. They would invest that money in purchasing a dilapidated motel or hotel. With their family members, they would operate the motel while fixing it up. When they had a profitable operation, they would sell the business in order to take the profit and buy a larger motel. At first, the entire family lived in one of the motel rooms in the rear. Each member of the family took their turns working the front desk as well as cleaning the rooms. This meant the business labor costs were minimal. The other advantage was that the operation generated a large amount of cash. Through their hard work and willingness to save, these families over time were able to accumulate large holdings of motels, which made them quite wealthy.

The **Govins** were a typical Indian family starting in the motel business and eventually were able to purchase the Studio Place Inn on Ventura Boulevard across from the world-famous Universal Studios. It was a great location because of its easy access to the theme park, which is one of Southern California's major tourist attractions. The motel was made up of several detached buildings that contained various rooms of the motel. It was timeworn and required considerable maintenance to keep it in operation. Mr. Govin had his family live in the back building of the units to save money. Even though this motel wasn't modern and very pleasing to the eyes, it continued to generate a consistent flow of money for the family, basically due to its excellent location.

Mr. Govin had two sons who took over his motel business after he retired. His son Victor (Verender) Govin continued to operate the Studio Place Inn and eventually was able to afford a respectable house just up the street from the motel. Father Govin's other son was Peter (Pravin) Govin who operated another motel for the family in Orange County called the Cyprus Inn. Business was good for both brothers, but they wanted to make even more money.

As to the **Kumar** family, both Gita and her husband Michael had come to America in search of the Good Life. They started out in Texas and eventually moved to Compton, California, where they bought a shabby motel in a less-than-desirable area. Just like the Govin family, they lived in the rear of the motel. They were very industrious, and within a short time they were able to turn around this Compton motel and make it profitable. In time, they were able to save enough money to buy the Universal City Inn with two other business partners. This was a dream come true for Gita and her family. As Universal Studios grew in popularity, their motel turned into a mini-goldmine. They made so much money they were able to purchase a very expensive house in the Hollywood Hills just a short distance away. The Govin and the Kumar families were typical of the upperly mobile Indian society that had migrated to America.

When the Govin's motel filled up with guests, they needed more room to park the guests' cars. The obvious place to park cars was on the old alleyway at the rear of the motel property. Eventually, Victor Govin had placed a barrier up to block any traffic from using the alley to go into the back of the neighboring Universal City Inn. Next door, Gita and Michael didn't have any objection, because it provided a greater degree of security to their back parking lot. All persons visiting the motel had to drive by the motel office. Auto thieves couldn't sneak into the parking lot by using the old alleyway entrance.

For years, both families were happy with the arrangement of closing off the alleyway. Over time, the Govins had erected large wooden barricades that made sure no one could use the alley as a thoroughfare. Years earlier, the Govin family had submitted a plan to the City to expand their motel. The City Planning Department had approved the plan on the condition that the alley would be permanently closed.

Each family needed the other's cooperation for them to succeed in their business. This was the beginning of what some people called the great 'Indian Motel Alley Dispute.' How were these Indian families going to resolve this dilemma?

CHAPTER 27 GOVIN-FIND AN INTIMIDATOR

Then the Govin brothers tried to come up with a plan to force Gita to sign the agreement. At first the Govin brothers asked others to help them to threaten Gita to sign. The idea was to have some "mean biker dudes" go with Victor Govin to Gita's house and confront her. The hope was that she would be sufficiently intimated by the threat of force that she would capitulate. At first, Victor Govin turned to his longtime friend, Carlos Alonso (Pseudonym), to see if he could help him out. Carlos wasn't big and despicable enough to carry off the plan. So Carlos got in contact with one of his buddies who knew some Mongols bikers who really looked rough and tough.

It was then agreed that Victor Govin with Carlos and two biker dudes by the name of Angel Noyes (Pseudonym) and Robert Somes (Pseudonym) would pay a visit to Gita at her spacious home in the Hollywood Hills. In carrying out their plan, Carlos would go to the front door and get Gita to open the door. When they all arrived at the front door, Carlos rang the doorbell as the others hid out of view. Someone inside asked who it was and Carlos came up with the story that he was a local resident who was circulating a petition for installing "Speed Bumps" to slow traffic on the street.

Gita, who was inside, opened the door a crack and glanced at Carlos. She must have been suspicious of the situation or of Carlos' story, because she immediately slammed the door closed. Carlos got cold feet and turned around and left. The other guys quietly retreated to the car. They discussed what they should do next, and they all agreed that conditions weren't right and they all drove away together.

There was considerable disappointment by all involved in this unsuccessful attempt. Victor Govin didn't get Gita to sign the agreement to give up their claim to the alley behind their motel. Nevertheless, the Biker dudes wanted to be paid because they had kept their part of the bargain by going up to the location. Victor wouldn't pay them because they hadn't done anything to frighten Gita, because she never saw them. One of the biker dudes tried to contact Victor's brother Peter and demanded to be paid. It would be a fair statement that no one was happy about this failed attempt to coerce Gita to sign the agreement.

Victor Govin wasn't going to give up, since there was too much at stake. He talked to Carlos about trying it again. The two biker dudes were so mad about not being paid that Carlos had to recruit some new accomplices. It isn't an easy task to shop for an "Intimidator." You don't open the Yellow Pages to "I" and find a listing for "Intimidators." It's difficult locating the right person for the job. All the person had to do was just stand there and look rough and tough. Some guys are just a natural for this part, especially around the Hollywood area.

But Victor Govin and Carlos had to find someone who they could trust to keep their mouth shut after doing the job. Next Carlos called upon an old friend who was a black man by the name of Droeger (Pseudonym). Carlos contacted him and he said he might be interested in helping out but he needed to scope out the location. Carlos arranged a meeting between Droeger, Victor, and himself. They all drove together into the Hollywood Hills to show Droeger Gita's house. Droeger looked all around as they were driving through the neighborhood. When the three of them returned to Victor's place, they asked him if they could count on him to do the job. To their surprise he declined by saying, "You know a 'Black Dude' like me would stand out in this white neighborhood and someone would end up calling the cops on me."

That was the end of attempting to recruit Droeger. By now, everyone was becoming leery if such a plan could be pulled off. So it fell on Carlos to recruit someone who wouldn't get cold feet and would definitely go through with it. Carlos contacted an acquaintance of his who he dealt with in the business of Repossessing Cars. His name was Alfredo Naranjo (Pseudonym). This time Carlos and Victor took Alfredo with them, hoping everything would go well. As they got up to Gita's house, they saw a minivan in the driveway. The three of them started talking about who could this van belong to. They couldn't decide whether to go forward with their plan. They believed that there might be several men who had come up in the van. Since there were only three of them, they decided to abort the mission to force their way into the house. After seeing what was involved in the job, Alfredo indicated that he wasn't interested in such a job.

By now everyone was disappointed in the lack of progress. Victor and Carlos couldn't find anyone who could help them. Part of the reason may have been the fact that they were looking for someone who would be more than a mere "Intimidator." Victor's brother, Peter Govin, was becoming more and more frustrated with his brother, who wasn't able to take care of business. Finally it was decided that the three of them, Victor and Peter Govin and their friend Carlos would have to do it on their own.

Into the house. After seeing what was involved in the job, Alfredo indicated that he wasn't interested in such a job.

[illegible]

CHAPTER 28 GOVIN-TIE THEM UP

The Govin brothers were desperate to exert pressure on Gita. Shortly, the City Building Department was going hold a hearing regarding closing the alley so they could receive a building permit for the addition to their motel. They knew that Gita had been out of the country to visit relatives in India. They had been told that Gita was returning from her trip the next day, May 4, 2002.

That date was selected to be the time for them to contact Gita and somehow force her to sign the document to abandon the alleyway. All that day, Peter was in contact with Victor, who was in contact by phone with Carlos. That afternoon, Victor and Carlos got together. Around 4:20 p.m., Victor went to a pay phone near a Rite Aid Drug Store and made a phone call to Gita's house. They knew by using a pay phone the call couldn't be traced back to any of them. When Victor heard Gita's voice on the phone he knew with certainty she was back home. He quickly hung up the phone and contacted the others, telling them she was there. Finally, around 6:30 p.m., Victor, Peter, and Carlos together drove up to Gita's house to check everything out. They wanted to know if Gita had visitors. When they drove by the Kumar house, they couldn't tell who was home. The Kumar house is set back from the street, and the front of the house is only partially visible from the street.

They decided that they would wait until dark. Carlos and Victor drove together over to a restaurant in North Hollywood for Chinese food. Peter followed them to the restaurant. They spent over an hour sampling various Chinese cuisines. At the end of the dinner they received their fortune cookies; however, they were in a hurry so no one took the time to read the messages in the cookies. Victor and Carlos drove directly over to the base of the hill up to Gita's house. Peter followed in his car, and when he got to the base of the hill, he parked his car next to the curb. Then the three of them piled into Carlos' pickup truck and drove up the hill to Gita's house.

This time Carlos drove slowly by the long driveway to Gita's house. They all looked to see how many cars were parked in the front of the house. Since they couldn't see all the way down the driveway, Carlos abruptly pulled down the long driveway to get a better look. There were two cars, but they couldn't determine how many occupants would be in the house. Since there were only three of them, they didn't want to have to confront a large group of people. They got cold feet and turned around, heading back down the hill. They couldn't be certain how many people were in the house; however, they agreed that they had to make their move that night.

It was almost 9:00 p.m., and they realized time was running out for them. They knew that most people won't answer their house door after 9:00 p.m. To show his initiative, Victor told Carlos that he wanted to test drive his truck and he asked for the keys. This time they got back in the pickup with Victor driving. Within minutes, they had raced back to Gita's house. Victor pulled the pickup into the driveway and parked behind an SUV.

Victor got out of the truck while Carlos and Peter remained in the truck. Victor slowly walked to the front door and nervously turned around as if looking over his shoulder. Not seeing anyone, he rang the doorbell. As he stood there, he waited for someone to answer. It seemed to take forever. Then a voice asked, "Who's there?" Victor hesitated as to what to say. With a muffled voice, he stated his name. Within a moment, the door opened slightly as Gita peered out. When she recognized him, she opened the door wide and motioned for him to come in.

Peter and Carlos remained seated in the pickup truck. They seemed frozen in their seats. After 15 minutes, they could see some type of activity at the front door. They could see the image of Victor stepping out of the door and walking toward them in the truck. He opened the door and stuck his head in. In a trembling voice, he reported that he had been able to determine that the only occupants in the house were two women with two older children. "Ok, let's do it." Peter reached under the seat and pulled out a ski mask and pulled it down over his head. At the same time, Carlos grabbed an old T-shirt and wrapped it around his head so his face was slightly covered. They both reached between the seats and pulled out two handguns.

As soon as they stepped out of the truck cab, they shoved the guns in their waistband.

The plan they had devised was that Peter and Carlos would follow directly behind Victor as he entered the door. They were to pretend that they were committing a home invasion robbery and treat Victor as one of the victims of the robbery. The idea of pretending to be robbers was going to require both Peter and Carlos to be convincing actors. They planned to wave the guns around and yell that it was a robbery. Peter and Carlos followed in Victor's footsteps as he proceeded back up to the front door. As Victor opened the outside security door, he turned around to nod to his two partners in crime whether they were ready. He saw his brother Peter wearing an old tattered ski mask with only his beady eyes peering out. Carlos didn't look much scarier with his dirty torn T-shirt tied around his head. Victor looked at his two colleagues and must have wondered, how are we ever going to pull this off?

Now you have a visual image of what was happening outside the Kumar's house, but one needs to know, who were the people inside and what were they doing? Victor was right in that, there were only four members of the Kumar/Patel family at home at that time. These individuals had no idea as to what horrific crimes were about to occur to them. Gita Kumar was a businesswoman who had worked very hard to make sure that her family was taken care of. Her two children were her pride and joy. She had raised them well. She stressed the importance of being courteous and respectful of others. She emphasized a strong work ethic having them work around the motel. What Gita was most proud of was how well they had done in school.

Her son, Paras, had excelled in high school and had exceptionally high grades, which permitted him to attend the prestigious University of California at San Diego, where he was presently attending. Since his mother had just returned from India, he made a trip from San Diego to his home in Los Angeles to spend the weekend with her. It was Saturday evening, and a good friend of Paras asked him to go out dancing to meet some girls. However, Paras told his friend that as much as he would like to socialize this weekend, he wanted to stay around the house to be with his mom. He promised his friend that the next weekend he would be back in LA and then they would get together. Paras had grown into a handsome young man and damsels took notice of him. He was very bright and a whiz on his computer. He could spend hours on the Internet or chatting with friends on the various blogs.

The Kumar/Patel family was an especially tightknit family, like many Indian families. The other pride of Gita's life was her beautiful daughter, Tulsi Kumar. She had turned 16 years old and was blossoming into a young lady. She was doing well in school and had set her sights on her transition to college. She was in the process of deciding on which universities to apply to. She was attending Reseda High School, and because of her outgoing personality she definitely would be placed in the category of one of the most 'popular' students on campus. Her future was amazingly bright, since she was one of those kids who was blessed with both smarts and good looks. She had stayed home this weekend because she wanted to spend time with her mother finding out about her relatives that her mom had visited in India.

The only other person in the house at the time was Gita's mother-in-law, Sitaben Patel. Like in many Indian households, it is common for in-laws to live with the family. She was always there to care for the children and do household chores. This assistance permitted Gita to have more time handling the motel business. Fortunately for the family, the mother-in-law had been living with them for many years.

When the Kumar family was able to move into this affluent neighborhood, they were well received. They were quiet and deferential of their neighbors. They would be described as being caring people and very considerate of others. They weren't the type of people who would be involved in any type of questionable activities or create any problems that would cause the police to become involved. When the Govin brothers and Carlos pulled into the Kumar's long driveway, there would be no suspicion by the adjacent neighbors. No one would have any thoughts of any criminal activity ever occurring at the Kumar house.

Victor knew the front door was unlocked, so he quietly turned the door handle and pushed open the door. He knew the women were in the living room, so he entered into the small foyer, holding the front door open so his brother and Carlos could get into the house. They all lined up behind Victor and pretended that they were forcing him into the living room. Both Peter and Carlos had their guns pointed at Victor.

They shoved Victor next to Gita and her mother-in-law, yelling that this was a robbery. The women were seated and looked more than surprised at these two masked men waving guns around. There was shouting, "Where's the money?" "Where's your jewelry?"

Peter and Carlos told Victor to put his hands behind him as one of them pretended to zip tie his hands together. The two Indian women looked horrified and seemed petrified as to what they should do. They couldn't help but see how their guest Victor had his hands and feet tied with plastic strips that are called 'zip ties.' Next the robbers took a roll of gray duct tape and ripped off a yard length of tape. One of the robbers went behind Victor and wrapped the duct tape over his eyes several times.

The women had seen what the robbers had done to Victor, so they understood what was about to happen to the two of them. In less than five minutes, Peter and Carlos had the women immobilized and blindfolded. Since neither of the women could see what was happening around them, Carlos went over to Victor and pulled him aside. When he was out of earshot of the women, Carlos tore off the duct tape and unloosened the zip ties on Victor. Victor could now switch out of his pretended role as a **victim** and be fully transformed into a **robber**.

Since Victor had been in Gita's house on several occasions, he was familiar with the layout of the house. Victor told Carlos the two adult children were in their bedrooms. Victor waved to Carlos to follow him and he would show him where their respective bedrooms were located. A short way down a long hall Victor pointed to the door of the son's room.

Carlos went up to the door and tried to listen for any sound from inside the room. Not hearing any noise, he motioned to Victor to get out of sight. Carlos turned the doorknob slowly so as not to make any sound. As the door opened, Carlos flung it wide open and charged in as he held the handgun out in front of him. He could see the body of the son lying on the bed as though he were asleep.

Carlos walked to the side of the bed so he could get a look at the son's face. In a loud harsh voice, Carlos told him that he was there to rob his folks. The son, Paras, who was 18 years old, looked surprised, but most likely, was more frightened, and he sat up on the bed. Carlos gave Paras a warning not to try to be a hero. He went on to explain that no one would be harmed and that they were there just for the money.

Without delay, Carlos told Paras to lie face down on the bed. Paras fearfully complied, not knowing what else to do.

Carlos pulled Paras' hands together and zip tied them. While Paras was laying on the bed he zip tied his feet together. Then he grabbed the roll of duct tape and started wrapping it around Paras' head, covering his eyes. To assure that Paras didn't break free, Carlos took a zip tie and connected Paras' hands to his feet together in a hogtie position. This had to be extremely uncomfortable to the point of being painful for Paras. Carlos' concern was they couldn't afford someone escaping while they went through the house looking for other people.

With the son restrained in his room, Carlos exited and reconnected with Victor, who was waiting in the hallway. Victor motioned for Carlos to follow him to the end of the hallway, and he pointed to another bedroom door. Victor whispered that was the daughter's bedroom. Carlos again approached the door, putting his ear against it to hear if the person might be on the phone or watching TV. Not hearing a sound, he leaned into the door and abruptly entered.

Although the room was dark inside, Carlos could make out the figure of a person curled up on the bed under the covers. He could tell from the colors and the large dresser with photos on it that this was definitely a young woman's bedroom and had to be the daughter, Tulsi, who was sound asleep. He had to shake her to wake her up. As she woke up the expression on her face was that of someone who had experienced a terrifying nightmare.

Tulsi offered no resistance, so Carlos made her lay face down while slipping on the zip ties to her hands and feet. By now, Carlos had become an expert using zip ties. Again he used another zip tie to hogtie her so she would be totally immobile. After covering her eyes with duct tape, Carlos left her in her bedroom.

CHAPTER 29 GOVIN-TIME FOR KILLING

With everyone secured, the robbers started to search the house for valuables. As the robbers scurried through the house looking for money and jewelry, they were soon disappointed. The three inexperienced robbers were dumfounded when they couldn't find anything of value. They agreed among themselves that they needed to get all four victims together in hopes that someone would reveal where the valuables were kept. At some point, Peter told Carlos to bring the children into the living room. Since both the children were 'hogtied,' Carlos started with Paras. Because of Paras' size, Carlos had to partially drag him from his bedroom to the living room. In the process, Paras' head and face were scrapping along the floor possibly, tearing some of the duct tape loose from his face. As to the transporting of Tulsi, Carlos decided it would be easier and faster to pick her up and carry her into the living room.

With everyone in the living room, Peter started to demand that Gita tell them where their home safe was located. She repeatedly said that they didn't have a safe. Her voice was that of a desperate person who was trying to be cooperative. She tried to explain that they had a security box but there wasn't anything of value in it. She continually stated that there wasn't anything in it. Peter wanted her to show them where the security box was kept. Because they had zip tied her feet together, she couldn't lead them to it. Carlos recognized that they had reached an impasse. He told the others that he would go out to his truck and get a pair of wire cutters. He quickly exited the house, walking outside to the truck. Anxiously, he rummaged through the tool box. As soon as he saw the wire cutters, he grabbed them and returned to the house. He directly went over to Gita and kneeled down next to her and cut the zip tie that had been securing her feet.

Now that she could walk, she led them to the master bedroom. Although she still had duct tape covering her eyes, she described where they could find the metal box. Just as she had said, the box was found and quickly opened. They realized that Gita was telling the truth, in that there was nothing in the box except some legal papers.

Peter was becoming frustrated in not finding any loot. He believed that if they used some force on Gita she would start to cooperate. Peter began to hit Gita and slapped her around, to which she screamed in pain. When Paras heard his mother in such distress he somehow had an adrenalin rush and was able to partially break free. He told the robbers to leave his mother along as he swung in the direction of the voices of the robbers. In a panic, Carlos lunged at Paras to pull him under control. Almost automatically he pulled out another zip tie and wrapped it around the son's hands and pulled it as tight as he could. Within moments Paras was moaning in pain and was no longer a threat to the robbers.

Gita clearly understood that her family's wellbeing was at stake. Being a businesswoman, she knew that if she could somehow appease these robbers this whole regrettable situation could peacefully come to an end. She remembered that she had some money in her purse as well as some cash placed in the back of the linen closet. She immediately explained where they could find some cash. They grabbed her purse and found several thousand dollars in cash and likewise the same was found in the linen closet.

This finding of money didn't satisfy the robbers; they only became more demanding as to where Gita's jewelry was kept. This had to be a hard decision for Gita, since some of her jewelry had more than intrinsic value. Some of the jewelry items had deep sentimental value attached to them since they had been in the family for generations. She pondered the desperation facing her children and was willing to give up all her family jewelry for her children's safety. She explained to the robbers that they could find her jewelry in a suitcase under the master bed. In an instant, one of the robbers rushed to the master bedroom and soon returned with a large suitcase. They quickly opened it and found that it contained a large amount of gold jewelry stored in small boxes and cloth bags.

Needless to say, Gita and her family were terrified as to what was happening to them. But now the victims had to feel some relief. After all, she had complied with all the demands of robbers. Gita had revealed where they could find thousands of dollars of cash and a bonanza of expensive gold jewelry. The members of the Kumar family must have thought that this robbery was about over, since the robbers had gotten what they had come looking for.

However, the Govin brothers had something else on their mind. Victor quietly went out to the truck and retrieved a gym bag. He removed from the bed of the truck a container filled with carburetor cleaner. Quickly he darted back into the house through the front door and went over to Peter and showed him the container. There was a short discussion as to the best way to use the fluid. It was decided that they needed to place the victims in a smaller room.

At that moment, Victor motioned to bring all the victims into a small room near the front door. Peter and Carlos pulled the victims into the small room and placed them in the far corner. Then one of the brothers started pouring the carburetor fluid on the sofa and chairs as well as splashed some on the drapes next to the long window. More of the liquid was poured on the bed and carpet.

Since the victims had their eyes covered, they had to rely on their ears and nose to understand what was about to occur to them. By now the smell of the carburetor cleaner had to be a bad omen of what was in store for them.

Peter had earlier placed a zip tie around Gita's neck and tightened it slightly to get her to cooperate and tell where the valuables were. Now that they were in this small room, Peter walked behind Gita and grabbed the end of the zip tie and started pulling on it with all his might. The sudden pressure of the zip tie tightening around her neck caused her intense pain. Within seconds, she started gagging as her lungs gasped for air. Her body began to thrash about as she desperately tried to find some way to breathe. Peter used both hands to try to pull the zip tie tighter. Then at some point Gita seemed to pass out as her body continued to twitch.

At that point, Carlos had seen enough and he said to the Govin brothers that wasn't what he had signed up for and he wanted out. Victor had the truck keys, since had to use them when he went to get the carburetor cleaner. Victor pulled the keys out of his pants pocket and threw them to Carlos and told him to wait in the truck. Carlos went outside through the front door and was momentarily surprised that his truck had been turned around with the front of the truck facing out. This was different from when they had pulled in and he wondered why Victor had done that.

Maybe it was for a speedier exit, but that was the least of his concerns right at that moment.

He looked around to see if there were any witnesses as to what they had been doing. Seeing no one, he listened intently and could only hear crickets chirping in the chilly night air. Outside everything seemed so serene as a slight breeze blew up the canyon with a hint of a sagebrush scent. Carlos didn't want to reflect on the HELL that was taking place inside the Kumar's lovely home on top of the Hollywood Hills. He opened the truck's door and sat himself down in the driver's seat. With his left hand, he slammed the driver's door shut and wondered to himself, "How did I get involved in this nightmare?"

The Govin brothers remained in the small room and tried to place zip ties around all the victims' necks. They tried to pull them as tight as possible in hopes that they would be able to suffocate the victims. By that time, the room was full of choking noises and bodies flailing in desperation to breathe. As the brothers headed for the door one of them took a lighter and clicked it. He took the lit lighter and placed it near the sofa, which was soaking with fluid. There was a large puff and a flame rose to the ceiling. The brothers turned and scurried out, slamming the bedroom door behind them.

As they reached the foyer, they rushed through the front door and ran past the small room's window near the front door with flames reaching to the ceiling. They ran further to the truck, where Carlos was in the driver's seat. As the pickup sped down the long driveway, the brothers

looked back at the house and could see massive flames consuming the small room containing the bodies of the four victims. When Carlos turned the pickup on to the main street it was exactly 11:02 p.m.

Carlos drove the Govin brothers down the hill to Peter's car, and from there they all drove to the Govins' motel. They went inside and divided up the spoils of the robbery. Carlos seized the American money, which totaled $17,000 in cash, as his payment for doing the job. He told the brothers that they could keep all foreign money and the jewelry for themselves, since he didn't want to be bothered trying to find a buyer for them. *On the following graphic page is a poster of the facts of the Govin case.*

Graphics Page

Although this was not used in the trial, it provides a summary of the case

CHAPTER 30 GOVIN-HOUSE ON FIRE

On that fateful Saturday, Michael Kumar, Gita's husband, had spent the day with his brother and nephew. He had driven the three of them up north to Bakersfield for a volleyball game his nephew was playing in. The trip took longer than he had anticipated. Proceeding down the 101 Freeway, he turned off on Lankershim Boulevard and continued on a surface street to their Universal City Inn, where his brother had parked his car. After dropping them off, Michael headed up the hill to their home.

As he pulled out of the parking lot of the motel, he had to think how far he and his family had come. For years they had struggled refurbishing old dilapidated motels into profitable businesses. He wondered how they ever survived the trials and tribulations while operating the motel in Compton. There he and his family had to deal with the gang violence and nightly shootings in the hood. He was so proud that he now owned and operated the large motel across from the main entrance to one of the biggest tourist attractions in Los Angeles. This Universal City Inn had changed their family's life. As a result, this motel had allowed his family to fulfill his dream of living high atop the Hollywood Hills.

He crossed the bridge over the 101 Freeway and navigated to the right onto Lakeridge Place, which paralleled the freeway for several blocks, coming to Lakeridge Road and winding up a hillside coming out on Lakeridge Drive overlooking the Hollywood Reservoir. The bulk of his neighbors were professionals, and many were involved in the entertainment business.

Even though it was late and there wasn't much traffic, he slowed down just to savor the moment of what a wonderful life he and Gita had made for the family. His son, Paras, was his pride and joy, while his daughter, Tulsi, was the apple of his eye. Besides all of this, he was able to have his beloved mother live with them. As he pulled his minivan into his long driveway, he felt like a man who had been blessed from above and LIFE COULDN'T BE ANY BETTER FOR HIM.

It was 11:08 p.m., a mere six minutes after Carlos and the Govin brothers had set the house on fire and left to drive down the hill. Michael was tired from all the driving, and when he stepped out of his van he was struck by a strong odor of smoke. Since the house is on top of a brushy hillside, Michael was use to the occasional mini-brush fires. He dismissed the smell as something the fire department was most likely involved in.

As he closed the van's door, he directed his attention to the front door, where he matter of factly put the key in the door lock and turned it. As he pushed in on the heavy front door, he was hit by a wave of scorching hot air. In disbelief, he stood there paralyzed, not knowing what to do. Where was his family? Were they inside? He started calling out in desperation their names and yelling for help.

Fortunately, at that very moment a guest who was visiting one of his neighbors looked toward where the yelling was coming from. That person noticed Mr. Kumar's distress and ran down the driveway to the house. As he came up to Michael, he helped him push in on the front door. By then the smoke and heat were overwhelming, and the two backed out of the front door. Michael had a dazed look on his face, traumatized with fear and not knowing what to do.

The Good Samaritan was only visiting a friend in the area, so he was unfamiliar with the addresses of the houses. So he leaned over to Michael and handed his cellphone to him. He uttered, "Call 9-1-1." Michael grabbed the phone and with his trembling fingers tried to punch in 9-1-1. Shortly thereafter a voice came on the phone line.

The 9-1-1 operator told Mr. Kumar that the Fire Department was on the line.

9-1-1 Operator- That's the Los Angeles Fire Department, give them the address.

Fire Dispatcher- Yes please

Mr. Kumar- 2933 Lakeridge Drive

Fire Dispatcher- What's the problem there?

Mr. Kumar- House is on fire

Fire Dispatcher- House is on fire?

Fire Dispatcher- Okay, sir we are on the way, Can you get out of the house?

Mr. Kumar- Yes, yes we are out of the house right now

Fire Dispatcher- We are on the way

Mr. Kumar- Please you know my family is inside really

Fire Dispatcher- Is somebody inside?

Mr. Kumar- Yes

The Fire Dispatcher had difficulty hearing Michael because the house windows were continuously being blown out by the intense heat from the fire.

Because the Kumar's house was located so far up the hills overlooking the Hollywood Reservoir, it took several minutes before the first firefighters could reach the Kumar's residence. By that time, the flames were already curling around the eaves. The windows near the front of the house had shattered from the heat, and blankets of smoke were billowing out, curling up in the jet black sky. The firefighters sprang into action, trying to figure out how to fight the fire. Since the house was set back so far from the main street, they knew it would take considerable time to connect to the city fire hydrants along the street.

At first, they used the water from the fire truck to try to stop the fire from spreading. The firemen immediately hooked up the hoses and started spraying water on the fire. They knew that they had a limited supply of water in the firetruck's water tanks. One team of firefighters approached the window curling out the most smoke and sprayed water through the broken window. Drenching the room with water seemed to check the flames, although a huge wave of white smoked burst out of the window.

One of the firefighters asked Mr. Kumar about the possibility of people being inside the structure. Mr. Kumar tried to explain that he didn't know if his family was inside or not. He pointed to his son's SUV parked in the driveway next to the front door as evidence that his son had come home from the university in San Diego. Gita's car was parked further down from the front of the house. At that point, the firefighters went into their rescue mode. A pair of firefighters pushed in the front door. One was holding a large flashlight to illuminate the dark interior of the house, and the other was pulling a small fire hose with a large nozzle on it.

They could see that the ceiling and upper portion of the walls had been blackened by the smoke. The firefighters proceeded through the foyer and could see a small board with a set of keys hooked on it that seemed to go to some vehicle. At this point, nothing seemed out of the ordinary. There was no evidence that any crime had occurred in this house, such as a residential robbery. Most of the flames were high up near the ceiling. Since the firefighters had been told that there might be people inside, they were shining flashlights in all directions.

When the firemen entered the living room, they couldn't find anyone. Everything seemed normal except for the swirling smoke. The firefighters glanced at the fireplace, which was built into the corner of the room. Next to it was a large screen TV at the far end of the room. The room was filled with three sets of oversize sofas facing the TV set. It was obvious that there had been people watching TV a short time earlier, because there was a bag of freshly popped microwave popcorn lying on one of the sofas.

What was uncanny about the living room was that everything appeared normal except for the soot covering the top of the walls and ceiling. The firefighters felt relieved that no victims so far had been found.

Then the firefighters proceeded down the hallway to the first bedroom. They pushed in the door to see a bed filled with several bags strewn on top of it. Again they were relieved to find no one was in the bed. This bedroom looked like a young man's room with a computer and stereo equipment. Again there didn't appear to be any fire in the room except for the intense heat and all the smoke clinging to the ceiling. However, the firefighters didn't see anything that would indicate that the fire might have been started in this room due to some type of electrical malfunction.

The next room they went into seemed to be a teenage girl's bedroom. There were numerous picture frames of photos of young teenagers. On the table tops were all sorts of mementos collected from trips or outings. There were giant stuffed animals and even a lava lamp. The firemen glanced around and didn't see any source of the fire or any victims in the room.

It was hard to grasp what had happened and why was the house on fire. But so far the firefighters had been lucky in finding that there were no one trapped inside these rooms. Then they entered the bedroom at the end of the hallway. It contained a large poster bed with several large dressers. This was clearly the master bedroom, and again no victim was found trapped inside. Over near the closet was a suitcase that appeared not to be fully unpacked.

Up to this point, the firefighters had found no victims. Also, they hadn't found any point of origin of the fire. They were trying to assess the situation. There was no direct fire in any of the three bedrooms and the living room and they could be eliminated as the source of the fire. They decided to cross over to the other side of the house and passed through the living room to enter the kitchen. They noticed several types of electrical devices plugged into the wall. The firefighters took note of it since so many house fires are caused by faulty electrical outlets. They swiftly looked around but didn't see any charring near the plugs or anywhere in the kitchen. They could tell that the stove hadn't caught fire, and it definitely wasn't an oil fire, which often occurs in kitchens when cooking oil overheats and ignites.

However, they did notice on the kitchen counter a cardboard pizza box with several pieces left inside. Since the box didn't have any charring on it, the firefighters discounted it as being the source of the fire. They discounted the possibility that the kitchen was the source of the fire. At that point, they directed their attention back to checking out the remaining rooms for possible victims.

CHAPTER 31 GOVIN-GRIM DISCOVERY

On the opposite side of the kitchen was a hallway with several doors. The firefighters approached one of the closed doors and could feel the intense heat. The door knob was red hot, so the one firefighter with the flashlight kicked the door inward and suddenly intense flames shot out from the open door. The other firefighter pointed the nozzle from the fire hose inside the room and pulled back on the nozzle handle, causing a gush of water to consume the room.

They had to spray a gusher of water to fully extinguish the flames. The smoke filled the entire room. At the same time, a pungent odor filled the air, similar to meat burning on a barbeque. The firefighters backed away from the door of this small room. It took several minutes for the smoke to dissipate enough so the firefighter could see inside the room. It was difficult to determine what the room had been used for. To the right side of the room there appeared to be the remains of a bed.

At first glance it seemed that the fire was so intense in this room that there was a likelihood that the fire had been set by some type of accelerant. The Arson Detail would be given the task to determine the origin of the fire. Everything in this room was completely incinerated, and nothing was recognizable except for the remains of a scorched dresser along one of the walls.

As the smoldering smoke began to subside, the firefighters started to check the debris on the floor. They could make out the charred remains of a human being. They removed more debris, and there was the eerie outline of another body. This was not what the firefighters wanted to find. A creepy feeling came over them. As they sifted through the remains of this small room, they found a total of four charred bodies that had been burned beyond physical recognition. With that discovery, the firefighters contacted the headquarters to have the Arson investigators respond to the scene of the fire.

The Arson investigators generally work for the fire department, and the main focus of their job is to determine if the cause of the fire was an accident or was it intentionally set by someone. If the Arson investigator comes to the conclusion that the fire was an accident, then that fact is written up in a report that the owner can submit to their insurance company in order to collect on their insurance. The arson investigator will try to track down the point of origin and determine if there was any type of accelerant involved in the fire.

In some situations, it might be the owner who sets the fire in order to collect from their insurance company. This could be a crime of fraud if the owner is trying to obtain money from the insurance company. It is a crime to set your own property on fire even if you aren't trying to defraud an insurance company.

However, when a person is killed as a result of the fire, the investigation can become more complicated. The Homicide detectives are employed by the police departments and will work hand in hand with the Fire Department's Arson investigators. This may seem confusing, to have two separate sets of investigators, one from the Fire Department and the other from the Police Department. Often it can be difficult to coordinate things, because both sets of investigators have different objectives in the manner in which they approach their job.

The Arson investigator may be digging around for samples to determine the origin of the fire. They want to determine if there was any type of accelerant, and if so, what was the accelerant: gasoline, lighter fluid, alcohol or some other type of fuel?

The Homicide detectives, on the other hand, are interested in any evidence that might indicate who set the fire causing damage, injury or death to others. So it is obvious that both sets of investigators have a different emphasis but the Homicide detectives want to follow up on whatever the Arson investigators uncovers.

In this fire, the Homicide investigators wanted to know whether it could have been caused to cover up the homicides. The ransacking of the house would be of interest to them. Also, if there is money or jewelry missing, this can be evidence of what happened in the house and that the arson was merely a means of covering up those other crimes.

This Kumar case may have started as an arson investigation, but when the four charred bodies were found all in one room with zip ties on their hands and feet it was clear that the Homicide detectives needed to be brought in. At first, the Arson investigators worked on the point of origin and the type of accelerant. Their findings were that the origin of the fire was in the small room and the accelerant was some type of common solvent that is used to clean carburetors. Based on those findings, the Homicide detectives took over the investigation of the case.

At the early stage of the Homicide investigation, no one knew what they had. When all the doors were checked, they all appeared to be locked from the outside. In other words, there was no forced entry, which meant that one of the victims had let the person in or someone with a key was able to enter. The detectives knew that Mr. Kumar had a key to the house, since he lived there. Also, the fact was that he was the only one to have survived while his entire family perished. Furthermore, he was at the crime scene when the fire department arrived. There were more questions than there were answers as to his involvement. Why wasn't he home at 11:00 at night when the fire occurred? Why was he away from his home and family that late at night?

The news media picked up the story that four members of an Indian family had been burned to death in a fire in their home in the Hollywood Hills. Often the news media ignores such stories that occur late at night because they can't be reported on until the next day. To report on such a fire a day later would seem to be dredging up old news. Since it was the weekend, there may have been slim pickings for fresh news stories to report on. The Fox Channel 11 News decided to fill time by using this story about the fire. The Fox news commentator reeled off the facts as they showed a video of the firefighters spraying water on the house in the Hollywood Hills. She ended her report by saying that the investigators suspected Mr. Kumar, the husband, to be the person who set the house on fire.

This story was not a piece of great journalism but a mere filler of TV airtime. However, if the news station hadn't stuck this little story in, most likely the Govin case would never have been solved. It just so happened that a Mr. Angel Noyes was watching the news. He heard the commentator mention about a fire in a house in the Hollywood Hills involving an Indian family.

Angel quickly tried to recollect a conversation involving an 'Indian Family' and 'Hollywood Hills.' His mind started to wonder if that could be related to something he had been involved in a while back. He tried to reconstruct in his head the parties who were involved in a strange request that had been made of him. A Hispanic man known by the name of 'Pedro' introduced him to an Indian gentleman by the name of 'Freddie.'

It had been over a month since he had been asked to act as an "Intimidator." However, in his situation there hadn't been any discussion about setting a fire or killing any of the residents of the house. But the fact that he had been asked to help out an Indian in a dispute involving Indian people living in the Hollywood Hills was enough to make him curious.

He thought long and hard about what the reporter had said. He was intrigued enough to take a short drive in his car over to the Hollywood Hills. After a few wrong turns, he figured out the right way to go up this curvy road. When he got to the top, he slowed down so he could spot the house he had been taken to. He kept glancing to the left and then to the right to see if his eyes could recognize something familiar. Slowly, he came upon a driveway that was set back from the road and looked familiar. He abruptly jammed on the brakes and his car came to a stop. He looked left down a lone driveway that led to a house. As he focused on the distant house, he could see yellow caution tape tied around the front of the house. Even from the street, he could see dark scorch marks on the plaster on the side of the house. He couldn't believe his eyes and was shocked that it was the same house he had been taken to in order to frighten an Indian family.

Angel's mind kept churning over the facts as to how lucky he was that he had refused to get involved. But he kept thinking about the situation and the fact that Mr. Kumar, the husband, was being suspected of killing his wife and children. Angel knew that it wasn't Mr. Kumar, since the person trying to put pressure on this family was a guy by the name 'Pedro.' To Angel, it didn't seem fair that Mr. Kumar should be accused of something he didn't do. Tragically, he was an innocent man who had just lost his entire family.

Angel Noyes was certainly no angel. However, his moral compass kept telling him he needed to do something to right a wrong that was happening to another human being. Because of his checkered background, he didn't feel comfortable going to the police about the matter. He thought that the fact that he had been recruited as an 'Intimidator' might get him in trouble with the law.

After considerable soul searching, Angel got up the courage to do something. He decided to contact the TV station and asked to talk to the reporter on the story. Eventually, he was hooked up with the reporter. He told the reporter that the police were wrong in believing that the husband was involved. The reporter told Angel that she was willing to meet with him to talk over more details about the crime. The two agreed on a time and place for such a meeting.

Meanwhile, the reporter thought over what Angel had told her. She had worked with police detectives on other stories, so she felt comfortable calling up the detectives on this story. She explained the phone call she had received from Angel and told the detectives that he sounded like he knew what he was talking about. She explained that this Angel didn't sound like a 'Wacko.' She related that she had agreed to meet him the next day. The detectives indicated that they were interested in the information and asked if they could come along with her to meet Angel. The reporter said she didn't see any problem with them being present.

The meeting occurred at a local restaurant. Angel recognized the reporter, since she was always appearing on the TV news. The detectives tried to keep a low profile during the first part of the meeting. They didn't want to frighten Angel away, but they wanted to see what he had to say. Angel was reluctant to say much because he had agreed to act as an 'Intimidator.' He stressed that all he wanted to say was that the husband didn't do it. When he was pressed for details, he said the real reason for the killings was over a dispute involving an alley in which an owner of one motel wanted the other motel owner to sign some agreement. He didn't know the true names of the parties he had dealt with. But he recalled that the man by the name 'Freddie' owned the motel next to the motel owned by the Kumars.

The detectives were listening carefully to what Angel was saying. They knew that the Kumars owned and operated a motel, but Mr. Kumar had never mentioned any dispute with the neighboring motel over an alleyway. Angel went on to describe another person by the name of 'Pedro' who was Hispanic. He was the one who had lined up the meeting. This person drove a gray pickup truck and had given Angel his cellphone number.

After the meeting, the detectives did some old-fashioned police work and found out the name of the motel owner next door. His name was Victor Govin, and they got a photo of him and placed it in a six-pack of photos of male Indians. They recontacted Angel and asked him to look at the photo lineup to see if he could identify anyone. He gazed over all the photos in the lineup and kept coming back to the photo of Victor Govin. Then he said, "That's the guy called 'Freddie.'" That was the beginning of the unraveling of a murder mystery.

Next the detectives wanted to see if they could determine who was the other guy named 'Pedro.' The detectives made some contacts about the phone number Angel had given them. The number was traced to a man who said that he had purchased the phone for a friend by the name of Carlos Alonso.

The detectives had then identified Carlos Alonso as possibly being involved and now were on the trail of Victor Govin. However, there wasn't anything pointing to Peter Govin. When the detectives pressed Angel, he said that when this 'Freddie' wouldn't pay him for going up to the house he got mad and demanded to be paid. He said that this 'Freddie' (who was really Victor) told him to contact his brother for payment. Angel was given a phone number and when he contacted the brother, he also refused to pay him.

The detectives asked for that phone number, and when they checked it out it came back to a Peter Govin, the owner of the Cyprus Inn. By that time, the detectives had three names to thoroughly check out: PETER GOVIN, VICTOR GOVIN, and CARLOS ALONSO.

The detectives were pleased they had some names, but first they wanted to see if there was any corroboration to support what Angel had told them. Angel didn't want to get his friend involved but told the detectives that he went with a Robert Somes to do the intimidation. When the detectives contacted Mr. Somes, he was able to verify everything that Angel had told them.

CHAPTER 32 GOVIN-BUILDING A CASE

To recap, the detectives had information that the killings might be a result of some type of dispute regarding two motels owned by two Indian families across from Universal Studios. One of the parties was called 'Freddie,' who was really Victor Govin. By tracing down a cellphone number, they found that a person who was called 'Pedro' was really Carlos Alonso who drove a gray colored pickup truck. Finally, by tracking down a cellphone number that Victor said was his brother's, the detectives located Peter Govin.

By this point, the detectives were getting a picture that this arson murder may have been committed by Victor Govin and Carlos Alonso, since they had tried to recruit Angel and Robert to intimidate the victim's family. The detectives, however, didn't have any evidence that they had been the persons who set the fire and murdered the four members of the Kumar family. All the police had was mere suspicion that they might be involved. They had to build a case with real hard evidence before they would be able to make any arrests.

The detectives had a dilemma. They didn't want to let Victor Govin know that they suspected him. The reason being he had strong ties to India and could easily leave the country, and it would be impossible for the police to ever be able to find him in order to arrest him and bring him back to California for prosecution.

One of the first things the investigators wanted to better understand was what was this so-called dispute between these two Indian motel owners was about. Angel had mentioned that it had something to do with a dispute over some type of alley. These were seasoned Homicide detectives. Neither of them had ever heard of someone being killed over an alleyway or any type of dispute over ownership of real property. It seemed more likely it must have been a dispute over one motel taking customers away from the other or taking employees away from the other motel operation. It seemed strange that two Indian business families would become so involved in such a dispute that it would lead to murder.

The detectives wanted to talk to Mr. Kumar, whom the media had originally named as a possible suspect of the heinous crime at the same time he was grieving for the loss of his entire family. It seemed outrageous to bother him with questions regarding such a bizarre idea. But on the other hand, if they were going to catch those who killed his family then he should be anxious to help them out.

The detectives arranged for a meeting with Mr. Kumar. They all sat down at this meeting and the detectives asked him some general questions. They cautiously asked him about any possible dispute that he might have had with the next-door motel owner, Victor Govin. Mr. Kumar seemed puzzled by the question and after some reflection said that he personally didn't have any disagreement with Victor. As Mr. Kumar was answering this particular question, the detectives noticed that he seemed to be pondering the question. He slowly went on to relate that his wife had mentioned that she did not sign an Agreement regarding the alleyway behind both of their motels.

Mr. Kumar seemed to be dumbfounded about the suggestion that the Govins were upset over the refusal to sign off on the alley. He didn't think the alley dispute was that big a deal, but he had to admit that he hadn't been directly involved in the negotiation since he had left the matter up to his wife to handle. Further, he stated that they had always gotten along with the Govin family. Since the Govins' motel was smaller and older than their high-end motel, they weren't really in competition with each other. After considerable discussion with Mr. Kumar, the detectives were getting the impression the alley dispute may not have been the motivation for the killings.

Now the detectives had their work cut out for them to contact the City to learn more about the possible alley dispute. They discovered that the City had scheduled to hold hearings in several days about the expansion plans of the Govins' motel. Even though Michael Kumar didn't see the magnitude of the dispute, the detectives now realized that the dispute could have been the motive for the murders.

The detectives knew at this early stage of their investigation that they needed to look at any and all possible motives that the killer might have had in committing such a heinous crime. First, the detectives looked at the two children, Paras and Tulsi Kumar. Could either have had some type of enemy who might want to harm them? Both were students. Paras was attending college at UCSD while his sister was finishing up at Reseda High School. Talking to the children's friends and teachers, they learned that both were excellent students. Neither had any type of discipline problems in school and certainly they didn't have any gang affiliations. According to everyone who was contacted, neither child had any involvement with drugs or the use of alcohol. The detectives were satisfied that the children weren't the source for the harm to the Kumar family.

Next they considered Sitaben Patel, who was Michael Kumar's mother and lived with the family. Again, the detectives quickly learned that this 63-year-old Indian lady had no enemies nor was she involved in any criminal activities. She was well liked as a gentle, passive grandmother type. The only other person in the house at the time was Gita Kumar. As indicated earlier, she was an extraordinarily hard-working businesswoman who wasn't into gang or any criminal activities. Even as a driven businesswoman, Gita's business associates and employees maintained that she always treated them fairly. Bottom line, Gita had no enemies who were out to harm her or her family. After their initial investigation, the detectives couldn't uncover any malice toward any member of the Kumar family. The only controversy or hostility involving the family was Gita's refusal to sign the Agreement for the Govin brothers to permanently close the alley behind their motel.

The detectives needed to find some solid evidence as to who was involved. After talking to the neighbors, they weren't coming up with anyone who had seen anyone coming or leaving the Kumar house around the time of the fire. One of the first things that detectives looked into was whether the Kumar's residence had any type of security cameras around their house. In this age of new video and digital cameras, home security has changed dramatically from door and window sensors and motion detectors. Security cameras have been developed that are so tiny that passersby aren't aware of them. Also, these new video cameras have become so inexpensive that practically anyone can afford them. After examining the Kumar house and speaking with Michael Kumar, it was learned that they didn't have any security cameras.

Upon learning that, the detectives were disappointed; however, they wondered if one of the Kumars' neighbors might have security cameras that captured the movement of traffic on the street. Again they were frustrated that the adjacent neighbors didn't have any such security cameras. However, in the process someone mentioned that one of the houses several houses down on Lakeridge Drive did appear to have security cameras.

The detectives immediately contacted that neighbor and asked if they still had images from the date of May 4th. The security cameras used a looping system that hadn't started erasing and writing over the images for that date. The detectives asked to see the video around the time that Mr. Kumar had called 911, which was 11:08 P.M. Sure enough, the detectives could see Mr. Kumar's minivan going up the street moments before his frantic 911 call. This verified what Mr. Kumar had told the detectives: that he was not at home and he had just driven up when he discovered the fire.

The police asked to look at the various vehicles that left the Kumar house just prior to Michael Kumar's arrival. They wanted to look for a gray colored pickup truck that had been described by Angel the 'Intimidator.' Even though the photos were only in black and white, it was possible to distinguish shades of colors. It didn't take long before they saw a grayish colored pickup truck coming down Lakeridge Drive at 11:02 P.M. This was only six minutes before Mr. Kumar had arrived home.

Next they looked to see when the truck may have gone up Lakeridge Drive to the Kumar house. Almost two hours earlier, they came across a photo of what appeared to be the same truck going up the hill at 8:59 P.M. That would mean the killers could have been in the house for two hours terrorizing the victims.

The detectives continued to look at the tapes and saw that the same pickup truck went up the hill at 8:14 P.M. and came down at 8:41 P.M. The police didn't know what that meant, but they thought maybe the killers were casing the house to see who was parked in the driveway.

The detectives were convinced that Victor Govin and Carlos Alonso were involved. From that neighbor's camera, it was clear that it was Carlos' pickup truck that had been used. But the photos weren't clear enough to reveal who was driving or an occupant in the truck. What the detectives needed was to conduct their own surveillance of this Victor Govin and Carlos Alonso and see if they made contact with each other or if they did anything suspicious.

Later on, the LAPD surveillance team followed Carlos in his gray pickup. He went to a pay phone and was seen making a call to someone. On June 5th, Carlos was seen going to a Denny's Restaurant. He appeared to meet someone there, and they went inside to eat. Later the two people left together and walked in front of Denny's.

When the police zoomed in with their camera they discovered that the person Carlos had had lunch with was Victor Govin. The two of them walked over to Carlos' truck and talked to one another. It appeared that Carlos was showing Victor some changes he had made to the truck. After their short conversation, Carlos drove off in his truck and Victor left in his car.

A number of days later on July 10th, the police surveillance team followed Carlos and observed him meeting with Victor Govin at his motel. Then Victor, Peter, and Carlos got into Peter Govin's Yukon SUV. They drove a short distance up the hill to a small park next to a cul-de-sac. They all sat in Peter's vehicle for a total of 45 minutes. Then they all left and drove back to Victor's motel.

At the same time the police were doing their surveillance, they had set up wiretaps on the various phones used by Carlos and Victor. The detectives listened to copies of the wiretaps, and it seemed that the parties were talking in some type of code. They were very careful not to say anything that could be considered incriminating. The wiretaps and the surveillance seemed to be fruitful, but they weren't revealing any so called 'Smoking Gun' evidence.

During all this investigation, the detectives had made contact with Victor to ask some general questions about his contact with the Kumars and their motel business. Apparently Victor and his brother were becoming nervous that someone might reveal the fact that they had a motive to harm the Kumars. After several days of the wiretaps, the detectives began to hear conversations between the brothers in which they talked about the need to eliminate Carlos, since he knew too much. The Govin brothers made it sound like they couldn't trust Carlos anymore.

This presented the detectives with a quandary. They wanted to continue the wiretaps and surveillance in hopes of obtaining some crucial incriminating evidence. However, they had concern that the brothers were about to kill Carlos. Did the police have a legal obligation to step in to prevent Carlos from being killed? The detectives were aware LAPD's motto was 'To Protect and Serve.' Did that mean that they were to protect Carlos, who was a suspect in a quadruple homicide? Even if the detectives didn't have a legal obligation to protect Carlos, at least they felt a moral obligation to protect him.

It was decided that things were becoming too dangerous for Carlos. So on July 25th, the detectives went to Carlos' house and arrested him. They took him in for questioning. They advised him of his Miranda rights. His reply was that he didn't have anything to hide and was willing to talk to the detectives. The interview started with general questions that Carlos was more than willing to answer. Gradually, the detectives started asking if he could help them out regarding some statements an Angel Noyes had told them about being hired as an Intimidator. They started asking him if he knew a Victor Govin.

This caught Carlos off-guard. His first response was to deny that he knew any Victor Govin. Then one of the detectives pulled out a folder that had photos in it. The detective nonchalantly dropped on the table several surveillance photos showing Carlos standing next to Victor, appearing to be talking with him. Carlos' eyes fixed on the photos. Carlos' face seemed to fade to ash white and he seemed taken back in thought. Then one of the detectives asked him about the photos that showed him in contact with Victor. At first, Carlos continued to deny knowledge of Victor.

The detectives began painting a picture that he was going to fall for the murder of four people. Carlos had been in trouble with the law in the past; however, he had gained 'street smarts' and had on several occasions learned he could save his neck by being a 'fast talker.' He was trying to assess the situation to see how he could save himself from a hard fall on the murder charges.

Could Carlos talk his way out of this predicament? Every time the detectives confronted him with some details, he would minimize his involvement. He didn't want to say anything that would incriminate him as to actually committing the killings. With all the so-called Intimidators pointing the finger at him, he realized that he had to admit to some involvement in the crime. He readily admitted that he did try to find some muscle men to force Gita Kumar to sign some type of document involving closing an alley.

Then Carlos could see the handwriting on the wall. He realized that the cops had enough to sink him for being involved in the murders. However, Carlos was smart enough to recognize that the detectives truly wanted to get the real masterminds behind the murder of four totally innocent people. Carlos knew that he could blow the whistle on the Govin brothers so they would fall for the murders. Carlos and the detectives were sitting in a drab police interrogation room looking at each other. Both wanted something from the other side. That was when they all agreed that this was the time for 'LET'S MAKE A DEAL.'

Carlos indicated that he was willing to lay out the involvement of everyone but that he wanted something for this information. All of a sudden, the ball was in the detectives lap. What sort of deal could they make to get Carlos to talk and cooperate? These were seasoned detectives, and they knew what they had to do to make a deal. They contacted the appropriate parties in the DA's Office to get a commitment as to what type of reduced sentence would be acceptable.

Finally, a deal was hammered out in which the prosecutors would be willing to accept a plea of guilty to four second degree Murder charges with a sentence of 15 years to life to run concurrently upon Carlos agreeing to testify truthfully in court about the Govin brothers' involvement in the death of the Kumar family. Now the detectives and prosecutors had what they needed to build a case against the Govin brothers.

CHAPTER 33 GOVIN-CARLOS TALKS

Once Carlos knew for certain that he would not be facing the Death Penalty and was guaranteed a sentence of 15 years in prison for merely telling the truth, he was ready to sing. The detectives had their tape recorder on, ready to record every word of Carlos' story. He started by explaining that he was a good friend of Victor Govin and that one day Victor was complaining that this woman was blocking his family from expanding their motel. Victor related that it had something to do with closing an alleyway to give them more room for parking in the back. At first Victor seemed to want to put pressure on Gita Kumar to sign this Agreement that had been drawn up by his attorney. But Victor became more frustrated when this woman, Gita, wouldn't sign off on the Agreement.

Then Victor asked Carlos if he would help him out in some way by pressuring this woman to sign the Agreement. Carlos at first didn't want to get involved. He didn't think of himself as some type of tough guy. Victor persisted in asking for help and advice as to how to get this woman to comply. Carlos thought about two guys he had contacts with and who seemed rough around the edges. One day when Victor was complaining, Carlos mentioned the names of Angel Noyes and Robert Somes as people who might be helpful. Victor latched on to those individuals and asked Carlos to have them come over to talk to Victor about this so-called 'job.'

That was when Carlos had them come over and go with both Victor and Carlos up to this lady's house. Unfortunately, that attempt to scare Gita didn't work out. However, these guys still wanted to be paid because they had spent their time going up to the house. Afterwards, Carlos explained to the detectives that he tried to line up others to act as Intimidators. But each time something prevented anything from happening. As he contacted more people, he discovered how hard it was to find good reliable people who would be willing to help out.

Finally, the lack of success caused Victor to turn to his brother Peter for help. After much discussion, the three of them agreed that they couldn't count on anybody else so they would have to do it themselves. By this time, Carlos was coming to the realization that the Govin brothers did no longer just want to put pressure on this lady, but somehow take care of her. Carlos recognized he was in over his head and was sinking into a quagmire that he had nothing to gain from. At that point, Carlos told the brothers that there had to be something in it for him. He felt he should receive something for all his trouble.

The Govin brothers, being businessmen, agreed with Carlos that he should receive something. They agreed that Carlos could keep a large portion of the loot they discovered in the Kumar house. The brothers believed that the Kumars kept a large amount of cash in a safe in their house. Also, the brothers believed that Gita and her mother-in-law had a considerable amount of gold jewelry in the house.

The detectives kept taking notes of what Carlos was telling them. Occasionally one of the detectives would check on the tape recorder to make sure it wasn't out of tape. The detectives realized that every word that Carlos told them would have to be corroborated. They wanted every detail he knew so they could verify it.

Carlos finally got to the point of the story of how they went about the killings. Carlos said it was agreed to do the attack on Saturday May 4th, since that would be the first night that Gita would be back from her trip to India. Also, it would be several days before the meeting with the City regarding the closing of the alley. On that Saturday, both Victor and Carlos drove by the Kumar house to check it out. During the late afternoon, Victor made a call from a pay phone in front of the Rite Aid Drug store. As soon as he heard Gita's voice on the line, he hung up. Victor then called his brother to meet for dinner at a Chinese Restaurant in North Hollywood. Afterwards, all three of them drove over to the bottom of the Kumar's street, where Peter parked his car. Then all three of them got into Carlos' pickup truck and drove up Lakeridge Drive. They slowly drove by the Kumar house. Carlos told the detectives that they were surprised to see an unfamiliar vehicle parked in front of the house. This spooked them, and they turned around and returned to the bottom of the hill.

They waited for some time but realized that they were running out of time and had to act. This time, Victor asked Carlos if he could drive his new pickup truck. Carlos had no objection and gave Victor the keys as Carlos and Peter got in on the passenger side. They headed up the windy road to the top of the hill. This time, Victor slowed at the entrance to the Kumar house and drove all the way down the long driveway and parked. The plan was for Victor to go to the front door as though he wanted to talk to her about their new building plans.

Victor told Peter and Carlos to wait in the truck until he came out to usher them in. Victor exited the truck and went to the front door and appeared to ring the doorbell. Carlos told the detectives that he and Peter waited for several minutes before Victor came back out of the house. He motioned them to join him. Before they exited the truck, Peter pulled a ski mask over his head and wrapped a t-shirt around his head to cover his face. Both grabbed a handgun from under the seats and then climbed out of the truck.

Over the next half hour, Carlos told the detectives all the details as to what each one of the suspects did during the crime. In the end, the two brothers had all the victims in this small bedroom. Carlos knew that they had poured carburetor fluid all over the room. Then Peter went behind each of the victims and pulled as hard as he could on the zip ties around their necks. It wasn't until the actual killings were taking place that Carlos state that he didn't take part in them. That was when he said to the brothers, "That's not what I signed up for." At that point, Victor threw the keys to Carlos' truck to him and told him to wait outside. Carlos grabbed the keys and turned and hastily left the house. He didn't look back, but he had no doubt in his mind what was about to happen. Thus began the final steps of one of the most horrific homicides in the annals of Los Angeles Criminal history.

As Carlos spilled his guts about his involvement in tying up the victims and moving them to the room where they met their brutal deaths, the detectives could have taken the approach that the case had been solved. For the LAPD statistical purposes, the Kumar case was officially listed as solved and they had a person in custody for committing the crime. At that point, the detectives could rest on their laurels that they had done their job. There was no need to spend more time and resources on this case, since they had nothing more to statistically gain in this case.

However, these detectives knew that the real culprits were the two Govin brothers, who planned the robbery and brutally killed each of the victims. These detectives were well aware that Carlos' admissions wouldn't be enough to convict either brother. They knew that they couldn't use his statement unless they came up with independent corroboration to support Carlos' statements of their involvement. This would take a mammoth task to build a case against the two brothers.

In going over Carlos's statement, the detectives remembered all the so called 'Intimidators' that Carlos had tried to recruit to put pressure on Gita. If they could get those 'Intimidators' to testify, that would help provide the corroboration they needed. The detectives again sat down with Carlos and pressed him for names, addresses, and phone numbers of these 'Intimidators.' Carlos was able to provide the necessary information to track them all down.

Next, the detectives began the process of locating them. They recognized how delicate it would be to try and gain the cooperation of the 'Intimidators,' who certainly wouldn't be anxious to talk to the detectives. The detectives' approach was that they couldn't intimidate these 'Intimidators,' or otherwise they would tell the detectives to 'pound sand.' So the detectives, with upmost diplomacy, contacted each of the 'Intimidators' separately. Initially, the detectives had to convince them that they weren't being considered suspects or even as an aider or abettor.

The easiest person to approach was Alejandro Villalobos (Pseudonym), since his only involvement was trying to find someone to help out his friend Carlos Alonso. Mr. Villalobos readily admitted that he was asked by Carlos to find some type of muscle man or a biker type who looked tough. Mr. Villalobos was forthcoming and explained that he was told by Carlos that he owed a favor to two Indian brothers. His understanding was there was some type of dispute in which they wanted someone to sign some documents. Mr. Villalobos' only role was to give Carlos the names of some tough guys. That was when he thought about some guys he knew by the names of Angel Noyes and Robert Somes, and he provided their information to Carlos.

The detectives had already talked to Angel Noyes and Robert Somes, and they had confirmed what Mr. Villalobos was just the middleman. The detectives now had people who corroborated Carlos' statement that the group of them went up to the Kumar home. Again, the detectives talked to Angel and Robert to obtain more details about the time they all went to the Kumar's house. They completely corroborated what Carlos had told the detectives about how he had gone to the Kumar front door and pretended he was trying to get a petition signed to put in speed bumps on Lakeridge Drive. Carlos even had a clipboard pretending he actually had a petition that he wanted Gita to sign. In the end, Gita closed the door, and that was when it was agreed to call off the confrontation they were going to have with Gita.

Next, the detectives contacted Droeger. He related to the detectives that Carlos had contacted him to provide muscle at a meeting at someone's home. He admitted that Carlos had talked him into helping out and going to a person's house in the Hollywood Hills with Carlos and Victor Govin. He said that he was uncomfortable with the entire operation. He told Carlos that he wouldn't do it because it was a white neighborhood and he would stand out. As a result, he backed out and had nothing else to do with Carlos or anyone else.

Another person's name that had been mentioned by Carlos was that of Alfredo Naranjo, the car repossession man. He substantiated what Carlos had told the detectives. Mr. Naranjo said he was contacted by Carlos to do a job in the Hollywood Hills regarding a dispute between motel owners. He was told that his only role would be to stand there and act as an "Intimidator." This seemed simple enough and he needed some money, so he agreed to go along.

He went with Victor Govin and Carlos up to the house. When they drove by the house, Victor noticed a van in the driveway and wondered how many people had come up in the van. Alfredo didn't like the looks of the situation, so he played up the fact that there could be numerous people who had come in the van and were inside the house. Because of this van and not knowing the number of people, Victor and Carlos agreed to cancel the confrontation. All of the parties the detectives contacted had corroborated everything that Carlos had told the detectives.

CHAPTER 34 GOVIN-VICTOR TALKS

After many days of tracking down witnesses and interviewing them, the detectives now had the corroboration they needed to go after the brothers. However, the big question was, how reliable would all this corroboration be? Unfortunately, none of these 'Intimidator' witnesses could be referred to as 'Choir Boys.' Every one of them had some type of checkered background. One might say someone who is willing to be an "Intimidator" most likely doesn't frequent one of the local churches, temples, or mosques.

On May 14, several days after the detectives had received word from Angel about the attempt to intimidate Gita, the detectives made contact with Victor Govin. Since this was at the early stage of the investigation, the detectives only asked some basic questions. At first, they started with small talk basically to gain Victor's confidence. Then they asked some more questions about how well he knew Gita Kumar. At first he acknowledged knowing her but not on a very personal basis. Then when asked if he had ever been to her house, he claimed that he had never been in the Kumar house. When further pressed, he indicated the general area where Gita lived.

The closest Victor admitted to coming to Gita's house was when he knew she was going to India and he called her up and asked her to take a large bottle of Aspirin to his relatives in India. He explained that she gave him the directions to her house but he was never able to find it. He was adamant that he never had been in her house, since he never knew its exact location.

The detectives spoke with other members of the extended Kumar family, and Sagar Kumar, a nephew, told them that he had seen Victor Govin in Gita's house several weeks earlier. Sagar was absolutely certain that he had seen Victor at the Kumar's house at least once if not more.

On July 17, the detectives again talked to Victor, and this time they asked if he knew a person by the name of Carlos Alonso. At first, Victor totally denied any knowledge of him. The most he was willing to admit was that he might have seen him a year earlier. The detectives continued to ask how well he knew Carlos, and each time Victor gave vague answers. When asked if he could describe the car that Carlos drove, Victor said that he thought Carlos' vehicle was white and had rounded headlights. When pressed, he said he thought it was a BMW type. Then the detectives asked if Carlos drove a gray Tundra pickup, to which Victor said that he didn't remember ever seeing him in a truck.

The detectives gave Victor ample opportunity to admit he had met with Carlos several days earlier. They asked whether his brother and himself met with Carlos and drove up to a park area above his house. Victor shook his head. The detectives tried to paint the picture with more details by asking if he remembered sitting in the car for almost an hour. All Victor was willing to acknowledge was a nonchalant "nope."

The detectives had in a folder several photos that showed Victor and Carlos standing next to Carlos' pickup truck. The detectives kept the photos stuffed in an envelope, and one of them held the folder in his hand and put his other hand into the folder as though he was about to remove the photos. They one more time asked about a meeting he had with Carlos at a Denny's restaurant. This time they asked if he remembered walking out of the restaurant and going over to Carlos' Tundra truck and standing there for several minutes looking at his new truck. All Victor said was that he thought Carlos had a white car with rounded headlights. After the detectives had given Victor enough rope to hang himself, the one detective reached into the folder and pulled out a photo showing Victor standing next to Carlos and his new Tundra pickup truck.

The detective said, "What about this photo of you standing next to Carlos and his truck taken a couple of weeks ago." There was a long silence as Victor's eyes fixated on the clear photo of him with Carlos. These are the 'GOT YOU' moments, and the detectives wanted to see the suspect's response. Victor could have denied that it was him in the photo, or he could have taken the approach that it just a big mistake. However, Victor remained silent and appeared to be deep in thought. The detective asked him if he ever saw Carlos with a gray pickup. The half-audible response from Victor was, "I didn't know if it was his truck." The detectives gave Victor additional time to dig his way out of the giant hole he had dug for himself. Even with further questions, Victor couldn't come up with an explanation why he had continually met with Carlos after the killings.

For some reason, Victor stuck to his original statement that he hadn't seen Carlos for over a year when the photos clearly showed them together at Denny's restaurant and all together in his brother's car at the park. These surveillance photos would be used in trial to show that he was lying as to his dealings with Carlos. Also, his denial of ever being in Gita's house would be countered by other witnesses who had seen him in the Kumar house on several other occasions. All the questioning and answers showed that Victor was lying and showed a 'Consciousness of Guilt.' However, it wasn't evidence that showed that Victor did the actual killings.

Victor may have cooked his goose by continuing to talk to the detectives. On the other hand, his brother, Peter Govin, may have been a little smarter, since he didn't agree to talk to the detectives. The detectives weren't able to obtain any statements against Peter. Why did one brother talk to the detectives and not the other? No one knows for certain, but it did become a major factor at time of trial.

The detectives had tried to obtain statements from both brothers, but neither was willing to make any outfight admissions and certainly not provide any confessions. The most they got from Victor was that he was a liar. Earlier the detectives had obtained permission from the DA's Office and a judge to used wiretaps to obtain conversations between the brothers and Carlos. Unfortunately, the results were less than helpful since the parties seemed to be talking in some type of code to each other.

All this hard work and incredible effort resulted in nothing useful for trial. However, the detectives were knowledgeable homicide detectives and they knew how useful cellphone records can be. First, they can show who has been in contact with whom. Also, it can show at what time they were in contact and how long they talked. True cellphone records don't reveal what was stated between the parties as in 'Wiretaps.' However, cellphone records may be even more useful than Wiretaps since they show the general area where both parties were located at a specific moment in time.

In this case, the detectives could rely on the cellphone records to provide the best form of corroboration that Carlos in fact contacted all the Intimidators on various dates to try to get them to help Victor out in intimidating Gita to sign the Agreement. Even better was the fact that the cellphone records could show how many times Carlos was in contact with the brothers.

On May 4th, the day of the murders, there were 20 phone calls between the three of them from 10:00 a.m. to 7:00 p.m. There was a verified call made from the Rite Aid phone booth to the Kumar house. When the three of them were together, there weren't any calls between them. After the murders, the three departed and went their separate ways, and then the phone calls between them restarted. In this case, the cellphone records were going to be vital, since neither brother could deny having substantial contact with Carlos on the day of the murders and for the week leading up to the killings.

The detectives were trying to build a case against the two Govin brothers based on Carlos Alonso's statements. They knew that the defendant brothers would try to claim that Carlos was out to get them. The detectives asked people who knew Carlos whether he ever said or did anything to indicate that he disliked the Govin brothers. What the detectives found out from others was that Carlos was a very dear friend of Victor Govin. Over the years they had had many business dealings together.

There were many people who said that Carlos had been close to the entire Govin family and on many occasions was invited to their houses. All agreed that Carlos had no hate or ill will toward the Govins—just the opposite. There was no reason for him to make up a story that they were involved in this murder. Carlos' only reason for testifying against them was not to be vindictive but to save his own neck.

CHAPTER 35 GOVIN-BROTHERS' TRIAL

Eleanor Hunter had worked with the two LAPD detectives, Jay Moberly and Vic Pietrantoni, on the Soliah case and had developed a good working rapport with them. When the Govin case came along, it was a 'no brainer' to have the DA's Office assign Eleanor to it. Eleanor's reputation as a heavy hitter had continued to grow. She had a 'No Fear' approach and was willing to take on the most difficult cases that were fraught with legal and factual problems. The famous Navy slogan by Admiral David Farragut saying ***'Damn the torpedoes, full speed ahead'*** could apply to Eleanor's approach to tough situations.

Eleanor gives the physical appearance of an attractive tall blond who many underestimate. Often Defense attorneys misjudged Eleanor as someone who could be easily pushed around. Those attorneys are soon surprised by her tenacity and attitude to take 'No prisoners.' She doesn't surrender but continues to fight for every piece of evidence in order to convict the culprit.

Major Crimes Division prosecutors are the best of the best who exude confidence in their ability to fight for justice. Eleanor fit the mold of a Major Crime deputy; however, she was certainly easier on the eyes than some of her male counterparts. Her self-assured approach was built on the fact that she knew how to relate to jurors. She understood the need to build a case from the ground up, which required incredible PATIENCE and PREPARATION.

After spending considerable time reading all the police and forensic reports as well as the coroner's reports, Eleanor was ready to start building a solid foundation for her case. Her experience using a PowerPoint slide show in the Koklich and Soliah cases had taught her how valuable a visual presentation could be in conveying to jurors the facts and law involved in a case. Eleanor collected all the photos and documents and came to my Trial Support Division and sat down with me to develop a comprehensive Opening Statement.

When Eleanor first explained the case to me, I could see that the facts were confusing and she needed several visuals to better convey to the jurors the facts they needed to remember. When she discussed the actions of Victor and Peter, I became confused as to who did what. I knew that the jurors could easily get confused, so I made a note to make some type of visual clarifying that. Next, Eleanor continued to discuss the dispute over the alleyway, so I wanted to make some type of visual display showing exactly what she was talking about. Another topic that needed to be illustrated was what happened at the motels and what happened at the Kumar residence.

Eleanor and I had considerable discussions as to how to show the burnt bodies of the victims. For prosecutors, charred bodies aren't shocking, since it comes with the territory of the job. However, jurors can be turned off by grotesque photos of corpses. The case law placed limitations on prosecutors from parading in front of the jurors gross photos of the remains of the victims. One way to prove the Cause of Death is to use the coroner's diagrams of the victims' bodies without showing the grizzly photos of the charred remains. No prosecutor wants to have a case reversed because an appellate court ruled that it was unfair to the defendant when repulsive photos of the victims were shown to the jury. However, this case presented some tough decisions for Eleanor.

She needed the jurors to understand exactly what horrific acts the defendants had committed. After considering all the options, Eleanor agreed that some of the photos were too graphic and selected photos that corroborated Carlos' statements, such as the photos that showed how the victims were zip tied around their neck and hands, as well as the photos showing the duct tape around the victims' heads. Some of these photos were not pleasant to look at, but it was necessary for the jurors to understand the facts of this case, in that four human beings had been brutally murdered. Eleanor would have to convince the judge that the limited photos she selected wouldn't unnecessarily inflame the jury.

Eleanor continued to fine-tune her Opening Statement, so I assigned one of my paralegals to work directly with her to incorporate all the changes she wanted to make with my draft of the visuals. Eleanor had learned how much more effective she could be by using a well-orchestrated slide show. This was why she spent endless hours preparing her Opening Statement, since she wanted to be concise but complete.

The day came for the trial to start, and Eleanor had done her homework and was ready for battle. However, her first hurdle was to see if she could select a group of potential jurors who would be willing to impose the Death Penalty in the appropriate case. This is a monumental task these days when the Death Penalty has lost much of its popularity. Jury selection was going to be a major issue in this case. Could Eleanor find 12 jurors who were ready and willing to impose the Death Penalty if they considered this to be an appropriate case?

However, Eleanor was faced with a much more daunting task, and that was that she had to find a jury who would be willing to convict two diminutive men from India. Most jurors would have a preconceived belief that the people from India were passive individuals who come from a culture not willing to 'harm a cow.' How could a person from India brutally kill four innocent people? Neither defendant projected the appearance of being the typical criminal who might be a gang member or a threatening person. Eleanor knew how delicate this subject was, so she had to temper her questions in order not to insult other cultural groups.

She knew that most jurors would have a sympathetic and supportive image of Indian people. She had to accept that as a reality. That might mean some jurors would require more proof to dispel their preconceived beliefs. However, what was of even more concern for Eleanor was the fact that she had overwhelming evidence against Victor but didn't have that much incriminating evidence against Peter. Whenever a prosecutor has to try several defendants together, it is not uncommon that jurors will have an expectation that there should be the same amount of evidence as to each one of the defendants. Some jurors use the proportionality approach, and if one defendant doesn't have as much evidence against him then they consider this lesserdegreeof less evidence to be the basis for reasonable doubt.

The jury selection process involved a lengthy questionnaire and numerous voir dire questions from the attorneys. After both sides exercised numerous challenges, eventually they agreed to accept the jury as it was then constituted. Now it was 'ShowTime.' The judge gave Eleanor a recess so she could set up the projector and could show her Opening Statement to the jury. When everything was set up and court was back in session, the judge asked Eleanor, "Does the prosecution wish to make an Opening Statement." Eleanor in a strong positive voice stated to the court, 'Yes, your Honor, the People do wish to make an Opening Statement in this case."

The following graphic pages are a sample of some of the 55 slides in Eleanor's Opening Statement:

Graphics Page

This slide was the title page for the Opening Statement

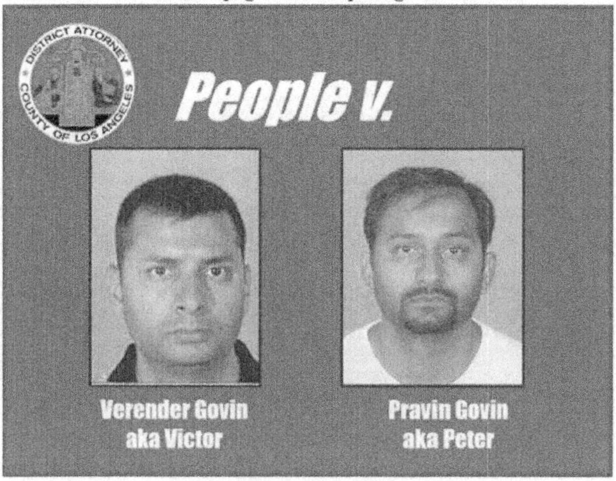

DA used this slide to introduce the victims to the jury

Graphics Page

This slide was used to show the front of the Kumar house

This slide showed the extent of fire in Kumar house

Graphics Page

This slide was a diagram of Kumar house where victims were found

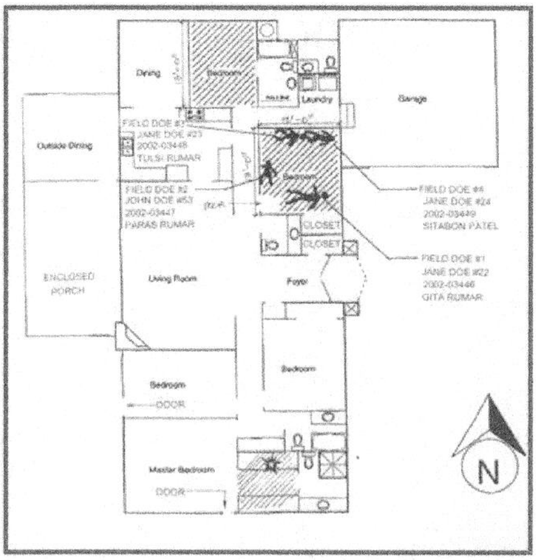

This slide showed the four victims who were killed in this small room

Graphics Page

This showed who owned each of the motels across from Universal Studios

This slide showed the alleyway and barricade behind the motels.

Graphics Page

This slide summarized what killers did to victims

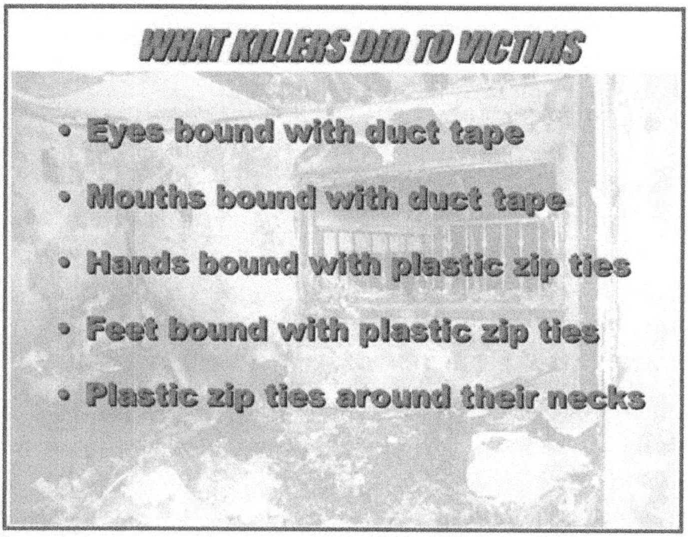

This slide showed the new plans of both motels with alley in the rear

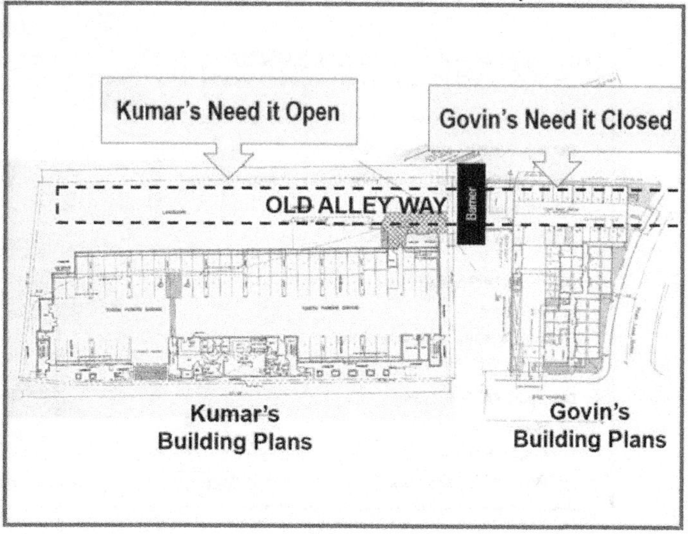

Graphics Page

This slide showed TV News report suggesting that Mr. Kumar was killer

This slide showed what information Intimidator gave to detectives

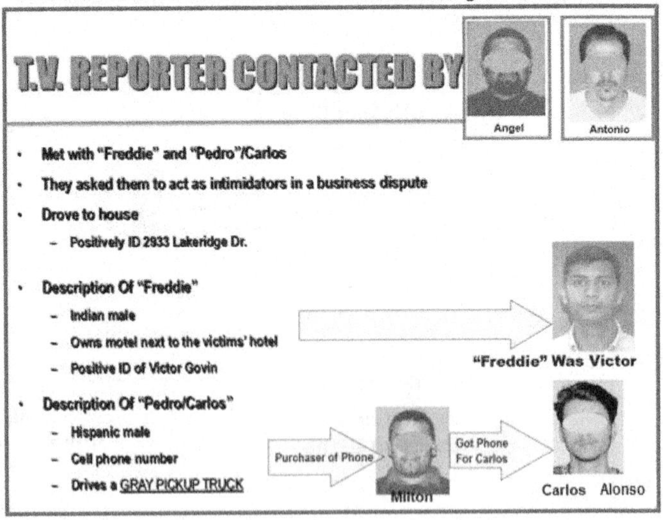

Graphics Page

Slide shows Carlos's truck going up street to Kumar's house &leaving

This slide shows Mr. Kumar driving up street to his house

Graphics Page

Slide shows how Victor lied about not knowing Carlos

This slide was used to show the planning of the killers

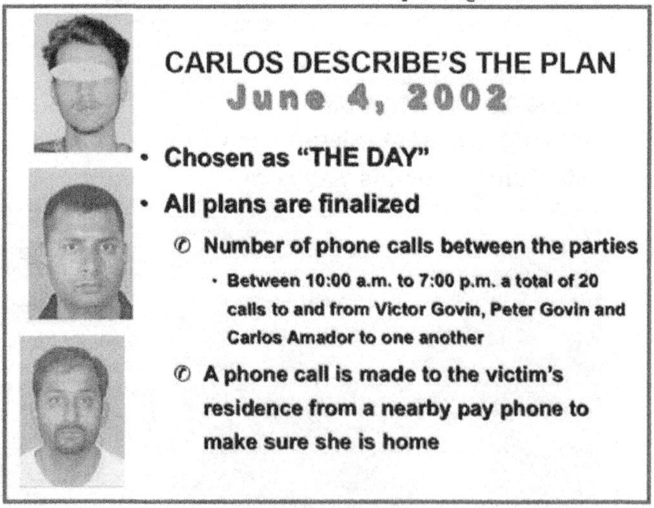

Graphics Page

DA wanted jury to understand what was & what wasn't the MOTIVE

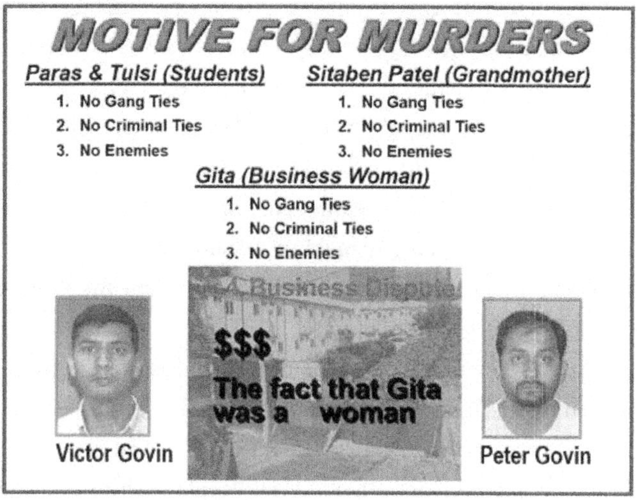

DA used this slide to show the jury all the charges against both defendants

Eleanor concluded her Opening Statement by reviewing all the crimes the brothers were charged with. She must have mentioned Carlos' name several dozen times. She kept saying that Carlos will explain everything to you as to what the brothers had done to the victims. She knew exactly what the Defense attorneys would be saying about Carlos as being the 'Judas of the group.' After the prosecutor had finished and sat down each Defense attorney in turn gave their Opening Statements. They attacked Carlos as a person who sold his soul just to save his own neck. They painted Carlos as a con man who couldn't be trusted to tell the truth.

The jurors must have thought from the Defense's description of Carlos that he was Satan personified as a human being, with horns coming out of his forehead. The two attorneys were like a tag team demonizing Carlos and suggested that the prosecutor had got it all wrong by making a deal with the real killer who had turned against his good friend Victor Govin to frame him and his brother for something they had nothing to do with.

Eleanor sat and listened to the Defense attorneys trashing Carlos. She realized that she had an uphill fight to convince the jurors that Carlos wasn't such a monster. The last Defense attorney had finished his Opening Statement and sat down. Then Eleanor with a composed voice stated, "The People wish to call CARLOS ALONSO to the witness stand.

Everyone in the courtroom could feel the tension as Carlos slowly walked up to the witness stand and turned to look at the clerk, who asked him to raise his right hand as she stated, *"Do you solemnly swear that you will tell the truth, the whole truth, and nothing but the truth so help you God?* He responded in a quiet, submissive voice the words, "I do." Eleanor stood up straight as a ramrod and took a few steps to the lectern and placed her notes on it. In a firm, self-assured voice, she started asking Carlos questions one by one. She wanted to try to put Carlos at ease so he would come across as a truthful person trying to explain what happened on May 4th at the Kumar house.

Eleanor walked Carlos through each step of the killings, starting with Gita. Carlos described that Victor placed a plastic strip around Gita's neck and pulled it tight to strangle her. While Victor was doing this, Peter repeatedly punched Gita in the head several times as she struggled to breathe. Carlos went on to describe that once during the process Gita's son somehow broke free and came after the killers shouting, "Don't hurt my mother!" They quickly subdued the son. At about this stage, Carlos stated he didn't want to be involved in the actual killing of the victims and he asked to leave. He believes that the brothers killed Gita first and then proceeded to kill Paras next. After they had strangled him, they then strangled his sister and finally the elderly grandmother.

Carlos then testified that afterwards they set the house on fire so the coroner wouldn't be able to figure out how the victims were killed. He explained how he saw them pour carburetor cleaner all over the small bedroom and other places in the house.

Eleanor asked extensive questions about all the Intimidators that Carlos had contacted to help Victor put pressure on Gita to agree to give up the alley. Eleanor recognized that the testimony about the Intimidators wasn't as graphic and interesting as the actual killings. Yet she knew that those Intimidators would be the foundation that she would rest her case on. She knew that she needed to CORROBORATE Carlos' testimony and was doing this by parading all the Intimidators in front of the jury. By calling all those witnesses, she would cement Carlos' testimony and create a solid foundation for the rest of the evidence to rest on.

When Eleanor had finished with Carlos, she picked up her notes from the lectern and took several steps to her left and sat down at the counsel table. She took a deep sigh of relief in that her direct examination of Carlos was over. However, she braced herself in her chair as the first Defense attorney started his cross-examination of Carlos. Eleanor knew that the next several hours were going to be hell as she listened to the Defense attorney try to undermine Carlos' credibility. All she could do was make an occasional objection to try to protect Carlos from being completely torn apart. As the other Defense attorney attacked Carlos, Eleanor was surprised that Carlos had enough street smarts to deflect the slings and arrows that were thrown at him.

Although the cross-examination seemed to go on forever, it eventually ended. Eleanor tried to use her re-direct examination to rehabilitate Carlos in some areas that needed clarification. Her objective was to get him off the witness stand as expeditiously as possible. It was time to call Mr. Kumar as the next witness. Eleanor knew that he would be the most sympathetic civilian witness she would be calling.

He slowly walked up to the witness stand with his head down, projecting the image of a man whose world had crumbled beneath his feet.

When Eleanor asked him why he didn't initially tell the detectives about the alley dispute, he slowly responded in his British accent, saying, "Victor had left documents to sign, but we decided not to sign them. Victor came by 10 days later and we told him we didn't sign since we didn't own the alley." But Mr. Kumar went on to explain that he didn't think that it was a serious matter. These may not have been the words that Eleanor wanted the jurors to hear, but it was the truth. In Mr. Kumar's world, he didn't like to think evil thoughts of his Indian neighbors, the Govin brothers.

When he was asked to describe what he saw when he arrived home on the night of killings, he stated, "I was shocked to see my mother's room was kind of burning. I tried going inside but couldn't go more than a few feet because the smoke was pouring out. I tried to call out for my family but no one answered. Then I called 9-1-1." Mr. Kumar finished up in very short order his testimony. The Defense didn't want to have him in front of the jury testifying, so their cross-examination was relatively short.

To shore up the prosecution case, Eleanor started calling the long list of Intimidators to explain their contact with Carlos. Each one had some type of baggage that the Defense tried to use to undercut their testimony. Eleanor was pleased to finish with the Intimidators and start on the forensic testimony, which included the coroner's testimony as to the cause of death being strangulation and thermal burns.

When it was time for the testimony about the cellphone records, the custodian of the phone records was less than stimulating and actually could be described as boring. Eleanor knew that as tedious as this testimony was, it would be up to her during Argument to connect all the dots for the jury.

Eleanor didn't know how well the testimony would go regarding how the brothers had divided up the loot that was confiscated from the Kumar house. She called Marti and his wife to testify that Peter had given them some items such as jewelry and some type of safe shortly after May 4th. The inference was those were some of the items that Carlos indicated were taken from the Kumar house. Also, a Govin relative was called to testify to receiving items from the Govin brothers that Mr. Kumar claimed were missing from his house.

The final part of the prosecution's case was putting the detectives on the witness stand to testify that Victor had spoken to them. They told the jury that Victor had maintained that he hadn't seen Carlos for almost a year. The prosecutor asked the one detective if photos had been taken of Victor and Carlos meeting together only days before his statement. The other part of the detective's testimony involved the fact that Victor claimed he had never been inside Gita's house. After the detectives had finished their testimony, Eleanor called witnesses who adamantly claimed to have seen Victor in the Kumar's house on several occasions.

The prosecution's case went well, and it was time for the Defense to present their evidence. Both brothers relied on the fact that Carlos couldn't be trusted because he had made a pact with the devil. The Defense called very few witnesses of their own. They basically relied on the cross-examining of Carlos and the Intimidators.

When it was time for Argument, Eleanor used the approach that she had used on her other cases. She initially discussed the law involved in this case. In order to make the case a first degree murder she told the jury that if they believed the defendants deliberated and premeditated the killing then that would sufficient. If that didn't exist then they could consider the Felony Murder Rule. She explained if the defendants were committing a felony like Robbery or Residential Burglary or even Arson and someone was killed during the commission of that felony, which would make it a first degree murder. Eleanor was concerned that one of the jurors might believe that the brothers were only planning to threaten Gita and not kill her. She wanted those jurors to understand that there was another way to get to first degree murder.

Next Eleanor wanted the jurors to realize there were three methods to move the case on to the Death Penalty phase. They could find that there were multiple murders. Even though this seemed obvious, the law requires that at least one of the murders was of the first degree. That was why Eleanor knew how important it was for the jurors to understand what constituted first degree murder.

Another way to move on to the Death Penalty was if the jury found that the murders were carried out for financial gain. That required the jury to believe that by killing Gita the Govin brothers would be able to remodel their motel, which would make it more valuable. Although that theory required a certain amount of speculation, the easier one was if the killings occurred during the commission of a

Robbery or Burglary. But what Eleanor was concerned about was that sounded very much like the requirements of the Felony Murder Rule. This can be very confusing for jurors to figure out.

After Eleanor was satisfied that she had sufficiently explained the law that applied, she moved on to the facts of the case. The testimony of Carlos laid out all the facts to prove the Govin brothers committed the murders as well as the robbery, burglary, and arson. Nonetheless, there was a giant hurdle she needed jump over in order to get a conviction, and that was that she needed to corroborate Carlos' testimony.

Eleanor read the law on CORROBORATION OF AN ACCOMPLICE to the jurors:

In determining whether an accomplice has been corroborated, you must first assume the testimony of the accomplice has been removed from the case. You must then determine whether there is any remaining evidence which tends to connect the defendant with the commission of the crime.

However, Eleanor knew that jurors can become confused believing that **every fact** of the accomplice's testimony needs to be corroborated, so she read further from that jury instruction as follows:

However, it is not necessary that the evidence of corroboration be sufficient in itself to establish every element of the crime charged, or that it corroborates every fact to which the accomplice testifies.

Eleanor's then began to argue all the points of corroboration that she had introduced through the testimony of others. First, she discussed all the evidence that had been presented regarding the 'Business Dispute' involving the alleyway behind both motels. At that point, she started to talk about the fact that the brothers had a strong Motive to eliminate their problem by doing Gita in.

At first, that was done by lining up Intimidators such as Angel Noyes, Alejandro Villalobos, Droeger, and Alfredo Naranjo. What substantiated these guys were the phone records showing the numerous phone calls among themselves.

Additional corroboration came from the neighbor's security camera photos of Carlos and the brothers driving up and down the street to the Kumars' house. Also, there were the surveillance photos of the three of them meeting together. Eleanor spent some time explaining how Victor lied to the detectives, which she claimed showed 'Consciousness of Guilt.'

She concluded her Argument by flashing two slides on the screen, one showing the amount of corroborating evidence she had presented as to both defendants. Eleanor knew it was risky to line up the amount of evidence against each defendant. What jurors will do is look to see if one defendant has more or less evidence than the other. However, Eleanor tried to make both slides appear to look like there was the same number of bullet points. In reality, she had tons of evidence against Victor, since he was the one who had the most contact with the so-called Intimidators, and much less evidence showing Peter's involvement. *On the following graphic page are copies of drafts of those two slides.*

Graphics Page

This slide was used to show the evidence against Victor Govin

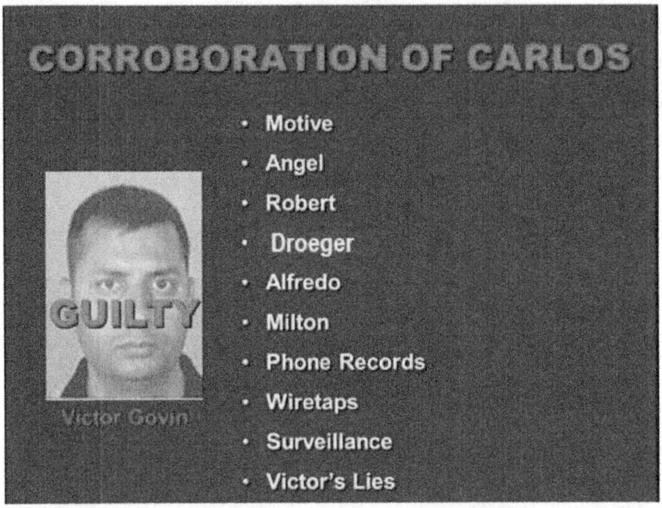

This slide was used to show the evidence against Peter Govin

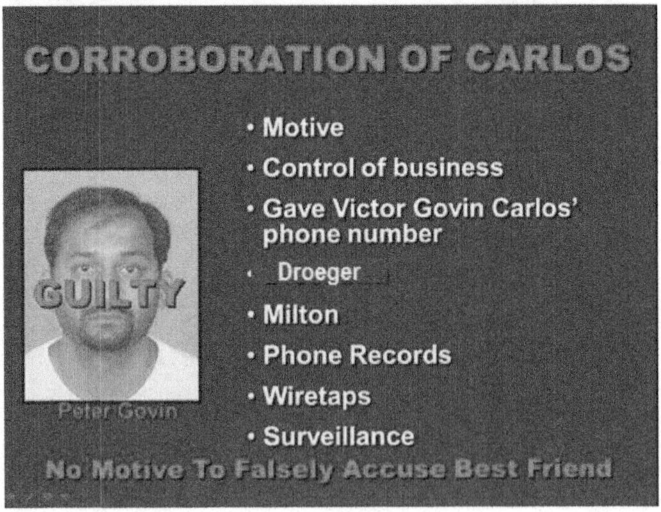

After using the two above slides, Eleanor finished her Argument with the slide she had used in her Opening Statement that showed the burnt bedroom with photos of the four victims overlaid on it. The only title on this slide was 'The Kumar Family.' This slide didn't use any of the gruesome photos of how the victims were burnt beyond recognition. As that slide remained on the large courtroom screen, Eleanor talked about the victims and how innocent they were. She wanted the jurors not to forget the victims.

Then it was the Defense attorneys' turn to argue their case. Each attorney argued separately, they stressed how the jury could rely on the testimony of an admitted murderer who agreed to sell his friends out so he could get his charges reduced to a second degree MURDER. They painted a picture of Carlos as a person who was willing to say anything in order to save himself. After they trashed Carlos, they went on to argue that the prosecution's case was so full of doubt that the DA had not sustained their burden of proving their case beyond a reasonable doubt.

The jury, consisting of ten men and two women, deliberated long and hard on the fate of the Govin brothers. After four weeks of deliberation, the judge called the jurors into the courtroom to see if they were likely to arrive at a verdict. The jury was unable to reach a verdict on any of the counts involving Peter. It was learned later that the jury was hopelessly deadlocked, with only three for Guilty and the remaining nine for Not Guilty. That resulted in Peter's case ending as with a hung jury to be continued for a later retrial.

However, in Victor's case all the 12 jurors agree to find him Guilty of all counts, including four counts of First Degree Murder as well as finding true all of the alleged Special Circumstances. As a result, the same jury went on to hear more evidence during the Penalty phase of the trial and ultimately agreed to impose the Death Penalty on VICTOR GOVIN.

After all the proceedings, the foreperson told a news reporter, "It's difficult to see what people are willing to do just for money. This case was all about GREED." Apparently, the jurors figured it all out, especially as to Victor Govin.

CHAPTER 36 GOVIN-PETER'S RETRIAL

What a mixed bag. Eleanor could rejoice that she had very skillfully proved the guilt of Victor Govin, but she had only convinced three jurors that Peter was guilty of the murders. How could nine jurors not be willing to convict Peter? What followed was typical of the prosecutors in Major Crimes Division, which is that Eleanor was as tough as any of her fellow teammates. However, the average attorney who had spent months preparing a case and endured an exhausting month-long trial would say, "Okay, I've done enough, now let's find some way to settle this case."

Conversely, Eleanor's reaction was **NOT** to wave the 'white flag of surrender.' Her response was more analytical in that she wanted to review every piece of evidence and see how she could present it in a more convincing light. She wasn't going to let one of the brothers escape her view of justice. Hung juries are a major disappointment for prosecutors, but it is amazing how the Major Crimes deputies are willing to pull themselves up by their bootstraps and willing to go back into battle. Eleanor was no exception.

Eleanor recognized that one of the areas she needed to shore up was the manner in which she presented the evidence of the cellphone records. She spent hours trying to find the best way to illustrate to the jurors all the phone calls that Peter made and received involving his brother and Carlos on the days leading up to the killings.

Next she needed to concentrate on the evidence that showed that Peter was involved in distributing the loot that they had taken from the Kumar house. Two people who were important in this regard were Marti and Susan Roberts (Pseudonym). Eleanor wanted the jury to understand the meaning of the items that Peter gave them shortly after the murders. Eleanor had a visual prepared showing a list of these items, which included a suitcase, travelers' checks, Indian jewelry, and a safe. These were exactly the same type of items that Mr. Kumar found to be missing from his home. Further, she wanted to show that Peter had given Marti a bunch of extra zip ties that were identical to the ones that were found on the victims' hands, legs, and neck. The one additional piece of evidence that Marti could supply was the fact that Peter had asked him to say that he and Marti were playing darts at the time of the killings. In other words, this false alibi showed a Consciousness of Guilt on the part of Peter.

Besides Eleanor being intensely focused on how to build a solid case against Peter, the detectives hadn't given up either. They went to work trying to learn more about Peter's background, especially with his business dealings. What the detectives uncovered was a similar situation in which Peter had some type of business dispute in which he tried to intimate the other party. Eleanor figured out how she could use that information in trial to show a pattern by Peter resorting to violent tactics to resolve business disputes. She had a graphic prepared that compared the similarity between the prior incident and the Kumar incident. *The following graphic page shows a copy of this slide she used in her Argument.*

Graphics Page

This slide was used to show jury that Peter had done it before

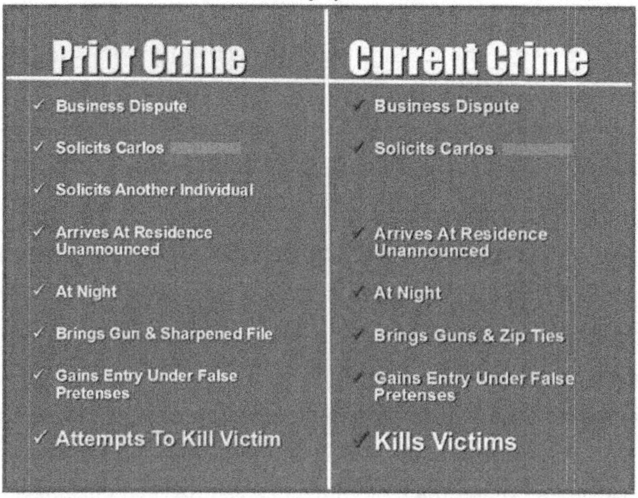

This slide was used to show that Carlos could be believed

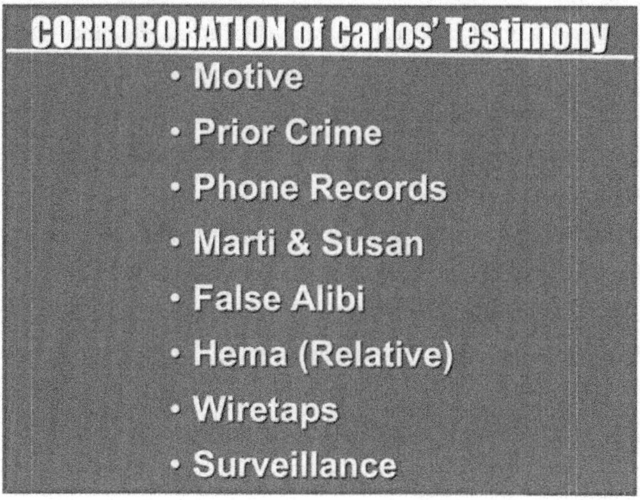

With all the additional pieces of evidence to her case, Eleanor felt that she could make a more compelling case against Peter. She knew that in a new trial involving only Peter, the jurors wouldn't be able to compare the amount of evidence against both the brothers. In the first trial, she had such overwhelming evidence against Victor that the jurors got the feeling that they needed the same amount of evidence against Peter.

There were numerous continuances that impeded the start of Peter's second trial. However, the delays gave Eleanor time to start the Sante Kimes jury trial. It wasn't until March of 2005 that the second trial of Peter Govin commenced. Eleanor knew how important it was to select a jury that this time would convict Peter. She knew that if this trial ended in a hung jury no judge would let her try the case for a third time. Therefore, she spent substantial time in picking this jury. She couldn't afford having a juror who couldn't get along with the other jurors. Eventually, she and the Defense attorney were satisfied with the jury panel and it was sworn in to hear the case.

Then it was again 'Showtime,' and the judge again asked Eleanor if she wished to make an Opening Statement to which she said she did. This time Eleanor rose up from her chair and turned her head toward the jurors. Her face was filled with a friendly smile as she greeted the jurors. Within seconds that smile had faded to a somber look of a woman on a mission. She scanned the entire jury, making eye contact with each one of them, and when she had their undivided attention she started her Opening Statement.

The tone of her voice was serious but sincere. She used her slide show to reinforce what she told the jurors. To some in the courtroom, her Opening Statement seemed like de ja vue, since it was basically what she had told the first jury nine months earlier. However, this time her presentation was more focused on Peter's role in the planning, the killing, and distribution of the loot. Eleanor use the following new graphics in her Opening to make sure the jurors understood the relevance of the cellphone records and distribution of the stolen property to friends of Peter after the killings. *On the following page are some of the new slides used in her Opening Statement in the Second Trial.*

Graphics Page

In Peter's retrial this slide was used to show all the cellphone calls

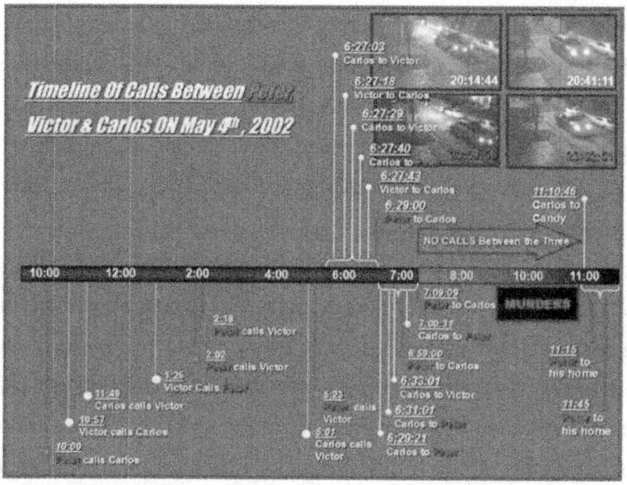

This slide was used to show what stolen items Peter gave to others

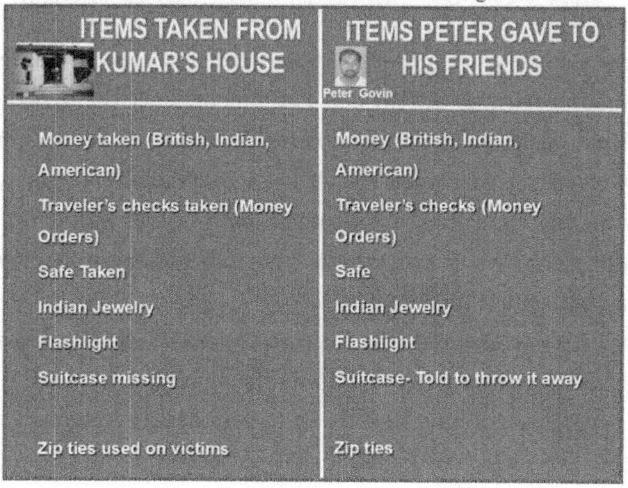

The actual second trial parroted the first, with similar testimony from Carlos, Mr. Kumar, the coroner, and all of the Intimidators. However, this time Eleanor spent more time with the custodian of the phone records to show Peter's involvement in the planning phase. When it came to the distribution of the loot, Eleanor went into more detail as to everything Peter did to get rid of the travelers' checks and foreign money, as well as all the Indian jewelry. The second trial was more finely tuned, since both sides knew what their strong points were. The prosecution plugged in witnesses to show that Peter was well involved in the planning and aftermath of the murders. The Defense attorney peppered their cross-examination of the DA's witnesses with all types of suggestive questions as to why Carlos's testimony couldn't and shouldn't be trusted.

After a contentious trial, it was time for Argument. This time Eleanor knew that she had to convince all 12 jurors of Peter's guilt. The pressure was on Eleanor to have a powerful Argument that would convince every single juror. After receiving input from the first trial jurors, Eleanor was convinced that they hadn't understood the legal concepts they had to apply to the testimony they had heard. She wanted this second jury to understand the legal concept of Circumstantial Evidence; the Felony Murder Rule; Accomplice and Corroboration.

As a result, Eleanor used several slides showing the text of those legal terms and highlighted the particular language the jurors needed to apply to Carlos' testimony. Often this is not a good way to start one's Argument, since the first five minutes is when the jurors' are most receptive to listening and remembering the attorney's Argument. However, Eleanor knew that if the jurors didn't thoroughly understand how to apply the law, the entire case would be lost. She was willing to take a chance in hopes that the jurors would continue to listen to her after her lengthy dissertation on the law the jurors must apply to this case.

After Eleanor was convinced that the jurors were thoroughly familiar with the law, she started her presentation, explaining the facts that had been proved during the trial. Although much of this was a repeat of her Opening Statement, this time she indicated to the jurors which witnesses had proved each specific point.

The Defense realized that they needed to counter Eleanor's strong Argument by undercutting Carlos' testimony of Peter's involvement. Peter's Defense attorney claimed that there was scant evidence presented by the prosecution that Peter was involved. All the Intimidators had contact with Victor and only one had a phone call with Peter in regards to getting paid. However, as to that one Intimidator, Peter's attorney argued that he was a member of the Mongols motorcycle gang, therefore he must be distrusted. In other words, his Defense attorney argued that there wasn't any real credible corroboration to support Carlos' testimony.

Then the Defense attorney focused on Carlos' issue of credibility. He argued, how could the jurors believe him, a self-professed MURDERER. During this second trial, the Defense had called witnesses who testified that Carlos had used his son's name to obtain a false identification. Further, other witnesses alleged that Carlos had been involved in a carjacking as well as an insurance fraud incident. In other words, the Defense was trying to show that Carlos was a flakey character who the jurors should disregard.

Additionally, the Defense attorney claimed that Carlos was motivated to make up the story to save himself. Then he added to that by saying that somehow Carlos was purposely out to get the brothers. However, there wasn't any evidence during the trial which proved that somehow Carlos had a grudge against either Victor or Peter. Next, the Defense attorney claimed that the brothers had no motive to harm Gita, since the alley dispute had already been resolved sometime before the killings.

During the prosecutor's Rebuttal Argument, Eleanor hammered hard on the fact that Peter had had numerous contacts with Carlos by phone. Further, she brought up the subject of the distribution of the stolen property by Peter. There was no real evidence presented by the Defense to explain why Peter gave away all the Indian money and Indian jewelry. Again, Eleanor asked why the Defense hadn't explained away the Wiretap and Surveillance evidence, which showed he was meeting and in contact with Carlos days after the killings.

To answer the Defense claim that the alley dispute had been settled, all the prosecutor had to do was show the jurors the letter from the Planning Department regarding a Public Hearing scheduled six days after the killing. The Alley Dispute was clearly not resolved. Finally, the prosecutor flashed on the screen the information about Peter being involved in a similar incident months before against other victims. This showed Peter in a different light, as someone who used threats of violence to get his way in his business dealings.

Eleanor finished with a strong Rebuttal Argument and sat down at counsel table. Then the judge gave the final jury instructions and the jurors started their deliberation. The agony for both the prosecutor and the Defense had begun. Day after day, the jurors dutifully marched into Judge Kenney-Powell's courtroom and disappeared into the jury deliberation room. After one week of deliberation, Eleanor was on edge as to what was going to be the outcome. She was convinced that the jury wouldn't come back with a Not Guilty verdict. Her biggest concern was what would happen to the case if it was another Hung Jury.

The stress factor on Eleanor was overwhelming. She knew that she had to stay focused. If the jury came back with a conviction with the Special Allegations True, she had to be prepared to commence the Death Penalty phase of the trial. That meant lining up witnesses and preparing her Opening Statement and Argument presentation. Generally, the judges give the attorneys one to two days before starting the Penalty part of the trial.

Then on the 14th day, the jury came back with a verdict of guilty of four first degree murders with the Special Allegations to be true. Eleanor was elated with the verdict, but it meant she had little time to celebrate a well-deserved victory for justice. Her undivided attention was on the most difficult phase of a trial, that being the Death Penalty. That phase has to be perfectly done, since if the defendant is ultimately sentenced to Death, the Supreme Court will be reviewing every step of the process. Eleanor knew that every 'i' had to be dotted and 't' crossed, since one mistake could cause the sentence to be reversed.

Peter's Penalty phase trial was similar to the one Eleanor used during his brother's Penalty phase trial. She started out explaining the Death Penalty law, which is unfamiliar to most jurors. It is totally different in that there is no burden of proof. Both sides present evidence. The prosecutor can present evidence that shows some form of Aggravation, which is *any fact which increases its severity which is above and beyond the elements of the crime itself.* While on the other hand the Defense can present evidence which shows some form of Mitigation, which is *any fact which is an extenuating circumstance in determining the appropriateness of the Death Penalty.*

Then Eleanor explained to the jurors that it would be their job to consider all the Aggravating and Mitigating circumstances and decide if the Aggravating circumstances are so substantial in comparison with the Mitigating circumstances that they warrant death instead of life without parole. Then the prosecutor recited a list of 11 factors that the law states that the jurors could consider to determine Aggravation and Mitigation. As tedious as all this legalese may seem, it was all important that the jurors approached their task knowing what they were permitted to consider.

The prosecution's evidence during the Penalty phase was basically Victim Impact witnesses. Relatives and friends of the Kumars testified as to what wonderful people they were. Gita was depicted as a fair-minded business woman that everyone liked. The witnesses heaped praise on Gita being a faithful wife and a caring mother to her two children. Likewise, young people testified what wonderful children both Paras and Tusi were. They were truly missed by all their friends from school.

The Defense, on the other hand, tried to present Mitigating evidence claiming that the jurors might have some type of lingering doubt. The Death Penalty was too final, especially in this case where the prosecution so totally relied on Carlos, who would say anything to save his own life. The Defense tried to paint a picture that Peter, as a person, was misunderstood by people who really didn't know him.

Then, after only several days of testimony, it was time for both sides to argue their case. Eleanor used a graphic that had all the Aggravating evidence listed on the left side showing that Gita was killed for money; abuse of position of trust; invaded sanctity of their home; and totally innocent victims. Then she added that the manner of death by strangulation and burning to death was totally an Aggravating factor. Then, on the right side of her graphic, she showed a short list of the Mitigating evidence, which showed the words that Peter had no prior felony conviction. Then Eleanor argued that Peter showed a total lack of remorse, which made it a negative Mitigating factor. Just by looking at the graphic, it was clear to see that there were many more items on the Aggravating side.

When the prosecution was finished, it was up to the Defense to convince the jury that Peter had redeeming qualities. Further, the Defense had a defendant who appeared to be a sympathetic Indian businessman. He didn't project the appearance of the typical criminal type. The Argument was that sentencing him to Life Without the Possibility of Parole was more than sufficient for this type of defendant.

Finally, both sides had a Rebuttal to each other's Argument. The judge asked Eleanor if she had any Rebuttal to present, to which Eleanor said she did. Eleanor stood up and in her confident manner went over to her laptop computer and started a slide show about the victims in this case. The first slide showed Gita, listing her birth date and date of death. What followed was a collage of 10 photos showing a happy Gita with her family. Next was a photo of Sitaben, the grandmother, with six photos of her in India and raising her family. Then there was a photo of Paras, with eight follow-up photos of him growing up, as well as photos showing how many friends he had in school. Finally, the last person shown was Tulsi, with ten photos depicting how popular and well liked she was with her classmates.

Then slide show paused for a moment as Eleanor indicated to the jurors what a wonderful individual each and every victim was. Then Eleanor displayed on the large screen Gita's photo on the left side, then on the right side of the screen an image appeared showing a photo of her burnt body. The stark contrast grabbed the attention of everyone in the courtroom. The next slide was that of Sitaben, with a color photo of her in life and on the other side a grab black-and-white photo of her in death with a zip tie around her neck. Similar slides were shown of Paras. The final slide showed Tusli, a vibrant, beautiful teenager with everything to live for, then on the right side several photos of her dead body, showing the duct tape over her eyes and mouth, as well of photos of her hands zip tied behind her back and a zip tie around her neck.

Eleanor finished by saying that those photos showed why the Death Penalty was the appropriate punishment in this case. She looked each juror in the eye and said, "Thank you for your attention." Deliberately she turned to her left and sat down. There was a silence in the courtroom that seemed like an eternity. Everyone except the defendant and his family was reaching into their pockets to find a handkerchief or anything to wipe away the tears rolling down their faces. The judge interrupted and said that this might be a good time to take a break.

After the short recess, the Defense attorney tried to rebut Eleanor's Argument. He tried to refocus the jury on any Mitigating evidence he could think up. But nothing he could say was going to change the facts of the case. Without a doubt, if any case called out for the Death Penalty, this was certainly it. The jurors deliberated for less than two days and returned to the courtroom with a recommendation for the Death Penalty.

Ultimately, the judge sentenced Peter to Death and the long journey for Mr. Kumar to see justice imposed was finally over. Mr. Kumar lost his loving wife, his two wonderful children, and his much-beloved mother. How was he going to restart his life without his family? Mr. Kumar struggled to find a new meaning for his life. He submerged himself into his hotel business, and things seemed to improve for him. Then several years later, he suddenly fell over dead. Sadly, he never got to enjoy the fruits of all his labor. Strangely, everyone involved in this case seemed to end up a loser not attaining their lifelong dreams of the GOOD LIFE.

Again, the DA's Office proved that their special **Major Crimes Division** truly stepped up to the plate and hit the ball clearly out of the ballpark. Was the DA's success due to the extraordinary job done by Eleanor or all the assistance she received from her support staff? In truth, it was a combined effort of everyone on the team. Eleanor knew how to use all the services available to her. She exuded confidence because she understood what was needed to get the job done.

An ancillary question is whether the **Death Penalty** has any purpose in our new, more Enlighted society. The old, worn-out cliché is that the Death Penalty makes us safer since it acts as a deterrent. However, in this case wouldn't Life Without the Possibility of Parole have deterred both brothers from committing a similar offense in the future? Likewise, others in society would be deterred from committing such crimes. In reality, very few people ever heard the final outcome of these murder cases, so how could the imposing of the Death Penalty be a deterrent?

However, the facts of this case are so repugnant that many people come to the conclusion that certain horrific crimes cry out for some type of punishment greater than Life Without Parole (LWOP.) The debate will continue as to the merits of the Death Penalty. Even those who are opposed to the Death Penalty admit this Govin case would be at the top of their list of the type of case deserving of the most severe punishment such as the Death Penalty.

CHAPTER 37

CONCLUSION

This book has exposed you the reader to some of the accomplishments of the Los Angeles District Attorney's Office's **MAJOR CRIMES DIVISION**. We have basically discussed one of the incredible prosecutors, **ELEANOR HUNTER**, as she as a member of this team quietly and without fanfare churned out one major case after another. She was just one of those amazing members who did astonishing feats for that group. To a lesser degree, we talked about Michael Latin, who assisted Eleanor as her co-prosecutor on two of her cases. I admire all the members of the Major Crimes team for their talent, courage, and tenacity.

Throughout history, we have seen glimpses of extraordinary elite groups such as the Delta Force, Green Berets, and Seal Team 6 performing incredible feats. Often these amazing groups go unnoticed because some believe that publicity will undercut and obstruct them from accomplishing their stated mission. That may be the reason why we seldom recognize the wonderful job done by such elite groups.

However, my approach is to shine the spotlight on some unique individuals who came together at one point in time to do a noteworthy job in prosecuting some of the toughest cases in the criminal justice system. They didn't do it for the publicity, to gain fame, and certainly not for the money. They believed in the American Judicial System, which states that **it is the government's job to prove that a person is guilty** of a crime.

In other countries, it is the accused who has the burden to prove he or she is innocent of the charges. In the USA, the prosecution has the task of building a case and convincing 12 members of the public that there is proof beyond a reasonable doubt that the accused is guilty of the charges. The vast majority of the cases are easily settled; however, there are those tough cases which require special attention, and effort in order to persuade a jury of the defendant's guilt.

Every District Attorney's (prosecutions) office has the difficult task of finding the resources and staff to take on those demanding cases. As stated earlier, the Los Angeles County DA's Office decided to create the **Major Crimes Division** to take on those most demanding cases. However, merely setting up a special unit to take care of those cases doesn't guarantee that justice will be properly served.

It's the remarkable people who came together and staff this special division that made it successful. ELEANOR HUNTER is just one of a long list of prosecutors who answered the call and caused the **Major Crimes Division** to accomplish its mission. What an incredible job she did in the above cases we have reviewed.

PEOPLE V. DAVID HELMS

Eleanor stepped in and took on a case in which the wrong person had been originally prosecuted. She had to deal with a situation where the medical examiner changed his testimony as to the time of death. When Eleanor got the case, it was several years old, and she patiently and diligently put the case together so that a little boy, Lance Helms, finally got justice.

PEOPLE V. KATHLYN SOLIAH aka Sara Jane Olson

Eleanor took on a case that was over 25 years old. She and her co-prosecutor diligently uncovered the witnesses and evidence to prove that the defendant, an SLA urban terrorist member, was involved in planting bombs under two LAPD police cars. The Defense delayed and continued the case for years. However, Eleanor's tenacity won out and the defendant pleaded guilty. What was remarkable about the case was that Eleanor, with the help of Michael Latin, built a murder case against the remaining SLA members. Although the bank robbery murder occurred in Sacramento, Eleanor and Michael fought long and hard to see that justice was done for Myrna Opsahl, the victim who was gunned down in the bank while making the deposit for her church's offerings.

PEOPLE V. BRUCE KOKLICH

It appeared that this real estate broker was going to get away with murder, since his wife's body was never found. The first trial ended in a hung jury of seven for not guilty. Instead of plea bargaining the case, Eleanor analyzed what was needed to make for a stronger case. She was flexible enough to change her strategy of the case, and with a new visual presentation of the evidence she convinced the second jury to convict the defendant for the murder of his wife.

PEOPLE V. SANTE KIMES

This defendant was a born con artist who with her son had left behind a path of crime and murder all across the country. Sante had been convicted of murder in New York and received a sentence of 120 years in prison. Eleanor could have said that was enough and not had Sante extradited to Los Angeles. However, Eleanor felt that justice required that this despicable individual be prosecuted for the killing of an old business partner, David Kazdin. Although it took years to ultimately convict her, Eleanor make sure that this defendant would never again be a menace to society.

PEOPLE V. VICTOR AND PETER GOVIN

Eleanor felt that what the Govin brothers did to four innocent people was so abominable that it deserved the Death Penalty. She recognized the difficulty in obtaining a conviction and receiving the Death Penalty against Peter, since he had little contact with the so-called Intimidators. After the hung jury in Peter's case, Eleanor went to work to build a stronger case against him. She recognized that she needed to find a way to explain the importance of the cell phone records to prove Peter's involvement. Also, she worked on ways to better illustrate how Peter distributed the loot taken from the Kumar's house. Eleanor diligently worked to find a way to prove beyond a reasonable doubt that Peter was just as guilty as his brother. Even though the victims, Gita, Paras, Tulsi, and Sitaben were no longer able to fight for their lives, Eleanor stepped in to FIGHT FOR JUSTICE.

I salute all the hard-working prosecutors who do an extraordinary job every single day. Fortunately, in Los Angeles County the sun, moon, and the planets all came together in perfect alignment to create the **Major Crimes Division** and staffed it with exceptionally gifted attorneys, and that is why it became known as the *DA Delta Force*.

Made in the USA
Monee, IL
04 November 2026

67376800R00187